S0-ABB-237

OUR CHURCH MOTHERS

Letters from Leaders at Crossroads in History

Gwen Ehrenborg

WESTBOW PRESS®
A DIVISION OF THOMAS NELSON & ZONDERVAN

Copyright © 2021 Gwen Ehrenborg.

All rights reserved. No part of this book may be used or reproduced by any means, graphic, electronic, or mechanical, including photocopying, recording, taping or by any information storage retrieval system without the written permission of the author except in the case of brief quotations embodied in critical articles and reviews.

This book is a work of non-fiction. Unless otherwise noted, the author and the publisher make no explicit guarantees as to the accuracy of the information contained in this book and in some cases, names of people and places have been altered to protect their privacy.

WestBow Press books may be ordered through booksellers or by contacting:

WestBow Press
A Division of Thomas Nelson & Zondervan
1663 Liberty Drive
Bloomington, IN 47403
www.westbowpress.com
844-714-3454

Because of the dynamic nature of the Internet, any web addresses or links contained in this book may have changed since publication and may no longer be valid. The views expressed in this work are solely those of the author and do not necessarily reflect the views of the publisher, and the publisher hereby disclaims any responsibility for them.

Cover images used according to permissions, courtesy of:
Judge Deborah, painted by Dutch artist, Jack Staller
Catherine Booth, Salvation Army Intl. Heritage Centre, London
Mother Teresa painting by Atula Siriwardane (Sri Lanka), courtesy of Amar Chitra Katha, Mumbai, Maharashtra, India
The writings of Mother Teresa of Calcutta © by the Mother Teresa Center, exclusive licensee throughout the world of the Missionaries of Charity for the works of Mother Teresa. Used with permission.

NIV: Scripture quotations taken from The Holy Bible, New International Version® NIV® Copyright © 1973 1978 1984 2011 by Biblica, Inc. TM. Used by permission. All rights reserved worldwide.

NASB: "Scripture quotations taken from the (NASB®) New American Standard Bible®, Copyright © 1960, 1971, 1977, 1995, 2020 by The Lockman Foundation. Used by permission. All rights reserved. www.lockman.org"

ISBN: 978-1-6642-4363-7 (sc)
ISBN: 978-1-6642-4364-4 (hc)
ISBN: 978-1-6642-4365-1 (e)

Library of Congress Control Number: 2021917630

Printed in the United States of America.

WestBow Press rev. date: 11/30/2021

What People Are Saying

"No one is better equipped to write a book on church mothers than is Rev. Gwen Ehrenborg. She has not only extensively studied these women, but has also lived them in her dramatic performances. Well researched, the book is engaging and accessible to those in ministry as well as lay people, male and female. Indeed, this is a volume for men as much as it is for women. We all expand our horizons when we come to grips with the lives of our fascinating church mothers."

Ruth A. Tucker, Ph.D.

Seminary professor and author of *Extraordinary Women of Christian History, Dynamic Women of the Bible, Katie Luther,* and more titles

"I am much impressed by the evidences of careful scholarship in Gwen Ehrenborg's work; and I can certainly commend the material on Katie Luther and Susanna Wesley—there being a not irrelevant tie between them created by John Wesley's evangelical conversion whilst listening to the reading of Martin Luther's Preface to St. Paul's Epistle to the Romans."

John Warwick Montgomery, Ph.D.

Professor Emeritus of Law and Humanities, University of Bedfordshire, England/UK; Professor-at-Large, 1517: The Legacy Project, Irvine, CA, USA; author, director, International Academy of Apologetics, Evangelism and Human Rights, Strasbourg, France

"*Our Church Mothers* is a significant read that I highly recommend. I was drawn in from the very first paragraph. The diverse group of women chosen provide substantial material, not only for learning history, but also for deepening one's faith. Hearts will grow warm in reading, and lives will be transformed. Rev. Gwen, as author, has an engaging way of writing. She is so good that I find myself wanting her to write about more and more women so that I might be edified by their stories and grow in faith."

Bishop Mary Ann Swenson
United Methodist Church

"As a former professor of church history, I'm well aware that churchwomen get little attention in most texts on the subject. *Our Church Mothers* gives readers a chance to "meet" and appreciate seven faithful women whose service to the people of God spans over three millennia. Author Gwen Ehrenborg's choice to introduce us to them by composing letters from them—based on serious historical research—makes her book not only pleasurable but also inspiring. It deserves wide readership."

E. Calvin Beisner, Ph.D.
Founder and national spokesman for the Cornwall Alliance for the Stewardship of Creation; Christian scholar, apologist, seminary professor, author, editor

"I commend Rev. Ehrenborg for her wise choice of avoiding the theological debate of the role of women in the church and the limits often placed on them and focusing rather on the common thread that united these church mothers in their desire to please God and serve their fellow human beings. Pastor Gwen skillfully identifies the unique qualities of the seven church mothers presented in the book that facilitated each of them to leave obscurity to find their influential place in the Body of Christ. Recognizing the sovereignty of God, these women, working with various coworkers, dramatically influenced the course of church history. It was a joy and pleasure to discover the many secrets that each of these leaders utilized to bear lasting spiritual fruit. I heartily recommend this exciting book to men and women alike, who are inspired by God's faithfulness in working through those who wholeheartedly yield themselves to Him."

Frank Hendrickson, Ed.D.

former professor, Oral Roberts University; school administrator, Kenya, Congo; professor of ESL and Bible, Bangkok, Thailand

"I am impressed by this unique book of fictitious letters from saintly women of faith, including two of my favorites, St. Clare and St. Teresa of Calcutta. Based on solid history, the author creatively pens would-be letters directly from these saints and saintly Catholic and Protestant women of God in a way that touches everyone across church boundaries today. It is very creative and effective in bringing these women to life for the modern reader today. I am happy to endorse this most creative work."

John Michael Talbot

Grammy- and Dove-Award-winning Christian recording artist, author, and founder, spiritual father, and general minister of the Brothers and Sisters of Charity, Little Portion Hermitage

"Most students of early church history are familiar with the early church fathers. Only in the last few decades has there been a growing interest and study of the important contributions of women of faith in the history of the church. In an area long neglected, Reverend Ehrenborg has provided just such a resource to help foster our appreciation for how God has long used both men and women to build his kingdom, with seven enlightening vignettes on women who have shaped church history in unique and enduring ways."

Jan Fekkes III, Ph.D.

Adjunct associate professor of NT, Fuller Theological Seminary

"Take a walk through history with a fresh and accurate examination of the experiences and feelings of seven exceptional Christian "mothers" who were totally dedicated to Jesus Christ and the promotion of His Gospel. They come alive in this book as living witnesses to our own heritage as men and women of faith. We read of steadfastness, courage, and dedication to

Christ as trustworthy examples for living in our present day. The author, Rev. Ehrenborg, has researched these historical figures in the homelands of their birth and imparts not only facts but also the very essence of their personalities. You will be encouraged reading these valuable accounts of women in history—women well worth knowing!"

Majors Clifford and Susan Jones
Western Territory Salvation Army, Stanwood, WA

"As I read this book, I felt that I was in the very presence of these women. It was as if each woman was in my living room talking directly to me about her days with God and encouraging me to keep serving him despite any obstacles I might face. I recommend this book to everyone who sincerely wants to live a life with great courage and effectiveness like these trailblazers of the faith, our church mothers."

Leah Switzer
Public relations consultant; founder, Cal-Pac UMC
Abolition Human Trafficking Task Force

"Catherine Booth comes to life in a most moving way. Pastor Gwen's careful research makes the Army's story compelling to follow, and most of all, she has caught the spirit of the Army Mother."

Frances Dingman
Salvation Army historian of the Western Territorial Headquarters

"Rev. Ehrenborg's characters are historically accurate, yet very much in touch with the realities of living for Christ today. They possess a balance of both strength and tenderness."

Martha Miser, Ph.D.
Professor, Whittier College, Whittier, California

"It's time for women in ministry to step out and take a leadership position confidently, standing alongside our church mothers throughout biblical history. Gifted and called women need to hear a voice that speaks truth over their calling and identity. This book will inspire a new generation of both young women and men to boldly face the future of kingdom work to the Glory of God."

Susan K. Abrams
AICI, Corporate Icon; author of *The Professional Image Toolkit*;
president, Supporting Women In Ministry International

To my beloved husband Rev. Todd Ehrenborg
in
"the School for Character"
(what Martin Luther called marriage)

Contents

Introduction

Church Fathers and Church Mothers

All through church history, the issue of the roles of men and women within the church setting have been observed, discussed, and also questioned. Even now in the twenty-first century, there is a wide range of positions as to how much a woman can serve in a leadership capacity. Ephesians 4 identifies leadership offices that Christ has given to the church as apostles, prophets, evangelists, pastors, and teachers, all to prepare God's people for works of service and build up the Body of Christ in unity. Rather than engaging in theological debate on if, when, or how women can fulfill these roles of leadership, I present a different approach. This book offers true-life stories of historical women who passionately loved God and found personal ways to serve him, their faith community, and their society as well. Follow how they quite naturally used their feminine characteristics, so often associated with motherhood, and successfully inspired other believers to follow their lead and, in so doing, dramatically influenced the course of church history.

In my first semester of seminary, I signed up for a church history class. Upon entering the classroom, I noticed a chalkboard filled with thirty names, only two of which I recognized. The first course assignment was to choose one church father listed on the board and give an oral report of his life and contribution to Christianity. That was the first time I ever heard the term "church fathers," but it would not be the last. Being an enthusiast of history and biographies, I studied the fathers with curiosity and great admiration. When I discovered Dr. Martin Luther had a wife, I began to wonder who Christianity's church mothers were. I believed there are many women of faith throughout Judeo-Christian history who would qualify for inclusion into such a category, but I have not personally heard this term in anyone's conversation.

What are the qualifications for being acknowledged as a church father? Certainly, no committee sat to create a formula for inclusion based on their contribution to the establishment of accepted theology and the *Canon of the Bible*.[1] Yet there is widespread acceptance of certain men as church fathers in Christianity's formative centuries.

Men led the church admirably in its early years, in line with the teaching and social structures of the times. Women were not recognized as leaders or theologians in the early centuries, so no attempt at finding counterparts of the same kind for church mothers was necessary. However, women have kept the faith and passed it on in numerous authentic ways: nurturing, counseling, organizing, creating, leading, and teaching.

The seven women recognized in this book were influential leaders chosen for their intense faith, godly character, and unique contributions to the direction of the church. God raised them up at crossroad moments spanning the history of his people, from ancient times to the present.

These women never attempted to replace male roles; instead they worked alongside their male counterparts as wives, mothers, helpmates, fellow disciples, and co-laborers in the vineyard of the Lord. Such team ministries can be seen in the New Testament in the lives of Phoebe with Paul (Ro 16:1,2), Priscilla with Aquila (Ro 16:3, Ac 18:1–4), Junias with Paul (Ro 16:7), and Tryphena and Tryphosa (Ro 16:12). The women leaders profiled in this book stand on their own accomplishments yet also worked in concert with their own co-laborers who were either husbands, mentors, children, and even a chosen warrior.

Wide Diversity among the Women

It is an engaging exercise to compare and contrast these seven women, because they lived in different centuries, countries, and cultures; spoke different languages; and had various levels of education. Despite never meeting each other, they have much in common. Quite naturally, they differed in temperaments, abilities, and spiritual giftings. Judge Deborah and Catherine Booth were both leaders of armies that were different in nature, one literal and one figurative. Deborah's soldiers fought their enemy, the Canaanite army, with weapons of copper swords and leather slings. Catherine's soldiers fought the enemy of poverty with the weapons of food, medicine, and the sword of the Spirit, God's Word. None of the women were born into abject poverty, but Mary of Nazareth, Katie Luther, and Catherine Booth lived very near that level. In an interesting reversal, Lady Clare and Mother Teresa intentionally chose to live in a state of poverty for the sake of identification with the poorest of the poor, in order to share the Gospel with them. Not surprisingly, these women also varied in their physical strength. Apparently, Deborah, Katie Luther, Mary, and Mother Teresa lived with good health and strong constitutions, while St. Clare and Catherine Booth lived most of their years affected, but undaunted, as semi-invalids. Some of these seven exceptional women were free to try new things, while others felt trapped inside the confines of the strict rules of proper behavior expected in their little sphere of society. The women who felt trapped would have identified with the feelings of the Englishwoman Florence Nightingale, who lived in the mid-1800s. Upper-class women in this time were seen as ornaments in the master's house. Miss Nightingale bewailed the expectation to have something respectable and lively to say morning, noon, and night. At the age of thirty, she wrote in her diary, "What is to become of me? I see no future but death!" Just as she eventually found her purpose in the world as the Lady with the Lamp during the Crimean War,[2] each of the seven women presented here managed to step out of obscurity when they saw a need and chose to fill it.

Several of the women were married and had children. Susanna Wesley, Katie Luther, and Mary of Nazareth, with dedicated hearts for God, centered their daily lives on caring for their own families. Two of the seven never married: twelfth-century Lady Clare of Assisi and twentieth-century Agnes Gonxha Bojaxhiu, known to the world as Mother Teresa. While Mother Clare and Mother Teresa took similar vows of poverty, chastity, and obedience, Clare remained cloistered for four decades, whereas Mother Teresa traveled the world. Yet they each held above all else the spiritual care of their sisters, always pointing them toward an intimate love of God and care for all humanity. In spite of these differences, all seven were directly addressed as "Mother," either by their birth children or by others due to spiritual relationships.

Judge Deborah was the wife of Lapidoth and is believed to have been barren. Nevertheless, as leader of her nation, she was respectfully called a mother of Israel. After Lady Clare and Sister Teresa founded their own monastic orders, they nurtured many daughters and sons in the faith. They were lovingly identified in the hearts of their children as their spiritual mother and were always addressed by that title.

Living a life dependent on God, each one of these mothers faced obstacles set before them with an undeterred forward stride, according to the perceived need of their day. They were not super human but ordinary women who had their faults, hardships, and heartbreaks. St. Clare of Assisi went to extremes, with long fasts that degraded her health. For almost thirty years, she spent much of the time in bed as an invalid. Mother Teresa prayed regularly, several times a day, and traveled the world with a smile on her face, and in spite of many years of difficulty, darkness, and spiritual challenges, she resisted living by her feelings and chose instead to cling to Jesus in pure faith and total dependence on him.[3]

Susanna Wesley suffered in her marriage with an often absent and obstinate clerical husband, who was disliked by parishioners, who viciously harassed their family. A friend said Katie Luther was stubborn, while others identified that characteristic in her as determination, tenacity, and reliability.

Two Common Threads

It is most enlightening to discover what these women had in common in spite of their vast differences. Though these mothers have been described with words like indomitable, astute, capable, resourceful, resolute, compassionate, and authentic, it can be stated above all that God was each woman's first love. They lived for God, to serve, worship, glorify, and know him. Observing their daily activities, it can also be said that they also loved God's children, their fellow human beings. Love for God was carried out in caring for others, often giving up their own comfort, wealth, position, or prestige. One Christmas Eve in England, the Salvation Army was given the honor of sending a speech around the world on the newly invented wireless radio. Due to technical problems occurring at the appointed hour for the broadcast, William and Catherine Booth's first Christmas message to their international Army outposts had to be shortened to only one word. What single word could be an encouraging sermon to their worldwide Soldiers of the Cross? They sent out the word: "Others." By this single word, the Salvationists listening would have known their co-founders' meaning. They were to assist others to find God and know him better so they also could become redeemed disciples of Jesus Christ. A Christian woman and mother is honored for her ability to nurture and care for the others within her particular sphere of influence.

Not one of these energetic women considered themselves anything like a feminist, but rather as a person who happened to be a female. The wives were partners and co-laborers with their husbands, content to take on different roles and responsibilities. In spite of the cultural norms for the women in their community, they were able to break through imposed restrictions and allow themselves to speak, write, and act with their own voice for the sake of the Gospel. They each tried something new, sometimes even radical, which affected the course of Christian history. By doing so, they found themselves on the cutting edge of what the Spirit of God was doing within the church.

Individual Achievements Making Crossroads in History

Overviewing the accomplishments of these remarkable women, they accepted their divine calling (God's planned purpose for their lives) in their appointed time, fulfilling God's plan for the church and humankind. In chronological order, we acknowledge each woman's unique contribution that informed the path of Christian practices in the development of the church. Discover for yourself the process that enabled them to achieve their influence and power as you read these incredible stories.

Judge Deborah

Deborah, of the village of Shiloh in Ephraim, is the ideal forerunner of feminine leadership for the Christian church. All women believers in the Judeo-Christian faith would learn from the ancient Holy Scriptures of this accomplished mother in Israel's history. Ask someone today to give an example of a famous woman leader in world history, and you will most assuredly hear the name Joan of Arc. Inspired by God, she led an army into battle and died a martyr for her cause and country. Judge Deborah, also directly inspired by God, called together an army from her nation and went to the battlefield with them. As Israel's prophetess during the turbulent era of the judges, she brought peace to the Israelite tribes and ruled as the solo judge and leader for forty years. Deborah stands out as Israel's only female national leader in ancient times. Beloved for her wise rule, she was called a mother of Israel. She is also credited with composing the first known poem recorded in world history.

Mary of Nazareth

When the fullness of time had come and all the prophetic circumstances of the Messiah's arrival converged, God chose Mary, a poor virgin in an obscure village. She would provide the home for the Son of God, who would be nurtured to manhood at her side. For over two millennia, Mary has been revered as the ideal model of motherhood and blessed among all women (Lk 1:42). No one else takes her place for her accomplishment of raising all her children to faith in God's redemptive plan—which she saw fulfilled by her firstborn son, Jesus. In her youth, Mary had found favor with God, and no woman could ask for more. In gratitude, she heard the prophetic words from her cousin Elizabeth, who proclaimed of her, "Blessed is she who has believed that the Lord would fulfill his promises to her" (Lk 1:45). Having said yes to God's plan for her life, she never wavered from her resolve, even though it included much suffering. If anyone can be identified as a church mother, it would be Mary, who was also present in the Upper Room when the church was born on the Day of Pentecost (Ac 2).

Mother Clare

When the wealthy Lady Clare was born, the Western Church of Europe, ruled by Rome, was in a terrible state of depravity being fed by wars, politics, and corruption. Inspired by a fellow citizen, Francis of

Assisi, Clare embraced a simple life of piety and poverty. She became the first woman in history to not only found but also write a unique "Way of Life" for a monastic order.[4] During her time, convents were comfortable places for pious noblewomen who continued to have servants and property. Clare's vision was different. She created a monastery that would neither own property nor make money. Inside, all classes of women lived as equal Sisters, serving each other. Mother Clare's Sisters, named the "Poor Ladies," were able to sustain their life of holiness, prayer, and service that continues to this day. A counselor and spiritual advisor to several popes, Clare, along with her counterpart Francis, brought much of the church of their day back to its roots and original purpose. Their actions counteracted much of the corruption and lethargy that had previously damaged the effectiveness of the church.

Katie Luther

In the age when Katharina Von Bora met the Great Reformer, Martin Luther, one-third of the populace of Europe was living in monastic life because the church taught it was the surest way to heaven. Luther's theology challenged so many teachings emanating from the Papal State that monks and nuns left their cloisters, with the understanding that celibacy was no better than marriage. Many saw the marriage of Katie and Martin, an ex-nun and an ex-monk, as a great scandal. Others saw the marriage as a true example of the freedom there is in the Christian life. Mrs. Luther's showed superior talent in managing finances over a bustling household of six children and an average of twenty houseguests a day, and she gave her husband twenty of the happiest and healthiest years of his life. Katie's marriage, during the dangerous times of the Peasant Wars (1524–25),[5] set the precedent for the next five hundred years of a married clergy for future Protestants.

Susanna Wesley

Born in one of the city rectories a few years after the Great Fire of London (September 1666), Susanna Annesley grew up her clergy-father's favorite, learning both Greek and Latin at his side. Intelligent and capable, she found herself married and isolated most of her adult life, in the farmlands of a reclaimed swamp. Giving birth to nineteen children in a twenty-year span (including two sets of twins), she suffered two house fires that left her family in constant debt, with little money for daily necessities. She saw herself as a simple clergy wife and mother, yet the mundane confinement of the four walls of the rectory included a methodically structured homeschool for her children. Her curriculum included systematic Bible study, reading, prayer, instruction, and an hour per week spiritual conversation with each of her children alone. Susanna's sons, the Revs. John and Charles Wesley, established the Methodist Movement in the British Isles that expanded over to the Second Great Awakening in America (1795 to 1835).[6] John ascribed his mother as the inspiration for the organization of his revival movement when she broke with tradition and led both men and women parishioners in joint Bible study, worship, and prayer meetings. These regular kitchen meetings in Susanna's home became the design for the classes and societies that would sustain the Methodist movement that exploded around the world.

Catherine Booth

It has been said, "Sometimes you don't find a career; a career finds you." In the early Industrial Age (1760 to 1840), the circumstances of life in the East End of London were so deplorable that Charles Dickens was moved to write his revealing novels about them. When the newlywed evangelist team of William and Catherine Booth observed the depravity and hopelessness of the souls living in the slums of the glorious Victorian Age (1837–1901), they found their lifelong mission. They would share the Good News of Christ with these forgotten people. Their quest would become an army of lads and lassies who preached salvation to the masses, accompanied with gifts of food, shelter, and clothing. The Salvation Army became the first Christian organization to recognize the biblical right of women to preach the Gospel, largely due to the teaching of Catherine, who was a brilliant published author and biblical scholar. At one point in the Army's growth, there were more women preachers and pastors than men. General Booth was once asked why he let women preach instead of men.

He shot back his answer: "Because, Sir, some of my best men are women!"[7] Aside from scholarship and writing, Mrs. Booth, the Army mother, was a devoted wife, highly sought-after preacher, and Bible teacher. She did all this while being a hands-on mother of nine children, all of whom served the Army, with one daughter eventually becoming its first female general.

Mother Teresa

While the Salvation Army found its way around the world and continues its work in Christ's name to this day, Jesus said the poor would always be with us. It is shocking, with numerous humanitarian organizations and advances in science and technology, that millions are still trapped in poverty. A simple Albanian nun serving as a principal of a Catholic girl's school in Calcutta saw the effects of World War II on her city and had to do something. Mother Teresa left her comfortable convent to live out her vow of poverty among the "poorest of the poor." This move evolved into the founding of a new Catholic Order, the Missionaries of Charity, which today has nine branches.[8] From a borrowed single-room apartment, she and a dozen fellow sisters began the first known "Home for the Dying." They let the once forsaken, living on the streets, die with dignity under a shelter while being truly cared for and loved. From that beginning, the little girl, Agnes Gonxha Bojaxhiu, became a household name in the world, Mother Teresa, identified as the greatest humanitarian of the twentieth century. As such, this Nobel Laureate influenced governments, addressed millions of people in speeches, met with world leaders, and even stopped fighting in war zones. Overall, she inspired in the name of God, not only churches and religions, but also nations to re-evaluate the care of the poor within their borders.

Women of Letters

At the 1972 Commencement Ceremony of Oral Roberts University, Kathryn Kuhlman, the celebrated American evangelist known for her healing ministry, was given an honorary degree of doctor of humane letters. Ms. Kuhlman was not famous for writing books and certainly not actual letters. Instead, the honorary doctorate was a degree of appreciation for her life's work of preaching the Gospel of Jesus Christ and changing the life, body, soul, and spirit of countless individuals. Many colleges in the United States and other countries recognize excellence by awarding honorary degrees to individuals with long records of achievements. The Doctorate of Humane Letters is one such degree, usually given in recognition of accomplishments in the humanities, literature, religion, or philanthropic work. The women whose stories are presented in this book would each qualify for an honorary degree of humane letters for their lifetime of service to the Judeo-Christian family. Yet none of these remarkable personalities envisioned a future for themselves with any fame or recognition in mind.

Mary of Nazareth never learned to read or write, according to the custom of her day, because only boys were taught these skills. Nevertheless, scribes listening to her personal stories eagerly wrote down her words. These records echo down the centuries like sermons for all of Christ's followers to read. Similarly, Judge Deborah of the Old Testament had her words documented on a scroll by a scribe who penned her experiences for posterity, including her Song of Victory, recorded in the fifth chapter of Judges. In contrast, Susanna Wesley was a careful correspondent, writing long letters to her three sons away at school, exhorting them to righteous living. Twice a day in study and prayer, she wrote in her private journals for her own exhortation, transcribing the spiritual truths she gleaned from Holy Scripture. St. Clare of Assisi seldom wrote lengthy letters, but when she wrote correspondence, her content often changed the opinions of friends, three of whom were ruling popes. Katie Luther stayed too busy to write many letters, overseeing the needs of a huge household in constant flux. She left that task to her husband, who is believed to have written more letters than any one person in history, and all with a goose pen. Dr. Luther's writings fill forty-four hefty volumes of print. Unlike Katie, Mrs. Booth's mastery of the English language is evident in her many highly praised sermons, published books, and articles. Mother Teresa resisted requests to write an autobiography, but wrote daily, answering requests to speak or start a new work for the poorest of the poor somewhere in the world. Whatever letters remain today from these seven women open the door for us to peek inside their innermost thoughts and hearts.

Church Mothers Address Us Today in the Following Letters

What would these Christian mothers say to their descendants and all Christian believers in the centuries after them, if they had the opportunity to give advice and share their personal faith? The best way they could accomplish such a task would be to put their thoughts and desires to pen and paper. It's a common practice for people anticipating death to leave their advice and requests for loved ones as a farewell address in a private letter. We are fortunate that we have many personal letters, eyewitness accounts, and biographies by friends and colleagues of these seven forebears of the faith that give us clear pictures of their character, thought, feeling, belief, and practice. From these primary and secondary sources, we can faithfully surmise what they would say to the church family living today.

The question is sometimes asked, "Why study the past?" The simple answer is another question: "How do you know where you are going, if you do not know where you've been?" While in Wonderland, Alice found herself at a fork in the road, with no sign pointing either way. She hesitated, not knowing which way to go.

Suddenly, a purple-stripped Cheshire cat appeared in a tree, so she asked him, "Which path should I take?"

"That depends on where you want to go," he advised her.

"I don't know," she answered.

"Then it doesn't matter which way you go," he replied, grinning.

As you can see, we need information to make wise decisions. We look back to the past to learn lessons from others, avoid making their same mistakes, and save time and effort in the process. Ancient wisdom tells us we need not reinvent the wheel, but we can build upon the past for a better future.

If these church mothers could somehow meet us, they certainly would want to do so. If they had been asked to give us their testimony and vision for Christian disciples in the future, they would stay true to what they practiced and believed. If they could communicate with us today, they would befriend us and encourage us from their own experiences. They do that now, in the spirit of Christian fraternity through the ages. The experiences of these mothers of the Christian church, of our common humanity, will encourage us to believe we can achieve whatever the Holy Spirit places on our hearts to do. Surely, we must take to heart the last recorded words of Mary of Nazareth, spoken to the servants at the wedding in Cana about Jesus. It is short but profoundly true: "Do whatever he tells you to do" (Jn 2:5, paraphrased).

A Mother of Israel

Introducing Judge Deborah

Over three thousand years ago, God brought his Chosen People into the Promised Land. However, instead of following him with their whole hearts, they began to take on the ways of the local inhabitants and worshiped their foreign gods and idols. The book of Judges explains, "In those days there was no king in Israel; every man did what was right in his own eyes" (Jdg 17:6 NASB95). This so grieved the heart of God that he let the enemies of his Covenant People oppress them while he raised up judges to lead them. These leaders did significantly more than judges do today. They were more like chieftains, heroes, and deliverers in times of war. But no matter how good the judges were, the people returned to their corrupt and idolatrous ways as soon as each judge died.

In the midst of this turbulent time, the Lord raised up a prophetess called Deborah, whose name means "honeybee."[1] Industrious and intelligent, she knew the awesome responsibility of conveying God's Word to his people. Historically named "the most courageous of the Judges,"[2] Deborah led Israel successfully for twenty years during one of the most oppressive captivities imposed by their enemies. She instilled confidence in her people and settled their disputes, not in an inner courtroom of a palace, but under a palm tree bearing her name. With unwavering tenacity in the revealed will of God, she rallied an army of ten thousand men to face a powerful opponent against overwhelming odds.[3] After leading a victory over the nation's enemy, she ruled the land with equity, which resulted in success and peace for an additional forty years.

Her prominence as a ruler in ancient Israel is rather remarkable, being the only woman to hold the highest leadership position. Affectionately called "a Mother of Israel" (Jdg 5:7), Deborah of Ephraim's life illustrates an important truth. One did not become a judge by birth like the Patriarchs, Abraham, Isaac, and Jacob. Least of all, no one would ever expect a woman in Deborah's day to be in such a role. However, despite the male-oriented society, this woman with exceptional personal and spiritual qualities did rise to leadership. It is not gender, but a close relationship with God and an anointed call to ministry that makes a spiritual leader, as was the case with Deborah.

Deborah can be remembered as the woman whose faith in God became the strength of Israel. This is reflected in the victory song in Judges chapter 5 that she and her people sang after a battle with the Canaanites. The poem is regarded as one of the finest of ancient Hebrew poetry and believed to be the oldest as well.[4] This song of praise, attributed to Deborah, reveals she seeks no personal acclaim but magnifies the Lord for his miraculous acts in caring for his Covenant People. Over the centuries, women have looked to Deborah as a forerunner and powerful example of women's leadership capability and acceptance in roles of governance. Moreover, she inspired and led her nation in spiritual matters with a recognized divine authority by her peers, both male and female.

An Open Letter from Judge Deborah

Shalom, beloved ones, peace and joy!

I salute you in the name of the Most High, King of the universe. It is a privilege as a Jewess to address you servants of God, who are carrying on the torch of truth of our Eternal Father. *Toda, toda!* That is, thank you for your faith in *Elohim* (what we used for your English word for God) and your desire to worship him as a fellow believer in the one true God. I am pleased that you want to know of life in Palestine four thousand years ago by reading this correspondence. Naturally, your day is different from mine, but then, it must also be similar in many ways. Knowledge increases, times change, but the nature of human beings does not.

I would like to tell you that I lived during a golden age of Israel's history, like in the time of King David, who ruled a unified nation from his palace in Jerusalem, but I cannot. Instead of a golden age, my time was more of a dark age. In the three centuries after Joshua entered the Promised Land, enemies on all sides threatened the nation of Israel. To really understand the time in which I lived and the ways of the Hebrew people, I must give you a little background and explain one very important thing.

The Covenant Relationship

In the ancient Eastern world, individuals, tribes, and kingdoms related to each other by means of covenants. You have treaties today where nations make agreements to trade with one another or to be allies in case of war, but these are not the same as we had. A covenant is more like a contract with negotiated terms between parties. Covenants in our day were very different because they were serious binding agreements made for a lifetime, and once made, they could not be changed at all.[5] There were two kinds of covenants. The first was a parity covenant between equals; two people or two tribal chieftains agreed to be each other's ally.[6] When you entered into this covenant, you became the same as if you were brothers, literally blood brothers, because you were then seen as family.

Most covenants in ancient times were not parity but suzerain covenant contracts between unequal parties, usually a conquering king and his newly defeated subjects.[7] Naturally, there were no negotiations between the two of them. The king alone decided all the terms of the relationship. There were several distinct parts to this kind of binding agreement. The beginning preamble named the parties involved. The second part identified what the lord had done to deserve the loyalty of his subjects. The third element listed the specific requirements expected of the vassal subjects. They might give loyal service as farmers, laborers, or soldiers. The next section of the covenant consisted of what were known as blessings and cursings.[8] Blessings were the benefits that would be bestowed by the king upon his vassals, if they followed the stipulations of the covenant. They would be given land, or provisions, and the king's protection from an enemy. The cursings, on the other hand, identified what would occur should the subjects fail in their responsibilities. After the terms of the covenant were publicly announced, it was ratified in blood, usually with the sacrifice of a valuable animal, hence the identification as a blood covenant.[9]

My kinsmen had a very unusual covenant relationship that was unique and different from all other suzerain covenants, because it was with the King of the universe, the Blessed Elohim. Furthermore, we were not a conquered people, but a Chosen People (Dt 7:6), who were all descendants of one man. We were the children of Abraham, to whom our God had revealed himself many centuries earlier. *Adonai* (our word for the English word "Lord") promised the man named Abraham that he and his wife, Sarah, would have many descendants who would live in a land he would give them (Ge 15:5–7). Furthermore, through their family, God would bless the whole world (Ge 18:18). All Abraham had to do to receive these promises was to follow the Spirit of Elohim on a journey, raise a son he would be given, and worship the one true God. These three things were all he was asked to do, and he did them.

Centuries later and over three thousand years ago, Elohim renewed his covenant with the descendants of Abraham on Mt. Sinai. One day at Sinai, called the mountain of God (Ex. 3:1), the earth quaked beneath the feet of a multitude of our ancestors (Ex 19:18). Fire and lightning flashed through the immense cloud that enveloped the entire mountain (Ex 19:16). By these manifestations, Adonai was making his presence known to us. Out from the mountain came a great and terrible trumpet blast, which got everyone's complete attention (Ex 19:19). It was like the deafening sound of a great many blasts of a shofar, which is a ram's horn.

Summoned to the top of the mountain, Moses received Elohim's spoken and written renewal of his covenant with Israel. We obtained from the very hand of God the new requirements by which we would live in partnership with him, known by us as the Decalogue. This Mosaic Covenant (named after Moses) began by naming the two parties involved: "I am the LORD your God," explaining that this agreement was between Elohim and the kinsmen of Moses (Ex 20:2). The words that followed reminded us why we should recognize God's Kingship over us: "I am the LORD your God, who brought you out of Egypt, out of the land of slavery" (Ex 20:2). It was followed immediately with the first requirement: "You shall have no other gods before me" (Ex 20:3). More precise directives followed in this section of covenant terms.

A Covenant People

We were descendants of Abraham's family, but now this covenant made us God's family. Like a perfect Father, Elohim would provide for us, protect us, and always love us. We were to simply obey his precepts and directives. The third section of this covenant listed ten precise laws that were commandments, telling us how we were to live, the first four with our God, and the next six with each other (Ex 20:3–17). Does God know what we are like, or doesn't he? He knew these laws were necessary for us. They were Adonai's gift to us, because he wanted us to know his will without us having to guess what it was. This law structure would form us into a unique nation, as well as a holy family. If we would keep all these commandments, we would be his beloved children, and life would go well for us and for our children's children forever.

Adonai also gave further instructions as to how this covenant would be ratified. On a designated schedule, our priests would offer unto the Lord God animal blood sacrifices performed in the Tabernacle courtyard. The Holy One had first shown us his glory and presence by the means of fire, light, sound, and smoke, and now he was revealing himself to us even more through this written law. Moses received 613 more detailed commandments that he recorded in the Book of the Covenant, written in the first five books of the Old Testament, which we call the Torah. Furthermore, God included all the details essential for the sacrifices, the priest's duties, and the building of the Tabernacle, where God's Spirit would continually dwell with us.

The Promised Land

The promise of a new land in which to live was a vital part of God's covenant agreement with us. I want to share with you the Word of the Lord recorded in the book of Exodus about the particular land Adonai pledged to give us. He explained his plan with this declaration:

> I will establish your borders from the Red Sea to the Mediterranean Sea, and from the desert to the Euphrates River. I will give into your hands the people who live in the land, and you will drive them out before you. Do not make a covenant with them or with their gods. Do not let them live in your land or they will cause you to sin against me, because the worship of their gods will certainly be a snare to you. (Ex 23:31–33)

God affirmed his will concerning this land in the Holy Scroll of Deuteronomy:

> However, in the cities of the nations the LORD your God is giving you as an inheritance, do not leave alive anything that breathes. Completely destroy them—the Hittites, Amorites, Canaanites, Perizzites, Hivites and Jebusites—as the LORD your God has commanded you. (Dt 20:16–17)

This was God's instruction to all Israel. We were not only to live in the land provided for us, my friends, but we were to also replace the tribal people who were living there before us. They were to be driven out completely. This meant war against the Hittites, Amorites, Canaanites, Hivites, Jebusites, and the parasites (I tease). We were also instructed to tear down their pagan altars, not to make treaties with them, and to smash their idols. Most emphatically, we were not to worship or sacrifice to their gods, which were really not gods at all.

Why drive out the inhabitants of the Promised Land? It is difficult for many people to understand why Elohim would order the destruction of people and nations. I know this is a very hard thing to accept. You may ask,

"Why did it have to be total destruction? Why would a loving, Holy Lord require complete annihilation?" The answer is based on the relationship between God and man. The first covenant relationship God established was not with Abraham but was with the first man, Adam, and his wife, the first woman, Eve. The terms of that suzerain covenant, designed for all humankind, were based on obedience to God.

Since the creation of the world, God has been clearly seen in what has been made, therefore, there is no excuse for not recognizing and obeying him. Although men knew God, they did not honor him nor give thanks to him. Apart from God, men and women become filled with every kind of evil, and then corruption becomes all-pervasive. God finds it absolutely necessary to eliminate those individuals for the preservation of all humanity. Like a cancer in the body, the diseased portion must be cut out before it destroys the whole body. The Canaanite societies were so depraved that God knew they would not change and, therefore, could not be changed.[10]

God judged the peoples occupying the Promised Land, just as the people were judged in the days of Noah. The Hebrew armies in Canaan would be the means by which that judgment was carried out, just as the floodwaters had been the instrument of justice in Noah's time. A just God cannot let guilty ones go unpunished (Ex 34:7; Na. 1:3). Evil must be overcome, and one day still to come, it will be destroyed completely. Adonai tarries in this fulfillment so that no one should perish. Elohim's execution of justice is not only necessary, but also wholly fair. Adonai's very words recorded in the ninth chapter of the Torah scroll of Deuteronomy explains his divine will by saying to Israel:

> After the LORD your God has driven them out before you, do not say to yourself, "The LORD has brought me here to take possession of this land because of my righteousness." No, it is on account of the wickedness of these nations that the LORD is going to drive them out before you. (Dt 9:4)

Disobedience in Entering the Promised Land

My ancestors were told to drive out all the occupants of the land in which we would live. Yet once again, from the history chronicle known as the book of Judges that you have today, you can learn what the tribes of Jacob's sons actually did instead of obeying Adonai:

> But Manasseh did not drive out the people of Beth Shan or Taanach or Dor or Ibleam or Megiddo and their surrounding settlements. … Nor did Ephraim drive out the Canaanites living in Gezer. … Neither did Zebulun drive out the Canaanites living in Kitron or Nahalol, so these Canaanites lived among them. … Nor did Asher drive out those living in Acco or Sidon. … Neither did Naphtali drive out those living in Beth Shemesh or Beth Anath. (Jdg 1:27–33)

You can keep reading the Holy Scroll to learn more of the same, but I am sure you have recognized the pattern. Did the tribes do what they were told? Apparently not. There was no earthly king ruling all Israel at this time because the Lord himself was supposed to be our only King. Each tribe concentrated on protecting their own assigned land, rather than being united as a nation, obeying the Lord's directions. The consequences of this failure to submit to God's commands would cost Israel dearly for many generations.

You may well ask, "Why did the Israelites not do what the Lord told them?" In the main, it was just easier not to. We think, *This much is enough.* So often, we don't want to give the entire effort that's required. We fall short of complete obedience to God. We don't want to pay the full price. We settle for less and miss the mark of completion, and then, yes, we have sinned. For example, it looked much easier to take the sparsely populated hill country in Canaan, rather than battle against the stronger villages settled on the plains. After forty years of desert wandering, our forefathers did not know dry-land farming techniques, and their crops in the new land came up quite poor and scraggly. The Canaanites had lush grain fields. Consequently, Israel made treaties with the Canaanites, who taught them how to plant better crops. But the Canaanites also taught my kinsmen how to sacrifice to the fertility gods, who they claimed gave them abundant spring crops. I am grieved to relate that these rites of sacrifice included obscene sexual practices and even human sacrifices. Sadly, the covenant people, step-by-step, compromise-by-compromise, sank into idolatry and gross immorality. In my day, there was no king ruling in Israel, and as a result, everyone did what was right in his own eyes (Jdg 17:6, 18:1, 19:25).

The depth of depravity to which humanity can fall is very deep indeed. Disobedience to God was a part of our Hebrew history that we, unfortunately, forgot to remember. I believe this came out of a sense of shame as well as much pride. It was certainly not discussed among ourselves. Nonetheless, Elohim has always had a remnant of faithful followers who love and obey him.

My Childhood Family Life

My parents were among those who wanted to be faithful to the Blessed One of the universe. My dear papa was a gifted storyteller who knew well the Holy Torah. He was always reading it, quoting it, and sharing its stories. Neighbors and friends would come in the evenings and sit with our family to hear the history of our people. How I remember my kinsmen crossing the Jordan River, the trumpets blast and the shouts of the people at Jericho. Ancestors like Isaac and Rebecca, Rehab and Caleb, Mariam, Rachel, Jochebed, and Joseph were my heroes and unmet family members. Their life stories remained in my heart.

Our life as a particular tribal people turned daily around faith in Elohim. We were extremely fortunate as a family to live in the village of Shiloh, where the Tabernacle of the Lord was permanently pitched from the time Israel settled in the Promised Land.[11] Lying in a quiet uninhabited valley a day's journey above Jerusalem, Shiloh became the center of worship for our people until the days of Samuel.[12] The Tabernacle was first called the Tent of Meeting when God had shown my ancestors his Shekinah Glory, in a cloud by day and a fire at night. Using these two supernatural guides, God led our nation through the wilderness after we left Egypt.[13] God had revealed to Moses back on Mt. Sinai the exact design for the Tabernacle[14] (Ex. 25:2, 8–9, 40; Heb 8:5, 9:24). The Tabernacle was not where everyone gathered to meet with each other and hear a long, boring sermon (I jest, of course.) We were taught the things of Adonai in our homes. You came to the Tabernacle to draw closer to Elohim, as it was his visible dwelling place on earth among us.[15]

We took personal offerings to the priests so they could make sacrifices as acts of devotion and worship on our behalf, consistent with the purpose of the blood covenant. In the Outer Courtyard of the Tabernacle, the priests performed daily blood sacrifice offerings on the Brazen Altar for sins and grain offerings according to the requirement in the law.[16] Due to human sin and God's absolute holiness, he could not physically coexist with human beings (Ex 33:20; Isa 59:2). Communing with God was only possible if there was a proper separation (symbolized by the curtains in the Tabernacle) and a sanctified place of meeting, which was the Holy of Holies.[17] Only the High Priest could enter the Holiest place once a year, on the Day of Atonement, as the appointed mediator to offer sacrifices on behalf of the nation.[18] Even so, any person was welcome to come and pray at the porch entryway of the Tabernacle and pour out their heart to the Most High, as often as they wished.

At the Tabernacle

One of my earliest memories as a child was watching flickering light shadows from the Tabernacle Lampstand dancing on the tent walls as though they were happy to be there. Like them, I loved being there too. It was a place like no other. Here in prayer, one sensed an unexplainable closeness to the Lord. One's soul soared high to touch the beauty of Elohim. You felt confident, without any cares and only sweet contentment because Adonai was near. In my day, this permanent tent location was truly the central symbolic dwelling place of the Most High on earth. People not only brought offerings to the Tabernacle for the priests, they also brought supplies to the Levites, whose job it was to care for its maintenance. Somehow, when I was still young, I was given the task of making the flax wicks for the individual lamps of the Golden Lampstand. This job was considered a menial task because even a girl could do it, but to me, it was my great pleasure.

I could not light the lampstand myself because that was the task of the priests. They alone could enter the Inner Court Holy Place, which housed the Table of the Bread of the Presence,[19] the Altar of Incense, and the seven-branch Menorah Lampstand.[20] I would deliver our family's offering of olive oil and my flax wicks on a certain day and time so I could listen to the *rabboni* teaching the boys the Holy Torah, just outside the doorway. Only boys attended school because they had to learn to read and write so they could know the Torah and teach it to others when they became men. Girls didn't have time to learn these skills because we were busy helping our mothers. Women controlled all the processes by which the families were nourished and clothed: bread baking, cooking, gardening, spinning, and weaving.[21] Yet all the priests knew me, and in my twelfth summer, they made me the Keeper of the Tabernacle Lamps.[22] I would clean each clay lamp, oversee the olive oil supply, and make the wicks. When I finished, I would stay behind to pray and listen for the voice of my Lord.

Becoming a Prophetess

In that holy place, the presence of the Blessed One became familiar to me. The sweet voice of God was growing ever dearer in my soul. After I was married, the prompting of the Lord within my heart became so strong that I had to speak it aloud from the *Ruach* (breath) of Elohim. A few words would come clearly into my mind, and I would open my mouth to share them. Once speaking, more words would quite naturally flow forth. I knew they were not my words, for they were specific things that I did not know or could not have thought of myself. Of course, I kept watch to see that whatever was revealed through these particular words came to pass in time. I did not want to attribute to God anything that came from my own mind alone. We must know how to recognize the voice of the Lord, and we can certainly learn to do so.

I noticed people began to refer to me as a prophetess, and then the priests did as well. This was not my role to claim, but others to identify. I knew what this meant. Prophets in my day received direct revelation from Elohim, which enabled them to interpret the past, give direction in the present, and announce the future.[23] They spoke the words God gave them and served as his mouthpiece. It would be dishonorable to the Holy One for me to withhold or deny this role from false humility or feminine shyness. If I withheld this gifting, I would be disobedient to Adonai, and he would surely choose another to speak for him.

Women in Israel

I'm sure you know that all ancient civilizations were patriarchal, where the role of men was prominent. In most cultures, women were little more than property, not permitted to inherit possessions, and much less did they have any authority. Israel was patriarchal too, but our women were not oppressed like other societies. We were not inferior citizens, but were valued, respected, and appreciated. While a woman's life focused on the home, she had areas of responsibility and freedom. For example, we could have our own business, arrange our time and workers, and make independent decisions (Pr 31:10–31).[24] You may remember that Abraham told Sarah to do what seemed best to her in managing her servants (Ge 16:6). More importantly, we could worship Adonai, to serve him, and, if called by God, to prophesy for him, just like the men.

My beloved husband, Lapidoth, encouraged me to constantly seek the Lord and act upon whatever I heard from the Spirit of God. For many years, people from all the tribes of Israel journeyed through the hill country of Ephraim on their way to the Tabernacle for the different High Holy Days. Alongside the roadway between Ramah and Beth-el in Ephraim, there was a large date palm tree that offered shade from the hot sun, where travelers would rest (Jdg 4:5). It was a well-known landmark, so people looked for me there because they heard we lived nearby. They came seeking a word from Jehovah from a prophetess because our harsh overlord, Jabin the Canaanite king, was oppressing them (Jdg 4:2). Above all else, my kinsmen really wanted to be given some hope. I was glad to pray with them and relate any word the Lord had for them.

When the Israelites came to me, sitting under the mighty palm for counsel or justice (Jdg 4:5), my dear husband was often nearby. Lapidoth, whose name means "light; to shine forth,"[25] was the best of men, with a deep love for God (Jdg 4:4). He was a wise and humble man. He never put himself forward, as he needed no public acclaim, accolades, or fame. He was not threatened by my apparent visibility or activities as either a prophet or judge. With a watchful eye, he talked to the people while waiting for their turn before me. At the end of a long day, he would always walk me home safely, so I continually felt his caring presence. I could not have done what God asked of me, throughout my adult life, were it not for the support of my considerate husband.[26]

Judging under a Palm Tree

The Spirit of Adonai called me to speak his words as a prophet by giving me an extra measure of wisdom and knowledge for individuals. In time, this caused me to be recognized by the people as a *shaphat* or judge.[27] The word *shaphat* means "lawgiver"; however, not as one who makes laws, but interprets them. Such a one arbitrates disputes between parties and executes judgments. For many decades, I did this every day, except on the Sabbath. For those who came for civil justice, I used only one method in my deliberations. I listened to what each person had to say. Everyone seems to rehearse their speech before a judge. I did not ask when, where, why, or how much was this or that. I was not a woman judge like some judges you have today. There is one in particular. What is her name, Judge Julia or Judith? Oh, I remember now. Her name is Judy—Judge Judy. I did not judge like her. When I mention her in this way, my listeners start laughing. They must not understand her either. I have to tell you that I do not understand your judicial system. You have so many laws that change from place to place in your country. We had only one law—God's Law. Remember, there are 613 commandments compiled by Moses and recorded in the Torah: the books of Genesis, Exodus, Leviticus, Numbers, and Deuteronomy.

I would ask the litigants who came before me, "Why is this troubling you so? Is not Adonai aware of your situation? What does the Holy Law say for this matter? What can you do in this circumstance that would please the Most High?" It's always best if people come to a solution for themselves.

Finally, I prayed, asking the Holy One to bring to my mind appropriate words from Holy Writ that applied to the situation under consideration. After rendering a decision, I sent them home with this same instruction: "Before you do anything else, forgive the one who has offended you." For twenty years, I judged our people while King Jabin cruelly ruled over us.

When his occupation ended, it was so much easier to serve my people with complete justice.

Cycles in Time

Something very distinct happened during the first three centuries my kinsmen lived in the Promised Land that explains why we suffered so much. Hebrew society was tribal, with no capital city or central government.[28] There were often struggles between the twelve tribes and their neighboring peoples, particularly with the Canaanite city-states. Beyond these occasional conflicts, we had a cyclical pattern of behavior that repeated itself over and over again.[29] There were five distinct stages in each cycle. At first, we were obedient to God's law. But then, we allowed ourselves to selectively decide just how much we would obey Adonai's commandments. Before anyone suspected, we had turned away from God to worship idols, the one main thing we were instructed not to do.

When you cast off the ways of God, you put on the ways of man. Soon we were mired in the second stage of rebellious apostasy, where we as a people abandoned our faith and loyalty to Adonai. This behavior thrust us into the third stage of experiencing cruel oppression by our enemies. You see, when you leave God's service, you leave his protection. Left to our own devices, we suffered the natural consequences of our choices, and we could not save ourselves. We learned our heavenly Father disciplined those he loved by allowing us to fall under the reign of neighboring aggressors. After a time of enduring shame and misery, we did the only thing that was left to do. We cried out to Elohim in the fourth stage, which was a much-needed repentance on our part. God in his great mercy ended our foolishness by choosing a leader (judge) empowered by the Holy Spirit, whose strength and wisdom would direct us to the final stage of deliverance from our persecutors.

This was the consistent five-part cycle pattern: obedience, rebellion, oppression, repentance, and deliverance. Appreciating God's deliverance, we would happily worship our true Lord, and we were then back to an attitude of obedience. If only we would have stayed in that place. But with the passing of time, it's common to take things for granted and get tired or bored, lazy or prideful; we rebel, and a stage of apostasy easily develops. Then, oppression by other kings and forces brings about the need for heartfelt repentance. Finally, God mercifully responds to our helpless dilemma by delivering us once again. This cycle repeated itself twelve times in the long span of three hundred years.[30] We are slow to learn and quick to forget. Fortunately, Elohim, our eternal Judge, has always had a remnant of followers, and for their sake, he is gracious and merciful, slow to anger, and abounding in steadfast love. Blessed be his Holy name!

Breaking through One Lifetime Cycle

Next to the territories of Naphtali and Zebulun was the grand city of Hazor, where King Jabin ruled over a coalition of Canaanite city-state kings (Jdg 4:2). When I lived, the current inhabitants hated us Jews most intensely because our forefathers had conquered Hazor and burned it down years earlier (Jos 11:10–14). Over the ensuing decades, the Hazor dwellers grew strong, and with revenge in their hearts, they easily overpowered us in our state of apostasy. We were scared of their advanced iron weapons, carefully forged with secret techniques known only to them.[31] King Jabin cruelly ruled over us for twenty long years because we were afraid of his strength (Jdg 4:2, 3). Besides harsh, forced labor and high tributes, there were constant raids on our people. Our enemy burned our crops and our homes, our vineyards and orchards, sometimes just for sport.[32] Women were dishonored, children kidnapped and slain.[33] After years of intense suffering, my kinsmen finally cried out to Elohim in sincere repentance. Yet, at the same time, an epidemic of panic spread throughout my people. Jabin's forces were growing stronger under their brutal Commander Sisera, and an invasion was imminent. Nothing was being done in response to this threat.

My people were cowering in fear, and we were the People of the Covenant, the Blessed One's children. These people were my children, too. I felt like a mother to all Israel. In their minds, they were coming to ask me for justice. But like frightened children, they really wanted to be comforted, to be consoled, and to be told everything will be all right. Sadly, we were stuck in unbelief, laziness, and cowardice as a nation. The mother in me was ready to take action (Jdg 5:7). I was administrating justice within Israel one person at a time. But why should I not implement justice for all Israel all at once? Suddenly, I was energized by this insight. I was angry at the situation and infuriated at myself for waiting so long. God had saved my people from armies and kings and the great Pharaoh of Egypt in the past, and he could do it again. What did it matter if Jabin's army had iron chariots? So what if General Sisera was brilliant? Our God alone was enough for us. Hope welled up in my spirit, and I said, "God alone is enough! Whoever has God wants for nothing at all!"[34]

Time to Act as Codeliverer

Elohim is enough, beloved friends, so it was time to act. I went to prayer and asked the Lord, "Who can deliver us from our enemy?" One name came immediately to mind: Barak. He was the son of Abinoam, from Kedesh in the northern territory of Naphtali (Jdg 4:6a). Barak was a well-respected man and devout believer. Our men would follow him. I summoned him. Yes, friends, I do mean summoned. My messenger asked him to come to me. Dutifully, Barak left his home in Kedesh and came in haste, because he respected my leadership position in the nation, as prophet and judge.

As soon as we met, the Lord gave me a word for Barak:

> The LORD, the God of Israel, commands you: "Go, take with you ten thousand men of Naphtali and Zebulun and lead them up to Mount Tabor. I will lead Sisera, the commander of Jabin's army, with his chariots and his troops to the Kishon River and give him into your hands." (Jdg. 4:6–7)

Barak was shocked. This was a military commissioning from the Lord, with full battle plans, complete with a promise of victory. Barak was quite willing to fight, but his answer to me revealed a hesitation on his part: "If you go with me, I will go; but if you don't go with me, I won't go" (Jdg 4:8). I was taken back. His answer was conditional. When do we add conditions to obeying God? Oye. Why was he asking me, in particular, to go with him? I do not believe it was fear of fighting on his part. A prophet nearby could give him assuring words from Elohim in a difficult battle. He didn't need me for that because God had already promised him victory.

Now a choice was before me. My response to his request was immediate. I didn't think about how to answer; the words just came out of my mouth:

> Certainly I will go with you. … But because of the course you are taking, the honor will not be yours, for the Lord will deliver Sisera into the hands of a woman. (Jdg 4:9)

Two are better than one, and three are better still. Especially when one is the Lord of Hosts. A cord of three strands is not easily broken (Ecc 4:12). Barak and I needed each other. We would work side-by-side and be stronger together. He would hold the sword, and I would speak the word. Ours would be a partnership. Israel had no standing army to defend itself. Instead, each tribe would call up a militia of all able-bodied men. Occasionally, neighboring tribes would join together to fight a common enemy.[35] So Barak and I dispatched a request to all the Israelite tribes for men to gather to fight.[36]

My Fear and Return to Faith

After Barak and I parted from that first meeting, I had plenty of time to think about the answer I gave him. I may have promised to go to battle with him, but they were not my words; they came from the Spirit of Elohim. Women did not go to war and enter into battle. They could only wait in fear for the return of their warriors.[37] Yet, I was going with Barak. At first, I wasn't aware of being afraid, but then maybe I should have been. General Sisera's huge army included nine hundred chariots of iron that had sharp scythes attached to the hubs of their wheels that slashed foot soldiers violently.[38] His soldiers were equipped with iron spears and shields and wore protective iron helmets and coats of mail.[39] Our men fought on foot with bronze swords, copper daggers, slings, and short bows and arrows, just as they had back in the days of Joshua.[40] Some might have a wooden shield, but no one had a spear or armor (Jdg 5:8). Our fighters were volunteers, farmers and artisans, not a well-trained standing army.

Was I actually going to stand beside Barak on the battlefield, watching men die in violent combat? I prayed, "Lord Adonai, what is your purpose for me?" I began to wonder and fret, and then, I caught myself. "I have no reason to doubt or fear. Has not the Lord himself expressed his will to us? Was this not an answer to our prayers for deliverance?" I had to trust Adonai. I will say to the Lord, "He is my refuge and my fortress, my God, in whom I trust" (Ps 91:2). A song welled up in my spirit:

Only in God is my soul at rest, in Him comes my salvation.
He only is my Rock, my Strength and my Salvation.
Only in God is found safety, when my enemy pursues me.
Only in God is found glory, when I am found meek and lowly.
My Stronghold, my Savior, I shall not be afraid at all.
My Fortress, my Savior, I shall not be moved.[41]

The words of this song restored faith to me; it was a gift from God. It came not from my own spirit, but from his.

Battle Preparation on Mt. Tabor

Within weeks, Barak assembled his new troops of ten thousand men on the steep slopes of Mount Tabor, which guarded the northern entrance to the dry Plain of Esdraelon below.[42] I joined a small detachment of fighters whose intention was to lure Sisera's army to the Jezreel Valley of the Kishon River,[43] just as the Lord had prophetically directed (Jdg 5:15). We were the bait in a trap, and it would succeed. When Sisera was informed about the assembled Israelites from six different tribes,[44] he mustered his entire army, numbering a hundred thousand, and marched for the fertile valley, well-known as the Bread Basket of Israel.[45] From the vantage point of the crest of the mountain, the size of Sisera's professional units of slingers, archers, swordsmen, horsemen, and nine hundred gleaming chariots raised fear in the hearts of our men. The leaders, too, were hesitant. How would you respond to ten-to-one odds? They wanted to move to a better place of safety, or run home, even if it meant returning to bitter servitude. Can you blame them? Nevertheless, this fear was not right. Adonai had given orders to fight, with a promise of victory. Courage is necessary to win in war.

One night, the Spirit of the Lord awakened me from sleep with another commanding word for Barak. I sent the message to him, saying, "Go! This is the day the LORD has given Sisera into your hands. Has not the LORD gone ahead of you?" (Jdg 4:14). In spite of the great odds, the victory was as good as won, because God had said so! All Barak had to do was begin. Suddenly, at first light, his forces swept down from the hill, taking Sisera's men by complete surprise. Such a move was never expected. Battles are fought uphill, never downhill.

The Battle

Dark clouds had been gathering through the night, with churning winds. At Barak's charge, freezing sleet and hailstones burst over the great plain from the east (Jdg 5:20–22). As Sisera's men and chariots roared forward to engage our troops, the freezing rain whipped directly into their faces. The beating rain disabled Sisera's slingers and archers. Barak had the force of the driving storm behind him and was not hampered by wind. The Lord can preserve his own while judging others, dear ones. The Lord can protect you in the midst of a storm.

Our men pushed forward with renewed hope and vitality. They could see the elements lashing the enemy, and they all knew this was the providential help of Jehovah. The Canaanites were stunned. Their chief god was Baal, the god of storms.[46] Had he abandoned them? It was the middle of the summer, and this was a winter blizzard! Floodwaters from the mountain rains were now racing down the Kishon River, which ran through the valley plain.[47] The heavy downpour caused the river to rise swiftly and overflow its banks, turning the battlefield into sticky mud.[48] So violent was the current that the heavy iron chariots toppled and sank deep into the mud, killing their riders (Jdg 21, 22).

Almost immediately, Sisera's troops chose to retreat and run for their lives. What was expected to be a lengthy battle was won in lightning speed. Hallelujah! Praise be to God! It seemed to us that Jehovah was making an obvious and bold declaration that Baal was, in fact, not really the god of storms or any god at all. He was miraculously demonstrating that only he, the true Lord, was in control of heaven and earth.

The Woman Jael

When Sisera saw the battle was lost, he abandoned his grand chariot and ran for his life through the pounding rain (Jdg. 4:15). At the edge of the plain, he saw several tents belonging to the Kenite tribe, who were currently at peace with King Jabin. Standing by the doorway of the first tent was a woman named Jael, who was the wife of Heber (Jdg 4:17). He was not an Israelite but a distant relative of Moses's father-in-law, and Jael was sympathetic to the plight of the Hebrew people. Heber was not at home, but away on business. Jael suddenly saw a man, near breathless from exhaustion, stumbling towards her. She invited him into her tent, breaking with all custom. A man never entered the tent of a woman except her husband (Jdg 4:18). Inside, Jael recognized who he was by his armor and insignia. Sisera asked for water. She brought him warm goat's milk (Jdg 4:19). He drank heartily. He was cold and water-soaked; she brought him a sheepskin mantel. He needed rest; she covered him with a rug behind a curtain.[49] Sisera ordered her to stand by the doorway and say, "No," if asked if she had seen him (Jdg 4:20). Pleased with his hiding place, Sisera fell into a deep sleep. Now, when the great general felt most secure, he was the least safe.

Jael was not a soldier and had no premeditated plan for heroic action. But these circumstances set a choice before her. Like Rehab of Jericho, who hid two Hebrew spies upon her roof, she quickly decided where her loyalty lay. In her home was the enemy of God's people, the embodiment of evil power and oppression. She was not a murderer seeking personal revenge, but she knew what she must do for the honor of God and the deliverance of Israel. She picked up a hammer and a tent stake, tools she knew well. In nomadic tribes, it was the task of women to pitch and strike the tents.[50] Tent stakes, called pegs or pins, fastened the tent to the ground. They had to be sharp to penetrate the rocky soil of Palestine.[51] Trembling, Jael cautiously and quietly approached the general and struck the stake through his temple, killing him instantly (Jdg 4:21).

God's judgments are great and deep, fair, and right. Jael went outside her tent and waited for Sisera's pursuers. Barak himself was the first to arrive.

"'Come,' she said, 'I will show you the man you're looking for.' So he went in with her, and there lay Sisera with the tent peg through his temple—dead" (Jdg 4:22). Inside, Barak found the slain Sisera, and the prophetic words he had heard earlier came immediately to his mind: "for the LORD will deliver Sisera into the hands of a woman" (Jdg 4:9). Beside him stood the woman who would be praised for her bold and shocking act. The Blessed One's prophetic Word had been fulfilled, just as it had been revealed. Barak's men pursued the enemy until all were gone (Jdg 4:16). King Jabin's death followed soon after, and the Canaanite tribe was never to battle Israel again.

The Battle's Victory Song

After the battle, there was one important thing still to do. We had to express our thanksgiving and praise to Elohim for his mighty deliverance. We did not express our joy with a victory parade, playing games, or drinking wildly. We sang praises to the Lord, by recalling his exploits. The Lord put a song in my heart, just like he had done years earlier for Miriam after Israel's deliverance at the crossing of the Reed Sea, which over time many called the Red Sea. With unrestrained joy, the sister of Moses had picked up a tambourine and led the women dancing and singing about what the Lord had done. We all knew the song because Moses had written it down for us. Miriam spontaneously sang:

I will sing to the LORD, for he is highly exalted.
Both horse and driver he has hurled into the sea. …
He is my God, and I will praise him,
my father's God, and I will exalt him. (Ex 15:1, 2)

In a similar way, a scribe recorded all the lines that he heard being sung in our victory song, which reported the battle story. I am told it will be placed in the written chronicles of Judaic history, and you are welcome to sing it any time you wish.

The Enemy of God

Beloved friends, I must remind you that you, too, have an enemy that wants to destroy you. This adversary doesn't come against you like a soldier, with iron spear and sword. His weapons are accusations, lies, guilt, and fear. He is the enemy of God. Furthermore, he is the arch nemesis of all that God does and all that God loves, and that includes you and me. You are not meant to do battle with this enemy, because he is not human. He is a created spiritual being who led a heavenly revolt against God and was cast down to the earth, with a third of the angels following him. You cannot fight this old serpent with a sword or spear. Instead, you can protect yourself with the firm knowledge of truth, to let his fiery darts of lies bounce off you. Be clothed in faithful righteousness as you live in obedience to Elohim's commands. Never think of doing combat with this one we call Abaddon in our Hebrew tongue, which means "destroyer." Simply stand and resist his harassment and persecution. Resist him, and resist him, and he will tire and flee from you, disappointed that he has failed to sway you to his purposes. Yet be wise; he will try again another day.

So fill your lamps with oil, and trim their wicks, beloved of the Lord. Wait and watch in readiness, and remember, the Almighty One has gone out before you (Jdg 4:14). Blessed is the Lord our God, King of the universe!

I am not a priest, but I leave you with this ancient blessing, given first by Aaron, the brother of Moses and Miriam:

Birkat Hakohanim: "The Priestly Blessing" (Nu 6:24–26)

Yevarechecha Ado-nai, veYishmerecha.
The LORD bless you, and keep you.

Ya'eir Ado-nai panav eilehcha.
The LORD make his face shine on you,

Vichunehka:
and be gracious to you.

Yissa Ado-nai panav eilehcha,
The LORD turn his face toward you,

Veyaseim leccha shalom.
and give you peace.

Amen,
Judge Deborah

Conclusion

Judge Deborah, the mother of Israel of her day, knew God through an intimate relationship with the Lord. She was chosen to lead, endued with power and wisdom from God, by means of a special anointing of the Holy Spirit. In the Old Testament or Old Covenant days, the Holy Spirit's empowerment was given to an individual for a particular purpose, and when that purpose was accomplished, the Spirit would depart from them.[52] The Divine Spirit would abide with a person for the duration of their assigned service, but if they disobeyed, the Spirit would leave them, as God left Samson. The idea that the Holy Spirit would be given to every believer and abide with them, as happened on the Day of Pentecost, would not have occurred to Deborah's kinsmen.

Today, there is no tabernacle, no temple, and no single dwelling place for Elohim. Neither is there an altar on which to offer sacrifices or an Ark of the Covenant to house stone tablets of the law. These things are no longer needed because God came and dwells among us through Yeshua, the Christ, and we have beheld his Glory. Today, the Messiah tabernacles in the believer, by means of the Holy Spirit. Today, the law of God is not written on stone or papyrus, because it is written on the human heart (Jer 31:33). The fullness of the breath of God, the Holy Spirit of Elohim, dwells in his followers, not in part, but in full. It abides there. As a result, we are never alone.

Throughout Deborah's years of ministry, the Holy Spirit remained with her, so the Hebrew people knew God's will through her prophecies, adjudicated wisdom, and leadership. Another major way the Israelites related to God was through the terms of his suzerain covenants. When

God made the first covenant with all mankind in the Garden of Eden, the blessing he promised was the gift of eternal life. The curse for disobedience in this covenant was death. At Mt. Sinai, God renewed his covenant with the Hebrew nation. He gave to Moses the law of ten commanded requirements that revealed his will and showed how he wanted his people to live with him and with each other.

Over many years of repeated cycles and wars, the Mosaic Covenant of the law demonstrated that we could never be good enough to live a holy righteous life on our own. So God, in his great mercy, offered to all inhabitants of the world a new covenant. Through it, the promised Messiah would fulfill all the requirements of the old covenant law. This is Good News, the best news, referred to as the Gospel. Now there is a far better and new covenant than in the days of the judges (Heb 7:22), This better covenant fulfills all the old covenants' divine promises (Heb 8:6–8). Jesus the Savior, the Father's only begotten Son, took the curse for humankind's disobedience onto himself when he was crucified and died on a wooden Cross. With the shedding of his innocent blood, Jesus ratified this new and better covenant, once and for all. Paying the penalty for human sins with the giving of his life, Christ eradicated the curse of death.

Whoever believes and trusts in the Messiah, Christ Jesus, is sealed by his sacrificial act and receives eternal life. In so doing, our Savior has graciously transferred his righteousness to us when we believe and trust in him. This awareness would have utterly amazed Judge Deborah, who surely could not have imagined such a thing. God had indeed previously promised in Genesis 3:15 that he would send a Redeemer-Deliverer for those who believed in him and his promise. In Deborah's day, the prophets Daniel, Jeremiah, Ezekiel, and Isaiah had not yet been born, and yet later, when God would speak through them, he would enlarge upon his promise and reveal more about his eternal redemptive plan.

The New Covenant has only blessings because there are no longer any curses for those who trust Christ. The ancient Israelites could not have foreseen such a complete gift of mercy. Divine forgiveness and eternal salvation are certainly enough, but there is more. Additionally, Christ gives to each one who believes his authority to minister in his name and continue his mission of reconciling humankind to Almighty God (Mt 28:18–20). This is not only an honor, but also a humbling responsibility.

It is foretold through the Old Testament prophets that at the end of days, great armies will gather once again beneath Mt. Tabor in the Jezreel Valley, known as Armageddon. Nations will assemble to do battle with Israel in an attempt to seize Jerusalem. But with the sound of a mighty trumpet blast, Yeshua Messiah, the Prince of Peace, will return as King of Kings and Lord of Lords in glorious victory over all the enemies of God!

Observing the world today, there is cruel oppression and intense suffering in so many places throughout the world, just as there has been all through history. Holy Scriptures declare that there will be wars and rumors of wars, nation set against nation, tribe against tribe, and neighbor against neighbor. We all know something of the state of affairs in these dangerous and uncertain times we live in. Nevertheless, believers know of God's redemptive plan for the world that he set in motion since the Fall. Jesus intended to comfort all his followers when he said, "In this world you will have trouble. But take heart! I have overcome the world" (Jn 16:33).

Can you imagine the unspeakable joy in Deborah's heart if she could have known of God's solution for redeeming humankind? How could she conceive of the mystery of God himself entering the world by means of a baby; the Creator coming into his creation? The incarnation is truly a mystery that can only be comprehended by faith. Judge Deborah did not have to comprehend this reality in her lifetime, but several centuries after her, a young farmer's daughter did. Living in a tiny backwater town, the Holy Spirit of God touched another chosen Hebrew girl's life to fulfill his plan. She is best known today by her Greek name, Mary, who lived in the tiny village of Nazareth. Her life would be very different from Deborah's. In the next chapter, we'll to get to know her better and examine her unique and demanding lifetime experiences.

Discussion Questions

1. Deborah's era was described as a time when "everyone did what was right in their own eyes." In what ways could this be said about today's world?
   In contrast to this behavior, how can Christians today demonstrate a lifestyle where they individually and corporately do what is right in God's eyes?

2. In the patriarchal society in which Deborah lived, what reasons can you identify which explain why she was accepted as a female leader over her nation?
   What challenges do you see for women to be leaders in the church today?
3. In the ancient world, a woman's expected role was to be a mother and raise her children. Since Deborah was barren, how do you think she adapted to this expectation?
   In what ways have you been challenged by the expectations of others?
4. When all of Israel was reluctant to address heir enemy, Deborah courageously took charge inspiring her nation to action. When have you been courageously moved to action by divine inspiration?

The Mother of Jesus

Introducing Mary of Nazareth

As the mother of Jesus, Mary stands apart from all women throughout history. Painters, sculptors, musicians, and poets attempted to capture her significance by creating masterpieces esteemed by countless admirers. No other woman in the world has been so honored or revered as the embodiment of all that is fine and noble in womanhood, in spite of the fact that much of Mary's life remains a mystery. Holy Scripture recounts only a few significant events in her and Jesus's life together. We can only hypothesize about the unrecorded years by studying in depth the culture of the society and the era of which she was apart.

Mary's greatness had modest beginnings. She was a simple peasant girl living in Nazareth, a small farming village twenty centuries ago. *Miriam*, as she was called in Aramaic, grew up with no expectation of anything other than an ordinary life of work and faith in the Hebrew God, as taught to her by her devout parents. We can only admire her faith-filled and sincere acquiescence to the divine will of God when she answered the angel Gabriel with the words, "I am the Lord's servant. … May your word to me be fulfilled" (Lk 1:38).

Miriam raised her family in relative obscurity and had no wealth, no status, and no acclaim. She never exalted herself but suffered as much as any other woman. Yet her suffering changed into exceeding joy at her firstborn son's resurrection from the dead. We leave her presence in the book of Acts, numbered among the hundred and twenty gathered with the disciples. If we listen, we can hear Mary's last recorded words about Jesus in scripture at the wedding in Cana, echoing down through the centuries, admonishing us to "do whatever he tells you" (Jn 2:5).

An Open Letter from Mary of Nazareth

Shalom, brothers and sisters,

I write salutations to you in the hallowed name of Blessed *Adonai*, who alone is worthy of all praise! I am grateful to be asked to tell you of our life in Galilee and of what it was like to be the mother of *Yeshua*. I will share with you some of my recollections, thoughts, and feelings through my learned friend, Lucas, whose excellent hand will record my words. Please forgive my awkward speech, because I am unfamiliar with dictating a letter. I have also asked Lucas, who is a trained scribe, to correct my words whenever it seems best to him. I cannot write to you in my own hand because I never learned to write or read, all my years in Palestine. These skills were very rare in our part of the world, and besides, I was a girl. We were not taught to read and write because we were too busy learning the work of women. I am sincerely grateful to have had the opportunity to be a wife and mother, and watch my firstborn grow up and fulfill his divine purpose on earth. I tell you true, it was not a privilege given me from any merit of my own. Instead, I was blessed from birth to have such honorable and devout parents, whose lives centered on the Lord Adonai.[1] He was our family's joy.

I liked growing up in Galilee because it is the most beautiful part of Israel—not as many rocks as Judea. My father, Joachim, and my mother, Anna,[2] were both descendants of the house of the great King David[3] (I called my parents *Abba* and *Imma,* which is Aramaic for "Papa" and "Mama" in English). No special privilege came with our heritage. We were considered peasants because my father farmed the land.[4] Nevertheless, my parents were well respected and loved by the townspeople. My village was rather ordinary, located about halfway between the Sea of Galilee and the

Mediterranean Sea. Many Jews did not like Nazareth, but not because it was small and unimportant. The empire of Rome had conquered all of Palestine sixty years earlier, and a garrison of troops had been placed in our town as an outpost.[5] Soldiers were everywhere. I learned at a very early age to watch for mounted soldiers when we played in the street. We never knew when horsemen would gallop through, yelling for us to get out of the way. Worst still was when they didn't yell. Sometimes, people were badly maimed or even trampled to death.

Jewish Life in the Pax Romana

The soldiers were officially in Israel to keep the *Pax Romana* for our "protection and benefit," but it was a "Roman peace."[6] Peace according to Rome meant that they were no longer at war. It was peace for them, but there was no peace in the hearts of my people. There was great anger toward these regents, which caused many political factions to form. Roman legions enforced the pax to keep down rebellion, but mostly to collect taxes. At least one-third of each man's earnings were taken for these taxes, and then we had the Temple tax on top of that.[7] When you traveled, you paid more taxes, and if you were a merchant transporting goods, you were charged for them again and again. Rome made us pay dearly, but there was something far worse. The empire showed no respect for Elohim.[8]

Jewish children learned in the streets of Palestine that Rome was our enemy. But from our parents, we learned of God, the Blessed One, and of our heritage as Hebrews. My people were awaiting a great leader, who had been promised from Adonai for many centuries, through the words of our prophets. The Messiah leader would be the anointed one who would rescue us from our oppressors (Dt 9:25). We were tired of being a conquered people, and I pray you will never be so. Our history was one of repeated fighting. First, there were the Philistines and the Assyrians, the Babylonians, and then the Egyptians, the Amorites, Jebusites, Hittites, and the mosquito bites (joking). The Messiah would establish a New Kingdom for us and restore Israel's glory.[9] He would become our King and bring justice to the world and even rule the whole earth (Ps 47:2, 7).

The soldiers learned of our beliefs, and when they wanted to mock us they would say, "Just imagine, a Jew ruling the world. How will he ever find Rome? Will your God come out of the sky and carry him in a winged chariot to Rome?"

We could not answer, but men would mutter under their breath, "Who says you have to rule the world from Rome? What is wrong with Jerusalem?"

There were other prophecies about the coming Messiah. He would greatly suffer (Ps 22) and be rejected by men and even killed (Isa 53:3). But these prophecies were ignored and forgotten over the centuries of waiting for him to arrive. Four hundred years had passed since the last spoken prophecy, and besides, most people were only interested in a military, political leader. Jewish mothers secretly hoped, and some even prayed, that one of their offspring would become the great Deliverer-King.

Life was difficult for my kinsmen because we were looked down upon as a simple tribal people with a strange religion. One thing sustaining us: the certain hope that "the consolation of Israel" (Lk 2:25), the Messiah, would come one day, because the Lord Elohim had promised. My admirable parents were true, pious believers, and I am glad. They taught their children the law with both words and their daily living, which modeled for us the joy of knowing El Shaddai, the "King of the universe" and "Almighty God."[10]

I have the best memories of the special, holy feast days from my childhood and later with my own family as an adult. They were such happy times of feasting, singing, dancing, and storytelling, all meant to be acts of worship. Our Holy Days were not austere times when one put on a serious face and behaved religiously. Instead, they were like parties, with Adonai as the guest of honor. There were seven special Holy Day celebrations a year. Then there was the weekly holiday of *Shabbat* (Sabbath), which was always on the seventh day of the week.[11] It is a sanctified day of rest because God rested from creating the world on the seventh day. Do you know Shabbat is the only holiday included in the Decalogue, the Ten Commandments, given to Moses?[12] From sundown on Friday night to Saturday evening, we are to remember and appreciate the things we are too busy to notice during the week.

Sabbath Worship

I want to tell you how we worshipped on Shabbat morning. A blast of the shofar, ram's horn, by the *Hazzan* ("Attendant" or "Ruler")[13] called all families to gather at the community's assembly building.[14] The Greek word for the assembly meetinghouse is "synagogue," which was best known to us Hebrews as the Place of Prayer.[15] This public building was usually one big room, with a few smaller rooms attached around it, used daily for classes, private prayer, and storing food and clothing for the poor. Worshippers entered the large room lined with stone seats against three walls and room to stand or sit on the floor in the center. In the middle of the fourth wall, a curtain was fixed which everyone faced. There were special seats of honor in the assembly room that were progressively elevated for greater importance; the highest was called the Moses Seat.[16] This seat, also called the *Bema*, was more like what you call a table that had prestige, more like a throne. (We did not make tables and chairs, because we sat on the ground, usually on mats.) From the Moses Seat, the Torah and the prophets scrolls were read to the people.[17] Before and after the readings, the holy papyrus was safely housed behind the curtain in the scroll cabinet, that we called an Ark.[18]

The celebration began with all assembled standing and facing Jerusalem. The service had seven simple parts, divided as "three threes," "one seven," and "three ones." I will explain. To begin, the Hazzan would stand before the Ark and recite aloud the *Shema* (call to worship): "Hear O Israel: the Lord our God, the Lord is One" (Dt 6:4). It was repeated three times as the people prayed in silence, and then together, we shouted a boisterous, "Amen!"[19] The ruler was not usually a priest or Levite, but one of the men of the congregation chosen by the elders. Other prayers were said. First, three "thanksgivings" and then three "praises" of *Jehovah* (another name we have for God), each statement affirmed with a loud "Amen" from the assembly.[20] The order was important. We are first called for worship. Secondly, according to the Word of God, we enter the Lord's gates with thanksgiving, and then, thirdly, we go into his inner courts with praise (Ps 100:4).

Next came the heart of the meeting: the reading of the Torah. Seven men stood around the Bema Seat and read in turn, being careful not to touch the Holy Books with their hands, so as not to soil the valuable papyrus. These Holy Scrolls contain the very words of the Most High. The law was read first and then the *Haftorah*, which are the words of the prophets.[21] Whoever read last chose the text and then gave a sermon, which was an explanation about the passage. When the preacher finished, he said a prayer and ended the service with a blessing over the people.

As each family left the building, it was customary to leave an offering on the porch for the poor—money, food, or goods, depending on your means to give.[22] No ritual sacrifices were ever performed at the synagogue. Only a priest at the Temple could properly offer them. Whenever we returned home from worship, my imma had special dried fruits to eat with a cold meal. It had been prepared the day before so as not to break the Sabbath by working. The rest of the day, we could play or do whatever we wanted. For me, the best thing about the Sabbath rest day was being together with all my family. We children were told if we got real quiet and listened, we could hear the soft, sweet voice of Blessed Adonai.

Growing up in Galilee

A Hebrew man, as the head of his household, was responsible for instructing his family in the ways of the law. Jewish sons learned about the Holy Law in school, where they were taught to read and write when they turned six years old.[23] By age ten, boys began the study of the oral law.[24] They also memorized scripture passages so one day, they could read and recite aloud the Torah to others.[25] Boys also learned the family trade from their fathers. My duty as a daughter was to help my mother with the women's chores. There was one expectation for a girl that was the most important. I'm sure you can guess what it was: become a good cook. This meant growing vegetables and herbs, collecting the daily supply of well water, grinding grain, and baking bread.[26] Several hours of each day were also spent preparing wool for dyeing, spinning, and weaving to make cloth. Then, there was the constant feeding of the animals and my least-liked task, the scrubbing of the clothes at the riverbank. It took skill to beat cloth with rocks and a little vegetable oil, without wearing it thin.[27]

The Betrothal

My life was a simple one, and according to custom, my parents arranged a marriage for me. It was always the practice for families to choose the spouses of their children. I know this is very different from the way others might do, but this means of selecting a husband worked very well. This way, you always got one. A husband was often older than his wife, up to ten or twenty years older. The average life expectancy in our day was around forty-five years of age.[28] A few lived much longer, into their eighties or even nineties, but that was exceptional. Women usually died ten years before men.

As soon as a daughter was mature enough to have children, her parents arranged the most beneficial marriage for her and the two families involved. Our weddings had two distinct parts. When the two sets of parents agreed upon a match, the *kiddushin* took place.[29] This was a formal betrothal that was completely binding, with the finality of marriage. Even if a marriage ceremony (the second part) had not occurred, a bridegroom could not break with his betrothed, except through divorce, and if he died, the bride would be his legal widow.[30]

The man my parents chose for me happened to live a few streets away from our home. The fact that he was older than me did not concern anyone. Joseph, the son of Heli (Lk 3:23), was considered an artisan because he had acquired the skills of carpentry and masonry. His was an honorable trade and considered superior to farming or herding. Because farms surrounded Nazareth, he made tools like cattle yokes, plows, sickles, and winnowing forks.[31] He had learned this skill from his father, who also made wooden parts for olive mills and winepresses.[32] Carpenters in Israel also built homes, which meant they also cut stone and, therefore, knew well the skill of masonry.[33] Wood was scarce and very expensive, and stones were scattered everywhere. Besides, stone buildings did not burn like wooden structures. I was so happy with Joseph as the choice for my husband, but not because he was praised for his handiwork in wood and stone. People said he was a righteous man who loved Adonai with his whole heart, and the town gossip also whispered that he liked me too.

At most kiddushin ceremonies, a settlement was made on a dowry, which identified the bride price.[34] A contract was signed, and vows were said with the drinking of a cup of wine, signifying the marriage as an unbreakable blood covenant.[35] The groom was then expected to prepare a home to which he would bring his bride. If the groom could not afford to build his own house, he would just add a new room onto his parents' house. This arrangement meant that the bride would be cooking, eating, working, and living with her mother-in-law, so it helped if you liked her. It helped even more if she liked you. The usual betrothal period was one year or longer, depending on the age of the bride.[36] The interval year gave a young groom time to plant his first field or vineyard to gain an income. Couples did not live together as man and wife until the wedding day, and only the father of the groom chose that date.

The Announcement

Joseph and I were already publicly promised to each other when a day came that changed our lives forever. I was alone when, without seeing anyone, I was suddenly not alone. I turned at the hearing of a kind voice saying, "Greetings, you who are highly favored! The Lord is with you" (Lk 1:28). As you can well imagine, I was startled and quite scared. There stood a messenger of the Lord Most High. If you think you would like to see an angel, do not be so sure. I could not think or move, and became stiff like a board. I had heard people speak of angels but never knew anyone who had seen one. Please understand, I did not worship the creature. However, I knew he was from the Lord because there was a sublime presence that I could not compare with any other feeling known to me.

The messenger sensed my great distress and said, "Do not be afraid, Miriam" (Lk 1:30). He said my name! I tried to take in the fact that he knew my name, but he kept talking, so I had to listen. "You have found favor with God. You will conceive and give birth to a son, and you are to call him Yeshua. He will be great and will be called the Son of the Most High." There was more: "The Lord God will give him the throne of his father David, and he will reign over Jacob's descendants forever; his kingdom will never end" (Lk 1:30–33).

These words thrilled me and confused me at the same time. How was this possible? I asked the messenger, "How will this be … since I am a virgin?" (Lk 1:34).

He gently explained, "The Holy Spirit will come upon you, and the power of the Most High will overshadow you. So the holy one to be born will be called the Son of God. Even Elizabeth your relative is going to have a child in her old age, and she who was said to be unable to conceive is in her sixth month. For no word from God will ever fail" (Lk 1:35–37).

The angel answered my question and then gave me a sign, something I could see for myself, that I might have confidence to believe. He seemed to be waiting for an answer. I did not think what he told me needed an answer, but apparently, a choice was before me. I did not need to consider anything. There was only one answer for me: "I am the Lord's servant. … May your word to me be fulfilled" (Lk 1:38). As soon as I stopped speaking, the angelic being was gone. I stood there dazed.

Visiting Elizabeth

I had seen only fourteen summers, and at my young age I had just spoken with an angel. Who could I tell of this encounter? Who would believe me? I had to find my mother. Imma was my strength, and she was ever so wise; she'd know what to do. Even if I had wanted to, I could not keep this encounter from her. Do you think I slept well that night? Would you have? The thoughts in my mind wouldn't stop turning. The words of the holy messenger rolled over and over in my mind until they were sealed in my memory.

Through the night, a desire to be with Elizabeth grew in my heart; I was compelled to go see her. Arrangements were quickly made so I could make the three-day journey[37] to my cousin, to see if she really was with child. Surely, this would be evidence for everyone that my story was true.

The distance between Nazareth and Jerusalem by today's measurements is about eighty miles. The journey to Zechariah's home, which today would be in the town of Ein Karem[38] just outside Jerusalem, seemed much longer than three days. When I finally arrived at the house, I saw no one outside. I called out a greeting at the doorway, according to our custom. We did not knock on a door, but announced our presence by stopping at the threshold and calling out a blessing: "Honor to this house and all who live here. May Adonai be praised by all you do in his name."

Elizabeth came running into the room, saying in a loud voice, "Blessed are you among women, and blessed is the child you will bear!" (Lk 1:42). She was so excited she kept talking, "But why am I so favored, that the mother of my Lord should come to me? As soon as the sound of your greeting reached my ears, the baby in my womb leaped for joy. Blessed is she who has believed that the Lord would fulfill his promises to her!" (Lk 1:43–45).

Elizabeth's excitement and prophetic words reached deep into my soul. Standing there became a holy moment for me. I had told her nothing, and yet she knew. Adonai had revealed this truth to her. Until that moment, I did not know that a child was with me, but now I knew myself. Elizabeth's words both announced and confirmed the wonder-filled truth. Many thoughts toppled over in my mind; excited, happy thoughts, even Holy Words from the Torah I had heard from childhood. I remembered Hannah's song of praise to the Lord for giving her Samuel, in answer to her prayer for a son (1Sa 2:1–10). Psalms of King David (Ps 21, 109) and promises of Isaiah blended together, and I could not hold back my joy. Words came flowing out of my mouth, babbling up like a spring of rushing water:

My soul glorifies the Lord
and my spirit rejoices in God my Savior,
for he has been mindful
of the humble state of his servant.
From now on all generations will call me blessed,
for the Mighty One has done great things for me—
holy is his name.
His mercy extends to those who fear him,
from generation to generation.
He has performed mighty deeds with his arm;
he has scattered those who are proud in their inmost thoughts.
He has brought down rulers from their thrones
but has lifted up the humble.
He has filled the hungry with good things
but has sent the rich away empty.
He has helped his servant Israel,
remembering to be merciful
to Abraham and his descendants forever,
just as he promised our ancestors. (Lk 1:46–55)

These words did not come from my mind; they came from the depths of my innermost being. Elizabeth and I believed the Holy One of Israel was doing something wonderful with these two babies he had miraculously given us. It was a thrilling time for us! We cried and laughed, clapped our hands, held each other, and giggled with glee like little girls at play.

It was wonderful being with Elizabeth the last three months she carried her child (Lk 1:56). She believed everything I told her about the angelic messenger's visit. Her faith encouraged me greatly. Those were the happiest of days. I waited with her until baby John was born because she asked me to stay. In truth, I wanted to be with her because her home was safe, away from questioning eyes. But it was time to go home. Joseph would have to be told. I could not tell my betrothed of my circumstance myself. It was not possible for me to go and talk with him at my own bidding. This was not done. My father would relay my situation to him. I naively convinced myself that Joseph would accept my story because Zechariah and Elizabeth believed me so readily. Surely with the miracle of Elizabeth's baby in her old age, the testimony of Zechariah's restored voice after being struck dumb (Lk 1:59–64), and my angelic visitor's announcement, there was enough evidence to accept my words. I prayed in earnest that my beloved Joseph would believe me, but it was just too incredible for him to readily accept. Had not other young women told a similar story to cover their infidelity, knowing what the consequences would be?

Joseph Obeys a Dream

Joseph could have refused to marry me. Because he was a righteous man, he could have sent me away with a bill of divorce, but he could also have me exposed or even stoned for adultery. These were legal under the law (Mt 1:19). I would surely be banished from Nazareth, from my family and friends, for the rest of my life. I was not to be Joseph's wife, and no Jewish son would ever be allowed to marry someone in my circumstances.[39] How would I live with a child as a single mother? Unmarried mothers were rejected in Israel and lived desperate lives in bitter poverty.[40] Would I be at the mercy of a distant relative who would be paid to take me in, so I would work for them as a servant? That would be the best for which I could hope. In spite of these things, it came to me that if Adonai had foretold that my child would be given the throne of King David, He would provide for us. I told myself I must trust Elohim. He would intercede on our behalf, and that is exactly what he did.

A few evenings later, Joseph lay awake, considering these incredible claims. He fell into a dream and saw an angel beside him who said, "Joseph son of David, do not be afraid to take Miriam home as your wife, because what is conceived in her is from the Holy Spirit. She will give birth to a son, and you are to give him the name Yeshua, because he will save his people from their sins" (Mt 1:20–21).

When Joseph woke up the next morning, he immediately followed the angelic direction. He was truly a man of obedient faith. The evening of our wedding, I went to his home willingly and joyfully, and as we talked of these things, he asked me for my forgiveness. Can you imagine that? Joseph asked me to forgive him for doubting me. It made me love him even more than I ever thought possible. I loved him for his deep faith, his attitude of submission to the Holy One, and his genuine concern for my feelings.

Decree of Caesar Augustus

Several months later, talk on the street reported that Emperor Augustus had ordered a census be taken throughout the Roman Empire. This census was not just to count the population, as was claimed, but to make sure everyone was paying their taxes. Caesar wanted more money. With Rome, it was always money! Men were required to return to the city of their father to register, no matter the distance. Rome did not care if you were ill or elderly; you just did what you were told. Joseph would travel to Bethlehem in Judea, because it had been King David's royal city. As his wife, I was required to present myself with him. The strenuous journey went over rugged roadways of steep hills and valleys, and it was quite cold at night. I was worried that my baby would come early in some desolate place. I wanted my mother and sisters around me, but Joseph and I knew that could not be so.

Before we reached Bethlehem, we understood it would be difficult to find a place to stay. There were simply too many people forced to travel for the census. It was a Jewish custom to offer your home to any relative or stranger passing by. If there was not room enough inside, you could sleep with the animals. Town inns often had stables, as did the wealthy. Stables were not wooden structures; wood was too scarce and costly because it usually had to be imported. Homes were made of either sun-dried straw, mud bricks, or most often stone, because rocks were plentiful, and they didn't burn like wood.[41] The stable of the only inn in Bethlehem was offered to us. It was a cave that had several caverns and connecting tunnels, with several families already camping there among their animals. But it was warmer than under the stars, and we could gather dry straw on which to sleep.

Yeshua Is Born

When my time came (days later, please know), several of the women helped me. Finally, my little one let out his first cry. He was washed with oil and wrapped tightly in bands of cloth in the same way our grandmothers and their mothers had done. We believed this gave the newborn needed warmth and a sense of security.[42] After wrapping, the infant was presented to the father to hold, so he might name the child. This was a father's right and responsibility that had been our custom for all generations.

When Joseph spoke, saying, "This child shall be called Yeshua" (that name is also *Joshua* in Hebrew and *Jesus* in Greek), he was obeying the instructions of the divine messenger who spoke in his dream months earlier. But Joseph was also, in that moment, claiming the baby as his own.[43] He would raise Yeshua as his son, knowing in his heart, as I knew in mine, who the baby's Father really was. Men gathered around my husband to give their verbal blessings and hardy pats of congratulation, assuming he was the baby's natural father.

Dear ones, I must tell you that Yeshua was so beautiful. What can I say? When a mother tells you her baby is beautiful, can you believe her? All babies are beauties, are they not? But this baby really was exceptional! I fell asleep with the warm, little bundle in a small feeding trough next to me that Joseph had filled with straw to make into a cradle. Deep in sleep sometime later, I heard Joseph's voice say, "Miriam, Miriam [that is what my husband called me in Aramaic, as the name *Mary* is Greek]. Miriam, are you awake?"

"I am now," I said.

"There are shepherds here who want to see the baby. They said an angel told them to come and see our baby."

Another angel? I thought. Angels were now a part of our lives. The sheepherders came in quietly, even reverently, and they wanted to see Yeshua's face. Some prayed, and others were eager to talk, telling us of what they had seen in the heavens. Apparently, while dutifully on their night watch, an angel spoke to them of a newborn baby nearby who is Christ the Lord. Then also, hundreds of angels, too numerous to count, suddenly appeared in the night sky (Lk 2:8–14).

These poor shepherd witnesses were so excited about their heavenly encounter that some of the families in the caverns were now awake, asking questions and marveling at their testimonies. I want to tell you what I think Elohim did that night in the open hills. The veil between the Kingdom of heaven and the kingdom of earth was lifted! Something unique and utterly marvelous had just happened. For just a brief moment, the unseen heavenly Kingdom was allowed to be viewed with human eyes. Never before that night had a multitude of angels been seen. Was my baby truly the promised Messiah Israel had been waiting for, the future Deliverer-King? This certainly must be. But I never imagined that his Kingdom was a spiritual one. None of us did. The sheepherders went away singing praises to the Most High. It was an extraordinary visit by ordinary people, but it was just the beginning.

Simeon and Anna at the Temple

We decided to stay in Bethlehem for several months because it was only a half-day's walk to Jerusalem. There, we could consecrate the baby to Adonai at the Temple, as the Law of Moses commanded. Three ceremonies were specifically required for a firstborn son. The first was the Ceremony of Circumcision, which the rabbi performed on the eighth day.[44] The second was called the Redemption of the Firstborn (Ex 13:2, 12, 15). A male child was presented to God one month after birth. The special ceremony included buying back the child, which is redeeming him through an offering. By doing this, parents acknowledged that their child belonged to Elohim, who alone has the power to give life. The offering was at least five shekels, which was substantial for a poor family. To be redeemed gave a meaning of great value to the child.

Joseph fulfilled these two ceremonies at the Temple without me, since I could not go. Women were considered unclean until the third ceremony, the Purification of the Mother, was performed (Lev 12:6–7). If a woman had a son, the purification rite took place on the fortieth day after birth and on the fiftieth day if it was a daughter.[45] The mother presented a yearling lamb or two young birds to the priest, according to what she could afford (Lev 12:8). He would offer the sacrifice on her behalf. On the fortieth day, our tiny family ascended the great stairs of the Temple to make my purification offering of two turtledoves. We noticed a very old man following after us. He seemed very gentle in spirit when he came up to us by the Nicanor Gate on the eastern side of the Court of the Women.[46] He told us his name was Simeon. I could not help but notice his brilliant eyes and beaming smile when he asked if he could hold our baby.

I would not normally give a complete stranger my baby to hold, but this man was so earnest that I could not deny his request. He cradled Yeshua in his arms ever so tenderly and then lifted him up to the heavens, as if making an offering. As he spoke praises to the Most High, his voice became stronger and robust, and he ended saying:

Sovereign Lord, as you have promised,
you may now dismiss your servant in peace.
For my eyes have seen your salvation,
which you have prepared in the sight of all nations,
a light for revelation to the Gentiles
and glory of your people Israel. (Lk 2:29–32)

He caressed and whispered to the baby, time and time again, and then turned to us, our eyes fixed upon him.

He blessed us, stared into my eyes, and said, "This child is destined to cause the falling and rising of many in Israel, and to be a sign that will be spoken against, so that the thoughts of many hearts will be revealed. And a sword will pierce your own soul too" (Lk 2:34–35).

When Simeon reluctantly gave my baby back to me, a prophetess who spent all her time at the Temple approached us and began thanking God for "this Child." Her name was Anna. She was the daughter of Phanuel, of the tribe of Asher (Lk 2:36). Everyone in Israel knew of her, for she was famous across Palestine for her devotion at the Temple. She was very old and had remained a widow after just seven years of marriage.[47] She never left the Temple area, and in the evening when the Temple gates were locked, she slept in one of the servant rooms across the way.[48]

As soon as they were opened at dawn, she would be waiting at the gate to begin her day's service to Adonai, with prayers and regular fasting.[49] Touching us, she began prophesying over Yeshua, saying that the Messiah had arrived. She continued loudly calling out to everyone who had been waiting for the coming of the Savior and the Redemption of Jerusalem (Lk 2:38). He was here, now, in the Temple, a babe in the arms of his mother. People quickly surrounded us, wanting to see our baby.

Magi from the East

After staying months in Bethlehem, it was time to return to Nazareth; one evening, we had the most unexpected visitors, maybe ten in all. They were men from the East, learned men called Magi, who were members of a religious community (Mt 2:1). They were men of high positions in Parthia, which was the land of ancient Babylon.[50] They had been traveling in caravan for over two years. They told us of a star that had led them for the past year to Bethlehem and even to the very dwelling where we were now houseguests (Mt 2:9–11). They told us of both old and new prophecies that said a very great King would be born to the Hebrews at this time, and they had come to worship the Child-King—apparently our Child!

These men were not all Magi; some were servants and others good friends and traveling companions. They were neither astrologers nor astronomers, but men of faith belonging to a priestly tribe who were known as dream interpreters.[51] The religious group to which they belonged had existed since the time of Daniel, the Jewish prophet, when he served in the Babylonian court. Their community had kept Daniel's prophetic writings and practiced the prophet's teaching, and from his day to ours, they had continued the worship of the Holy One. Some were Hebrew descendants, but not all of them.

These visitors went to their knees before Yeshua. They prayed and gave us gifts for him: fine expensive perfumes used for offerings in temple worship and myrrh (anointing oil for burials). They presented gold as well, something that could only be possessed by royalty throughout the known world. After blessing the house and each one of us living there, the great men returned to their caravan encampment outside the city wall to begin their trek home. They had promised King Herod to tell him when they found the child they were seeking, but warned by God in a dream, they chose not to do so and left quickly by a different route (Mt 2:12).

Flight in the Night

We continued making preparation for our journey back to Nazareth, when one night, Joseph had another spiritual dream. An angel appeared to him and ordered him, "Get up … take the child and his mother and escape to Egypt. Stay there until I tell you, for Herod is going to search for the child to kill him" (Mt 2:13). Within minutes, we left in the darkness for the trade road nearby, praying that we might find a caravan moving from Beersheba to Egypt. Our trip to Bethlehem had been a summons, but this was flight. The terror I felt eased when the main road came into view, and we could see a caravan breaking camp in the early light of dawn. We paid the fee to join their company with some of the gifts from the Eastern visitors. The hard journey took over a month before we reached Heliopolis, just inside the border of Egypt, where there was a community of Jewish immigrants.[52] Among them, we could speak Aramaic and buy familiar food, and Joseph could work at his trade. Yet it was not home; we were refugees with an unknown future.

After two winters passed, my husband had another message from the Lord in a dream, telling him it was now safe to return home. King Herod was dead, and the Child would now be safe. We headed for Judea, but then another dream directed my husband to go to Galilee instead. I was more than delighted. We would go back to Nazareth, our home. I was anxious to learn of my family's well-being and live among friends and relatives again. Moreover, my children could all be Nazarenes. Thereby, Yeshua fulfilled the words of our ancient prophets who said of the Messiah, "He would be called a Nazarene" (Mt 2:23).

My Firstborn's Childhood

I am asked if Yeshua was a normal Child. Actually, it is the question I've been asked the most. What a question to ask a mother, especially a Jewish mother like me. Dear friends, do you know what is a genius? I will tell you: A genius is a normal child with a Jewish mother. I tease, of course. For me, being a mother is the greatest joy in life. I am also asked, "Did Jesus do all the common things children normally do?" Yeshua was a happy baby and had several toys, as he grew older. Fathers made rattles for their babies and toy animals on wheels for toddlers.[53] Children had balls, hoops, and spinning tops, and they played games that looked much like hopscotch and jacks.[54] Adults had different board games to pass the time pleasantly too. My son was a good boy, strong and handsome in form, happy and well-liked. He was very curious, always asking questions, day and night, asking questions. He learned his lessons rapidly and could speak Hebrew and Greek, as well as the Aramaic we spoke at home.[55] He spent many hours listening to the learned men at the synagogue discuss the law and the difficult issues of the day, as men like to do. People often remarked how my eldest was wise beyond his years.

Nevertheless, Yeshua was different, too. When most children are told on Sabbath morning to rise to dress for worship, they protest, "Oh, Mother, do I have to go?" I didn't have to prod Yeshua. Even as a small child, his favorite place was the Temple in Jerusalem and then the study rooms at the synagogue. He also liked the open fields, where he often went to pray.

Joseph did not always grasp his singular ways. He would often come into the house and ask, "Do you know where Yeshua is?"

"Yes," I would answer, "don't worry, I know where he is." When my trusting husband would leave the room, I would say, smiling, in a soft voice, "He's somewhere … in Galilee." But I did know where he was: in the fields, alone with his heavenly Father.

I want you to know that my eldest son did not perform miracles as a child, as legends have claimed. I have heard strange stories. One of them said he shaped birds out of clay from the river bottom, prayed over them, and tossed them in the air, and they became real and flew away. I never saw him doing anything of that kind. Such a thing would be magic, and our son never used any incantations or sorcery tricks, and he certainly did not accept money, as some healers did. (The first miracle I witnessed was at a wedding feast in Cana, when Yeshua was thirty years old.) He was a normal boy and yet unique at the same time. But he wasn't always easy to understand.

The Temple at Twelve Years Old

I remember well the Passover Festival when my first-born son reached his twelfth spring, which was the year of entrance into manhood. Every year, we traveled with our family and friends up to Jerusalem for the holy feast days of Passover (Lk 2:41). Our eldest son at that age was considered a young adult, so he did not spend a lot of time with Joseph or me, since we were busy with our younger children. When the week was over, we started home in a caravan, because it was much safer to travel in a large group for protection from wild animals and robbers. It was the practice of women and children to walk together at the front of the caravan, away from the accumulating dust cloud of multiple footsteps. The men walked together in the back, with all the animals, that would leave soft, little presents on the ground in which you might step. A twelve-year-old boy could be in either group.

The first night trekking home, Joseph and I discovered that Yeshua was not with either of us. We each assumed he had been with the other parent. We hunted for him in the caravan among our relatives and friends (Lk 2:44). When we realized he was truly missing, we turned back to Jerusalem, leaving our younger children in the care of cousins. I felt like a bad mother. Imagine misplacing a child. Had he been kidnapped from the caravan? Had he fallen, or was he hurt, lying along the roadway? Was he hungry and thirsty? Or worse still, had he been captured and sold into slavery? All this was possible. I would not allow myself to consider that he might be dead.

We desperately searched in the city for three days, going to the homes of all we knew. By then, I was sick in my heart with worry, so I went to the temple to pray. In the Court of the Women, I suddenly saw him with a group of elders under the colonnades (covered porches that ran the length of the outer courtyard, where the scribes and the Pharisees taught the law and held their debates).[56] My son was just sitting in the shade, as if an equal with the teachers of the law, discussing spiritual questions. I was angry but also relieved to see him there. However, I did not know what to think of this.

I went straight up to him, ignoring decorum, interrupted the rabbis, and scolded him, "Son, why have you treated us like this? Your father and I have been anxiously searching for you" (Lk 2:48).

His answer completely disarmed me. With a look of innocent and wonder, he said, "But why did you need to search, Imma? Did you not know that I would be here at the Temple, in my Father's house?"

Oye! Of course! If I had only thought calmly for one peaceful moment, I could have guessed where he would be. Had I forgotten? Joseph wasn't his paternal father. Yeshua was trying to tell me that the Lord of the universe was his true Father. I did not have full understanding of what this meant, but I know now that Yeshua understood on that day who he truly was. My eldest son was placing himself under his heavenly Father's will, not just under the roof of a religious house of stone.

Joseph and Our Eldest Son

It may be hard for you to understand why, after all the prophetic words given over Yeshua and the angelic encounters, neither Joseph nor I completely realized who he was. Saintly Anna had called him "the Son of God," and Simeon, the "Savior" and "Messiah." The angel had told me his Father was the "Blessed One of heaven," and yet, we did not fully understand. But before you judge me too harshly, allow me to ask this: How many people have heard the story of Yeshua's life, have grown up worshiping God with their family, and still do not believe who he really is? The evidence is before the world, the testimonies of the witnesses and the *Ruach-breathed*,[57] written testaments, and still many do not believe. At twelve summers, Yeshua knew that his Father was the Supreme One of heaven and earth. Yet he still obeyed his earthly parents and returned to Nazareth and lived in our home for eighteen more years (Lk 2:51).

My beloved husband died a few years later, when Yeshua was still a young man. Many people mistakenly thought that my firstborn son did not marry because he assumed the responsibility of the eldest son to lead the family in his father's absence. From Joseph, Yeshua had mastered the skills of woodworking and stone cutting. He dutifully taught his younger brothers the same craftsmanship. I loved my eldest son dearly and relied on him throughout my middle years.

But then, one day shortly after his thirtieth birthday, Yeshua closed the shop door for the last time and sat down by me as I was working. He said words I knew were coming but did not want to hear.

"Imma," he began, "I am going away tomorrow, and I will not return to this house."

My heart tightened within my body as I heard his firm voice. It was like a knife bluntly stabbing into my chest, but it was not because he was leaving. I just had a feeling of foreboding about the life awaiting him. Though I knew nothing of what it would be, I feared for him. And I did not know it, but I was never to hear him address me as "Imma" again.

A Miracle at a Wedding in Cana

My son said good-bye the next morning, without saying where he was going. Months later, I heard he was staying with friends in Capernaum on the north shore of Lake Gennesaret, also known as the Sea of Galilee. In his absence, an invitation to a wedding of a niece of mine who lived in the village of Cana arrived for the entire family. I sent word to Yeshua, and he returned a message that he would attend. I was anxious to see him. When he arrived at the wedding festival, he had several new friends with him: a young man named John and his brother James, and two more sets of brothers, Simon and Andrew, and Philip and his older brother, Nathaniel.[58] There was music, dancing, storytelling, children playing, and much food and drink.

The festivities were merry, but on the third day, I noticed the wine was almost gone. It was much too soon. This was a poor family who had not realized how many friends would attend the weeklong celebration. All I could think to do was tell my eldest about it (Jn 2:3). I was so used to going to him whenever there was a problem. I did not think about what he could do to solve the situation.

But I remember his strange answer: "Woman, why do you involve me? My hour has not yet come" (Jn 2:4). These were strange words. What did they mean? I thought him serious but not unkind. I believed he was about to teach us something. You do not live with someone for thirty years without getting to know his ways.

My son rose from his seated position as if he would do something.

So I told the servants, "Do whatever he tells you" (Jn 2:5), and stepped aside.

Nearby stood six stone water jars used for ceremonial washing (Jn 2:6), each large enough to hold twenty to thirty liters of water. Yeshua instructed the servants to fill the jars with water. So they filled each to their top. Then he said, "Now draw some out and take it to the master of the banquet" (Jn 2:8).

One servant reluctantly obeyed his instructions, and the host sipped the water that had now become wine! He was overtly pleased with the taste, but he did not know where it had come from. His eyes searched for the bridegroom, and finding him, he exclaimed, "Everyone brings out the choice wine first and then the cheaper wine after the guests have had too much to drink; but you have saved the best till now" (Jn 2:10).

Those of us who witnessed the miracle were utterly astonished. The commotion around the stone jars was almost comical. The six companions and the servants had to see and taste the wine for themselves. There was real wine in all the jars, and it was absolutely delicious. There had been miracle workers in the past, but never like this. The making of wine begins with planting a vineyard, not with the collection of water. Grapevines must be properly planted, pruned, and watered, guarded from sunburn and foxes.[59] Grapes must be picked at the right time, pressed and stored properly.[60] We believed this singular event to be a sign from Elohim; the Lord of Hosts was with Yeshua. Only a few people that day witnessed the marvelous glory of the Blessed One manifested through Yeshua. We did not know this was the first of many signs and great wonders that he would perform. His disciples believed in him that very day and would not leave his side for the next three years (Jn 2:11). What a perfect first miracle for Yeshua to perform, turning water into wine, which would become the very symbol of his own shed blood upon the Cross.

Yeshua's Ministry and Rebuke to His Family

As the days turned into weeks and months, then a year, conversations about Jesus could be heard anywhere. Some called him a great prophet. Others said he was a mighty miracle worker. There was nothing unusual about being a miracle worker, for there were other men in Israel who performed healing and miracles. Several of them had proclaimed themselves to be the Messiah, and each in turn would gain some followers for a time. Their fame would rise and then fall. But the people said Yeshua was different. A few said he was strange, but more said he was full of the Holy Spirit of Elohim. He was always addressed directly with the respectful title *Rabbi*, meaning "Teacher" or "Master." Though opinions varied, there was no doubt in anyone's mind that Yeshua genuinely healed the sick.

Some people were skeptical about Yeshua because he was not a typical ascetic prophet, like his cousin John, who was called the Baptist.[61] You remember, John was my cousin Elizabeth's son. John lived austerely, apart from society, avoiding the pleasures of life. Yeshua, to the contrary, attended parties and banquets, and could comfortably enter into a festive mood (Mk 2:18–20; Jn 2:1–12; Lk 19:1–9).

But there was more. My son associated with the derelicts of society, dined with tax collectors, and openly talked with prostitutes and known sinners. He broke tradition by choosing his own disciples by inviting them to be his student-followers. It had always been the custom for a student to choose his own rabbinic instructor in the law. In point of fact, just about everything Yeshua did broke with tradition in some irregular way. For example, he had never sat under the tutelage of a rabbi before being acknowledged as one himself, and he even allowed women into the wider circle of followers who sat under his teaching (Lk 8:1–3). He deliberately limited the number of his student disciples to twelve, corresponding to the twelve tribes of Israel.[62] It was a subtle statement of his importance, and the temple leaders certainly did not miss this symbolism.

The most obvious difference between Yeshua and other prophets was what he said. Our honored prophets brought forth utterances from the Lord, beginning with the phrase, "This is what the Lord says." Yeshua, however, would say, "I tell you the truth," as if he was speaking on his own authority. "You have heard that it was said, 'You shall not commit adultery.'

But I tell you that anyone who looks at a woman lustfully has already committed adultery with her in his heart" (Mt 5:27, 28). He would preface the difficult points in his teaching by repeating a call for the listener's attention, saying, "Truly, truly, I say to you." He even taught things that were radically different from what the elders taught as divine law. Things like, "I have come to turn a man against his father, a daughter against her mother" (Mt 10:35). Such an idea would make a skeptic question how a representative of God could say something so unnatural and ridiculous.

The Son of Man

There were other peculiar things Yeshua said that no one understood. He referred to himself as the Son of Man, a title none of us recognized. It was a name that referred to the Messiah in a prophecy written by Daniel when he was in captivity in Babylon (Da 7:13–14), but even the learned Jews over us had long since forgotten it. My eldest used this term so often, it ran through his speeches as a repeated theme. There was also a statement he used that caught everyone's attention, sparking hope that he might be the promised Messiah. He said something like, "Truly I tell you, some who are standing here will not taste death before they see that the kingdom of God has come with power" (Mk 9:1). My dear friend, the Kingdom of God is still at hand upon the kingdom of earth, and it is making its power felt in the hearts of men and women. Never doubt it. The Lord sits on his throne in the heavens and rules the universe. Everything that the Holy One has said will surely come to pass in its appointed time.

We did not comprehend how Yeshua's kingdom was making its power felt in our lives. We thought he was referring to how Elohim had always been the one true Lord of the Jews. We did not know that it was in Yeshua's very own body that God's Kingdom was on earth, in a way it had never been before. When he started to explain that he was the Son of Man, my kinsmen recoiled at the very idea that he could be such a one. I watched the hearts of people turn against him in an instant. News reached me that he and his friends were coming to Nazareth. To welcome him, the ruler of the Assembly of Nazareth invited Yeshua to read the *Haftorah* and give the sermon on the Sabbath. The whole town was excited with curiosity.

It would be my first time to hear my son preach since he had performed many signs and wonders.

At the time of the seventh reading, Yeshua stood up and was handed the scroll of the Prophet Isaiah. Unrolling it to a passage he was allowed to choose himself, he found where it is written:

> The Spirit of the Sovereign LORD is on me,
> because the LORD has anointed me
> to proclaim good news to the poor.
> He has sent me to bind up the brokenhearted,
> to proclaim freedom for the captives
> and release from darkness for the prisoners,
> to proclaim the year of the LORD's favor
> and the day of vengeance of our God. (Isa 61:1, 2)

When he finished the short passage, he rolled up the scroll, gave it back to the attendant, and sat down. All eyes in the synagogue were fastened upon him, and he began by saying, "Today this Scripture is fulfilled in your hearing" (Lk 4:21). People smiled approvingly and settled comfortably into their seats, anticipating more gracious words that would please them. This passage referred to the deliverance of Israel from exile in Babylon, much like a year of Jubilee, when all debts are mercifully cancelled. Perhaps Yeshua was about to speak about a forthcoming deliverance from our Roman masters. Men asked one another, "Isn't this Joseph's son?" (Lk 4:22).

Yeshua began, "Surely you will quote this proverb to me: 'Physician, heal yourself! Do here in your hometown what we have heard that you did in Capernaum. Truly I tell you, no prophet is accepted in his hometown" (Lk 4:23–24). He continued in the same vein, with examples of Elijah and Elisha the prophets, recalling how their listeners abused them. Soon the people became incensed at Yeshua's criticism of them. They jumped to their feet, yelling insults, and pushed him out of the synagogue and through the streets to the edge of the hill on which the town was built. Several men wanted to throw him off the precipice (Lk 4:29).

These people were my neighbors, and some were even relatives. Others were friends of my children with whom they had once played, my first-born included. How he escaped the mob, I never knew. I feared for his life and prayed to the Lord of heaven to protect him from harm. The danger was real. Many self-proclaimed prophets, sages, and miracle workers had been killed for their pretense and the disturbances they caused. They were not just deemed nuisances by the empire but were seen as political threats, disturbing the peace among a volatile people.

The Opinion Tide Turns

Yeshua was acceptable as a good rabbi, as long as he worked miracles and healed the sick brought to him. However, the mood turned one day when he forgave a man's sin. That was too much. Only the Lord of Hosts himself can forgive sin. Now the people in Galilee were laughing at him, and some said he was mad. His brothers laughed too at first, and then the ridicule started to affect all four of them.

One day, they came together to persuade me that their elder brother was mad and needed our help, saying, "We must bring him home for a rest."

I protested vehemently. It was not so. James, Joses, Judas, and Simon (Mt 13: 55–56) all argued reliable reports said that their brother was not eating because he fasted for days at a time and often prayed through the night without sleeping. His face was drawn, and he looked ill. If this was true, perhaps I should weigh their arguments. All he needed, they reasoned, was rest and a few days of his sister's chicken broth. It was good soup, actually, very good soup. What harm could rest and loving care do?

I set out with my sons for Capernaum (Mk 3:21), where Yeshua was teaching. By then, it was never hard to find him, for someone always knew his whereabouts. I confess that I had started believing that my eldest had fallen into an extreme way of thinking. But I could not believe anything more than that. Once you are a mother, you never stop being a mother. I wanted to help my son in his difficulty. When we arrived, the house was overflowing inside and out with people. We could only send a message to him: "Your mother and brothers are standing outside, wanting to speak to you" (Mt 12:47).

Staring into the faces of the crowd, our son answered our request with a question: "Who is my mother, and who are my brothers?" (Mt 12:48). He pointed to his disciples and said, "Here are my mother and my brothers. For whoever does the will of my Father in heaven is my brother and sister and mother" (Mt 12:49–50).

I had addressed him as my son; he answered me as the Messiah. It was painful to be dismissed like that. I was shocked by his words, as were my sons. But I knew not to take offense because he was teaching us something beyond our natural understanding. He was not criticizing family relationships but revealing a larger spiritual community that went beyond earthly boundaries. I knew, standing outside the house, that Yeshua was no longer mine. I was his mother, but he did not belong to me. He belonged to the world and everyone in it, though I did not realize the extent of what that meant at the time.

Passover Week

The greatest pain of all was yet to come. I am often asked if I knew what was happening to Yeshua the last week of his earthly life. I was in Jerusalem that year, staying with my sister for the Holy Days of Passover. I knew my firstborn would be in the city with his closest friends, but I did not know that he was spending nights in Bethany. Nor did I know of his arrest or of the illegal night trials when they were occurring. I am glad for that. There was much confusion among Yeshua's followers, and some of my friends decided not tell to me what was happening. They wanted to save me from worry. Still, I learned later exactly what transpired once the special meal was finished that Yeshua hosted for his disciples. Apparently, for months, the highest temple leaders had laid aside their strong rivalry and temporarily united with a plot to kill Yeshua. It had to appear as if they were not responsible for his death. When the private Passover meal in the upper room ended, my son led his friends to a favorite prayer place outside the city gate, on the Mount of Olives. While all Jerusalem slept in their beds, Yeshua prayed to his Father. Even I, his mother, slept peacefully that night, completely unaware of the tormenting struggle burning within him. A choice was before him. I am sure that Yeshua (recall that this name means "Savior") knew precisely what awaited him, and he had known for some time. He had the power to stay or flee that night. He had the power to choose his destiny. As the evening wore into the early hours of the morning, the choice having been made, a detachment of armed soldiers and officials from the chief priests marched into the olive tree garden and arrested my son.

Standing beneath the Crucifixion Cross

When you hold your baby in your arms, cuddle and sing to them, it never occurs to you that one day, that babe could be called a criminal. How could I imagine that I would stand at the foot of a Cross and look up at a Man who was my son? It is not conceivable. What did I feel standing there? Dear ones, I did not feel anything. I could not feel because I was numb in utter disbelief. Neither could I speak, for what was there to say? What had he done? My mind was confused, trying to accept what my senses were telling me. Surely this was not happening. Five of us huddled together, supporting each other to stay on our feet. John, Mary Magdalene, Mary the wife of Cleopas, and my sister were all with me (Jn 19:25–26). It was important for each of us to stay with Yeshua and to stand for him, unashamed in spite of the taunts and curses hurled at him. There was a din of sobbing and wailing in the air by the Daughters of Jerusalem, who always accompanied crucifixions.

Seeing us beneath him, Yeshua struggled to speak. Was he speaking to me? He whispered, "Woman, here is your son" (Jn 19:26). Then, to his beloved friend John, standing beside me, he said, "Here is your mother" (Jn 19:27). Now, even now, in this moment of anguish, he thought of me, his mother.

I found my voice, and my tears broke. Dying in naked shame, in unspeakable pain, his concern was for me, for his imma. I must explain to you what meaning these pronouncements had behind them. They were the final severing of our tie as mother and son. Yeshua was putting me in John's care, and John understood perfectly. He would care for me like an eldest son in Yeshua's place. I had four other sons, and they were good men and would have cared for me according to our customs. But this was the start of a different family on earth, a spiritual family begun by Yeshua himself.[63] He was laying the seed of a holy family that was to come, the *Ekklesia*, the "called-out ones," which eventually became known as the church. It would be his spiritual body on earth, a new family that would be birthed in a short while.[64]

In answer to our earnest prayers, death came quickly for Yeshua. Had he not been badly flogged, he should have lived for several more days. But when the ninth hour came, with all the strength he could gather, he cried out in a loud voiced, "*Tetelestai*," which actually means, "The debt is paid in full." What debt was fully paid? This word was used only in legal matters, a forensic term in jurisprudence. This was a strange saying to those left in his hearing. Knowing that his mission was complete, he said, "I am thirsty," so that scripture would be fulfilled (Jn 19:28).

The Daughters of Jerusalem had brought with them a mixture of strong wine and myrrh to give to those dying, to deaden pain and consciousness; it was raised to Yeshua's lips from a saturated cloth at the end of a long pole. With a few more words spoken directly to his Father in heaven, he gave up his spirit and let his body die. This was the hour for which heaven and earth had waited. His hour had come! This was the hour about which he spoke to me at the wedding in Cana three years earlier.

The ground beneath our feet began to shake, and the sound of the earth itself rumbled louder than any quake I had heard before (Mt 27:51–52). All in Jerusalem were frightened by the sounds that day, but more frightening to me had been the darkness from the sixth hour of the day (Lk 23:44). The sky grew blacker than a starless, moonless night, and yet it was still day. Was this not Adonai's displeasure? For it is he alone who makes the sun to rise, the wind to blow, and the earth to bring forth its life. Nature was grieving. It was as if the earth knew what humanity had done.

In my heart, the Blessed One was speaking. The Mighty One of the universe did speak, for at that moment in time, the seamless curtain in the Temple, barring the Holy of Holies, was torn from its top to its bottom (Lk 23:45). It tore in two, in the center, the same way the animal was cut in a blood covenant ceremony.[65] Like the open curtain, there was now direct access to the King of the universe; anyone could freely enter into the Holy Presence of Elohim. Burial tombs were opened, and righteous dead inside them rose up and came into the city and were seen by many (Mt 27:51–53).

God's Provisions

On the hill of Golgotha, in spite of the darkness, there was an immediate problem of concern. The Sabbath was to begin at sunset, about the eleventh hour. Jewish law required that a burial take place the same day of a death[66] (Dt 21:22–23). The rites of preparing a corpse for burial took time, and no work could be done once the Sabbath began. Worse still, Yeshua could not be buried with honor because he had been condemned by an order of a Jewish court. Our heavenly Father cares about our every need, small or great, and he was at work placing a solution in the hearts of two men. Ironically, these men were members of the Jewish Council, who appeared on their own initiative to take care of Yeshua's body.

Thankfully, not all of the Sanhedrin agreed with the council's findings. Joseph from Arimathea was a wealthy man who had a recently hewn stone tomb that he offered as a burial place for my son (Lk 23:50–52). The elderly Nicodemus came with him to accomplish all the necessary tasks, for he was an admirer of Yeshua and believed in him (Jn 19:39). Soldiers balanced ladders against the Cross and lowered Yeshua's body into my arms that I might hold my son one last time. Somehow, it consoled me to hold him. He was my Child, my innocent, well-loved Child. The frightened little boy who once cried out, "Imma, Imma," for me to comfort after being stung by a bee, now lay across my lap, a dead man.

The need for haste, heightened by fear, made everyone anxious to bury the body. I wanted to attend the burial party but was constrained not to go. Jewish law forbade me from burying my son myself because he was a condemned criminal.[67] What did I care of that? Still, it was Preparation Day, and the Passover Sabbath was about to begin (Lk 23:54). There was no time to think, just obey. We hurried back through the city gate before it was locked for the night. We had to entrust the burial of my beloved son to the two learned men. There was nothing to do but wait, breathe, live, and endure.

On that Sabbath, I never knew the depth of sadness could be so bitter. I had mourned deeply for my husband. When he died, I felt ripped apart, as if a piece of me had died. I mourned for each of my parents, fully aware that much of my life was a reflection of theirs. How I grieved for them, but this time, my mourning was different. I grieved for Yeshua as my son, but there was something greater to my sorrow. I was grieving for my people and for Israel. I was despairing for a world without peace and the promised Kingdom that would not be.

Beside my pangs of grief, there was also agonizing confusion. What about the angelic visitations and the prophecies? He was Yeshua, the Savior, the one who would save his people. He was supposed to have David's throne, and the reign of his kingdom was not to end. Is that not what the angels had said more than once? I struggled in my mind for some kind of explanation that would give me relief. Was God wrong? No, He cannot be, but wasn't he? Had Adonai's will not been done on the earth because of the interference of men? Was it that simple? Yeshua could not rule over us now. There was only utter disappointment and dead hope.

In desperation, I asked the Lord of Hosts to grant me mercy in my bitter sorrow: "Give me some measure of understanding that I might have peace in my heart." Very soon, my thoughts began running along a different path. Had there not been many holy prophets who had died in the service of God? To the world, Yeshua was just one of many. Then I started to remember different means of provision over the centuries by Jehovah Jireh—the Hebrew name for God the Provider: a ram caught in the bushes for Isaac, deliverance out of Egypt through the Red Sea, manna to eat in the wilderness, and a water spring for Hagar and Ishmael in the desert. Moreover, there was all the good Yeshua had done; he had healed the lame, the deaf, and the blind. He had cast out unclean spirits, restoring the infirmed to their families. He had raised the dead and taught marvelous ways of our heavenly Father. Had he not turned many toward obedience to the Holy One of Israel? Yeshua's life did have meaning; he had made a difference. I had a child knowing no man, and Elizabeth bore a son in her old age; what the Mighty One had done once, he could do again. If my son was not to be the Messiah, Elohim would raise up another. A kernel of hope lived again in my heart.

The Resurrection Is Reported

Yeshua had raised people from the dead, but to raise himself was not expected by any of us, even though he indicated several times that he would do so. No one among us, I say it again, not one of us understood what Yeshua meant when he said he would rise. It is amusing that the only ones concerned that he had said something about rising from the dead were the chief priests. They didn't believe him, of course, but they still asked the procurator to place a Roman seal on his tomb (Mt 27:62–66).

On the morning of the week's first day, Mary Magdalene, Joanna, and Mary the mother of James and John, announced amazing news (Lk 24:1–10). Yeshua was alive! Mary of Magdala had seen him and talked with him. He had risen from the dead. "Risen from the dead" meant one thing to me: He was with us. I did not try to comprehend the manner nor the teaching of such a miracle, as the learned men might do. I simply believed it and was consumed with blissful joy.

In the days and weeks that followed, Yeshua appeared many times: to his disciples as they were eating, to men walking to the village of Emmaus, to different size gatherings of people, some as large as five hundred. He continued to teach his disciples about the Kingdom of God. New insights of the disciples were circulated among the believers. I never saw him myself. I didn't need to. Yeshua never came to see me. Why should he? He owed me no special favor. He was not my son alone; He was my Kinsman-Redeemer and my Lord, the Anointed One who saves. I am just like you: a human sinner in need of a Savior.

Parting Exhortations

My dear friends, each day for many weeks now, Lucas and I have met together to put to paper this correspondence to you. And now, the papyrus scroll is nearing its end. Lucas chose the longest papyrus roll that is made, thirty-three feet to be exact. He tells me that's why no literary work from our day can be found that is longer.[68] I chastised him when he brought it that first day of our dictation. I was convinced it was too long, for I thought I did not have that much to say. But he knows the ways of a woman better than I realized. He has written with great speed, some hundred lines a day, but then no more is possible. He has worn away at least a dozen reed pens and made his own ink of soot and gum glue.[69] Now there is but a short space left for me to share my heart with you.

I have testified to you in this letter all these things for only one reason: to affirm to you what I have seen and heard myself, that these reports are true, so that you might believe. I want you to believe these accounts so you will believe Yeshua. When Jochebed nursed little Moses for the princess of Egypt, she did not neglect to teach her son about Adonai. This good mother did not teach her son to merely believe *in* the Hebrew deity of Elohim. She taught him to believe him.

Please, do not let the fact that these things happened so many years ago dissuade you from believing them. Yeshua is the living Christ, the only and begotten, eternal Son of God, who died to pay in full the penalty for sin, both yours and mine. He did this that we all might be redeemed, that is, purchased back by his death so we will live forever with him. It is your privilege and mine to tell everyone we meet this greatest-of-all Good News. Blessed are you who believe in Yeshua as the Christ, for you have not witnessed these things yourselves, and yet, you believe by the word of our testimony. You please Elohim, for you have believed by faith and not by sight.

Dear brothers and sisters, I say to you what I said to the servants at the wedding in Cana so many years ago: Do whatever Yeshua tells you to do, whether it is great or small. What has the Holy One placed in your heart to do? Be obedient to Christ, and allow him to perform miracles in you and through you. For did not Yeshua say that his disciples would do greater works after he went to the Father (Jn 14:12)? Love one another, dear children of the Most High, that the world may see your righteousness and be drawn to the love of Christ. Always remember that what I have witnessed, I pass on to you as of first importance: that Christ died for our sins, that he was buried, that he was raised on the third day, and that we beheld his Glory! We are the people of the risen Christ, who is alive forevermore.

The blessing of the Lord of Hosts be upon your lives.

Shabbat Shalom,
Miriam of Nazareth

Conclusion

The last time Mary appears in the New Testament, she is in the Upper Room with the People of the Way. Christ's followers had dutifully assembled there to pray in obedience to Jesus's directive to "stay in the city until you have been clothed with power from on high" (Lk 24:49). Mary's presence there during the Festival of Pentecost speaks to us of the esteem they had for her. She was not there as an object of worship or as the directress of the infant church,[70] but as a believer, praying and waiting for the promised gift of power. After the church was born, we can safely surmise that Mary was sought out and asked to share her experiences as the mother of the Savior. Who else could better share the details of the Nativity than she? We can easily admire her character and contribution to the church and the nurturing of Jesus.

When God chose Mary for her unique purpose, he must have seen her pure heart and known how she would respond. She immediately submits with profound humility. Her question as to how such a thing could happen is not skepticism but curiosity. Knowing the customs and penalties of her day, Mary responds in simple faith, "May your word to me be fulfilled" (Lk 1:38).

Another girl might have said, "I'd rather not; could you pick some other virgin?" Doesn't that sound ridiculous, after knowing what really happened? Mary yielded not only her body, but also her future to the Lord, which would include both joy and pain. In so doing, she was used in the miracle of the Incarnation, revealing the two natures of Jesus Christ: as the son of Mary, his humanity, and as the Son of God, his Deity. By this means, Jesus fulfilled the purpose for coming to earth when he took the sins of humankind upon himself on the Cross and won the victory over death.

Examining "Mary's Song," spoken upon learning that she was with child, reveals a character of strength and wisdom beyond her years. We see her depth of faith when she instantly praises God as if the fullness of the miracle was already accomplished. What she does in this prophetic poem, we can do as well. First, she rejoices in the privilege given to her. Then she glorifies God by declaring his power and mercy, taking delight in his greatness. Mary next looks forward to his blessing the world through the Messiah, and finally, she exalts in God fulfilling his promises. These four things remind us that we too can glorify the Lord every day in these ways.

Hearing Mary's heart explains why she has been so revered over the centuries. There is so little to fault in her and so much to admire and emulate. Undoubtedly, many countless women living after Mary have taken her fine example to heart. Just as the Magnificat proclaimed, all generations have called her blessed, by seeing her humility and lifetime of holy living. The new family of God that the apostle John and Mary began at the foot of the Cross and established at Pentecost grew and spread throughout the world, in spite of much struggle and persecution. Through the succeeding centuries, the church grew exponentially, sharing the Good News. In the next chapter, we will fast-forward to the twelfth century, where we will witness the church in great need of renewal and a return to the basic tenets of repentance, simplicity, humility, faith, and agape love. The grand Lady Clare of Assisi joins a converted reveler, and together they will transform the church with their wholehearted love for Jesus Christ.

Discussion Questions

1. How does Mary's response to the angel's announcement of God's will for her compare to Moses' response to the revelation from the burning bush concerning his future role?
2. What life experiences have you had whereby you can relate to Mary? What emotions can you relate to that Mary underwent in her lifetime?
3. Mary pondered in her heart the unusual things that were happening concerning her firstborn son. How do you ponder the things of God in your heart?
   How does this help you to live day by day for God?
4. Mary joined others in the upper room on the day of Pentecost when the Holy Spirit filled the believers with his presence and power.
   How do you cultivate your relationship to the Holy Spirit?
5. What do you admire most about Mary, the mother of Jesus?

The First Franciscan Mother

Introducing St. Clare of Assisi

St. Francis of Assisi stands out as one of the most loved and respected men in all of world history. His universal appeal was grounded in an awe-inspiring faith in the goodness of a loving God. Lesser known was his spiritual counterpart, the Lady Clare di Offreduccio: intelligent, attractive, wealthy, noble by birth, with a reputation for good works, holiness, and virtue.[1] The fervor between these two friends was consumed in their mutual, intense love for Jesus Christ. At sixteen, young Clare began two years of secret meetings with Brother Francis that would seal dissatisfaction with her privileged life and guide her to her destiny.

In 1212, Lady Clare turned eighteen years of age; on the night of Palm Sunday, she escaped from her palace to receive the rough Franciscan habit from Francis. In so doing, she began the second Order of Franciscans, known today as the Poor Clares. While Francis's quest to preach the Gospel took him to the courts of Rome and as far as Spain and the Sultan in Egypt, Mother Clare lived out her vows in the convent of San Damiano in literal poverty, constant prayer, and hard work. In contrast to the Middle Age's worldly goals of riches and success, Francis and Clare each chose to embrace a simple life in poverty to imitate the life of Christ as closely as they could. To their great surprise and delight, many others joined them in their radical way of life.

Clare's life was as rigorous as any peasant farmer's wife. At twenty-one, Sister Clare reluctantly consented to the role of Abbess, at Francis's insistence, though she never used the title or the word "nun," choosing "Sister" instead, for she saw all her companions as equals. Neither did she ask her Sisters to do anything she would not do herself. Apparently, according to another Sister, Mother Clare washed the mattresses of the sick in the infirmary herself, "not running away from their filth nor shrinking from their stench."[2]

While Francis was unable to maintain the "Privilege of Poverty"[3] within the Franciscan Brotherhood, Mother Clare fought all her life for it and won. She became the first woman in history to write an officially approved rule or Form of Life by which monastics organized their daily lives. Mother may also be the first woman to succeed in gaining a goal through a hunger strike. After the Lord Pontiff took away the right for the Friars Minor to preach to the Sisters, she said, "Let him now take away all the Brothers' service [providing the convent with food through begging] since he has taken away those who provide us with spiritual food."[4] When Pope Gregory heard the Brothers no longer supplied food to San Damiano at Clare's request, he rescinded his demand and allowed them to preach and serve the 147 houses of Poor Ladies throughout Europe. Since then, Poor Clare communities continue to follow the rule of their beloved foundress, with nearby Franciscan monasteries providing priests and Brothers for their spiritual support and kinship, as their Father Francis had promised them.

An Open Letter from Mother Clare of Assisi

Buongiorno, Pax et Bonum, Pace e bene, the Lord give you peace and goodness.

I greet you in Italian, Latin, and English with the salutations St. Francis and the Brothers Minor used to bless people as they walked through the hills and valleys of Europe so many years ago.[5] It is the most exceeding pleasure for me to write to you of the goodness of Almighty God. Friends have insisted that I must recount my spiritual journey throughout my life for other people. This is uncomfortable for me because I prefer to speak only of the things of our Beloved Lord God. However, they believed the telling will honor the Holy Spirit, who directed my life even before I was born. Since my story is so intertwined with that of my spiritual Father Francis, I am pleased to oblige this request and share both of our stories of God's Grace.

Growing up in Assisi

Francesco di Bernardone and I were each born in the town of Assisi, nestled on the eastern slope of the Umbrian valley in the heart of *Italia*. He was twelve years older than me, and we did not grow up in the same circles because my extended family consisted of seven wealthy knights, who were sons of my grandfather, Offreduccio.[6] My excellent mother's ancestry could be traced back to King Pepin and his father Charlemagne, the first Holy Roman Emperor.[7] This might have helped impress my father, Lord Favarone, to choose the noble and wealthy Lady Ortolana as his wife. My *madre* (mother) was highly respected as a devout woman known for her piety and abundant charity. Her heart was drawn to take spiritual pilgrimages to Rome, Spain, and the Holy Land, in spite of the hardships of these dangerous journeys. Madre was my champion and model, and I was blessed to grow up in her shadow, minding the ways of such a godly woman.

I heard of an experience Madre shared, with the greatest of care, that caused me to recall it reverently at special moments in my life. When she was about to deliver her first baby, she became frightened of the possible dangers involved. One day, seized with fear, she knelt in prayer before the church altar, asking God to sustain her life. Madre distinctly heard these words: "Do not be afraid, woman, for you will give birth in safety to a light which will give light more clearly than light itself."[8] She wanted her daughter to have a name that signified light and one that would remind her of God's promise to her. At my christening, I was given the name *Chiara* (Clare), which as you might guess means "bright light."[9] Names were to reflect a person's character, but how could I live up to such a designation?

I learned to pray at regular times of the day from my madre, who also taught her three daughters music, needlework, reading, writing, spinning, and caring for the poor, according to the lifestyle of aristocratic women of society. Feudal laws were still observed, and obligations were due to the emperor and to the lords, the *majores,* as all noblemen were identified, in contrast to the *minores,* who were the common people.[10] As also expected, *Madonna* Otolana[11] had gathered around her noble women and female relatives as a support circle of intimate friends, who spent much of their time working and socializing together. As the head of a large household, Ortolana was *Domina,*[12] who had responsibility over all the servants, musicians, guards, and ladies-in-waiting. We were a family of majores, probably the wealthiest in Assisi and living in the largest palace.

The King of Youth

In spite of the separation of these two classes that seldom mixed together, one could not live in the town of Assisi without hearing about the lad Francesco di Bernardone. While his father was in France, his wife Pica had her newborn son baptized Giovanni di Pietro di Bernardone, after John the Baptist. When Padre Pietro di Bernardone, who loved all things French, returned, he renamed his son Francesco, "the little Frenchman."[13] The town folk called him a scamp, observing him as a spender and charmer who was always singing, day and night singing, especially at night singing. Yet he was so likable with his pleasant manner that he was forgiven his many antics. I think it was his happy laughter that won your heart. He had many nicknames. He was the "Lord of Revelers," the "King of the Youth," and the "Lord of the Rumpus,"[14] because he loved to party, night after night, week after week, and month after month.

It was no secret that Francesco enjoyed the life of the rich, though he was still considered a minore and, as such, not of the ruling class. Yet Francis's father, Pietro Bernardone, had one consuming passion: the making of money. He was a merchant of textiles, carrying only the finest and best fabrics for the wealthy majores. Ours was a time in European society when money was becoming more than just a medium of exchange; it now was a goal in itself. By it, one could obtain power and improve one's rank in society. Wanting these things for his family, Padre Pietro had great plans for his talented, firstborn son. Naturally, he would inherit the family business. He would learn all aspects of the trade. Talking to customers was an art, and Francesco had natural finesse. His padre indulged him with the finest clothes and lots of spending money, believing it was good for business with his son's friends. Francesco learned to read and write in both Italian and Latin, and he would speak French at his father's insistence. His mother, Pica, an excellent, pious woman, oversaw his religious instruction and had him attend the parish school nearby.

Our two families did not attend the same church. I lived in the upper part of town in our family's palace, which faced San Rufino, the Cathedral of Assisi. The Bernardone shop and home was one large building in the middle of town. Assisi claimed twenty-two thousand inhabitants, not including the residents of the monasteries and the German garrison.[15] It was built on the site of an old Roman city, and the churches were built atop the ruins of the ancient temples of the Etruscans and the Romans. Our little portion of Italia had its wild woods, crystal rivers, and deer-grazing meadows, all proclaiming the glory of God with their beauty. Assisi in Umbria was an ideal place to live.

In our day, there were at least 150 religious holidays a year in Italia,[16] any number of which you could celebrate if you wished. So with much free time and money in his pocket, Francesco would grab his lyre or shepherd's pipe, and out the door the troubadour would skip, with a trail of friends behind him. There would be much food and drink, dance, and revelry until the light hours of the morning.

But the events in the outside world invaded this carefree life. The thirteenth century was a dark age, alight with the fires of constant wars, most of which were really local battles between city-states. Life was short because diseases and death were everywhere. Emperor fought emperor, towns fought towns, and the peasants fought the lords. Traveling troubadours brought news of current events. In the year of our Lord 1187, Europe learned that the Great Sultan of the East had captured Jerusalem. All Christendom reeled with this news. The princes of the West boastfully vowed they would go on crusade against Saladin, but only one emperor attempted to keep his promise. On his way to the Holy Land, Henry VI suddenly drowned, and Europe erupted into petty fighting.[17] These feudal wars were our way of life.

War between Perugia and Assisi

In January 1202, a war broke out between Perugia and my city of Assisi. Naturally, the King of the Youth would have to be with the knights. But the glorious battle of Collestrada turned into a total massacre.[18] Only the knights were spared, taken as prisoners for one purpose: money. By God's grace, Francis was mistaken by the victors to be a knight. Had this error not occurred, he would have been killed with all the regular soldiers. If you owned armor and you owned a house, and that meant you could afford to pay a ransom. For a year, Francesco languished in a damp, unlit dungeon and suffered high fevers from malaria. After Padre Pietro paid the ransom fee, his son returned home at the age of twenty-two with tuberculosis.

Francis's skilled mother nursed him faithfully, and many months later, he left his sickbed, leaning on a cane to amble down old, familiar Assisi lanes. They were the same, but he was not. In time, however, memories of war fade, and Padre Pietro persuaded his son to accompany the famous knight, Count Gentilia, on a holy Crusade. He could earn a knighthood and bring glory to the family name. Moreover, the honor of Christendom was at stake. What could be more admirable than reconquering Jerusalem? Francesco would have a complete suit of armor, a horse with all its equipment, and he would serve a great knight on the battlefield and return an invested knight himself. The sum of this regalia was tremendous, the price of a farm.[19] Pietro di Bernardone would gladly pay it all, for his son's success would be his own.

The Fourth Crusade, preached by Pope Innocent III, proved to be another fiasco[20] and not just for the troops, but the Bernardones as well. After a one-day ride, the knight and his new squire took lodging at Spoleto. That night, Francesco took sick, tossing and turning in his bed. Burning with fever, he thought he heard a voice call out, "Francesco!" Who was calling his name? He heard his name again, "Francesco," then once again, "Francesco!"

"Yes, my Lord?" he answered.

"Who can give you more? The master or the servant?"

"The master, Lord."

"Then why are you leaving the master for the servant, and the prince for the vassal?"

"What do you wish me to do, Lord?" Francesco asked, trembling.

"Return to the place you were born, and you will be told what you will do."[21]

Return home, to his father? Surely not. Yet the voice was kind and had to be from God. Hiding his pride and with daydreams of chivalry shattered, he gave away his armor to a poor nobleman he passed on his trek home. He would have to work hard in the textile store to repay his irate padre.

Francesco di Bernardone's Conversion

The love of fun had not quite left Francesco. His old friends came back. He would give them more songs, free food, and silly laughter. Yet he often sought times to pray and grew more and more quiet. One night at a party, he was playing the great lord of the banquet, like he had done so many times before. His companions crowned him "the King of Youth," placing a stick in his hand for a royal scepter. They spilled out into the street, heading for the main piazza to sing their drunken songs. Frances chased them with the fool's baton in his hand, calling, "Felippe, Angelo, Rafino, wait for me!"[22]

Suddenly, he stopped as they ran ahead. In one moment, the Person of Jesus Christ was with him, even while holding the baton in his hand. He saw himself as God saw him. God was calling Francis to himself. For years, he had been struggling with something, or rather someone, and abruptly that one overwhelmed him with the power of his glorious presence. Jesus Christ, the very Son of God, was now the Lord of his heart. Francis was twenty-five years old. In spite of his new joy, there was still more to come.

In the streets of Assisi, Francis gave alms to every beggar he met. If he was out of money, he would give the beggar his cap, his belt, or even his shirt. He would go off by himself, often in a cave, spending many hours alone, weeping over his sins. People dismissed him as silly, but I did not think so. He may have been alone, but he was with God. I understood, and so did his madre. When you are truly in love with God, you will not care what other people think about how you express your love for him.

In the eyes of a world that knows not God, you will probably look rather ridiculous. *Sì?*

Prayer at the Cross of San Damiano

One day, Francis had walked a distance in the fields outside Assisi when he came upon an ancient chapel that had fallen into ruin. This church, called San Damiano, was named after a great man of God, a preacher, healer, and miracle worker. A life-sized Byzantine Crucifix hanging above the altar attracted his attention. The figure of Christ had a faraway look, as if watching for someone. Conscious of standing on holy ground in the presence of Almighty God, Francis fell to his knees. There before that cross, he realized as never before what Jesus Christ had suffered upon his wooden Cross for Francis and for every human being. The pain and the spiritual agony of Jesus's soul in that moment became real to Francis, and he wept uncontrollably.

While weeping, to his astonishment, he heard these words: "Francis, go and repair my Church which, as you see, has fallen into ruin."[23] It was a message from the Savior to the redeemed sinner. Francis was overjoyed; he had heard from God! He had work to do, work for God. In his usual capricious nature, he took this message literally. He would repair this church of San Damiano.

This project would take money and lots of it. There was much to be done. He ran home to the storeroom and took several bales of expensive scarlet material, mounted a fine steed, and sold them all (bales and horse) in the neighboring town of Foligno. He then tried to give the money to a priest to rebuild San Damiano, but when he would not take such a great sum, Francis realized what he had done and began to fear his father's anger. So he actually hid in a cave for a month, afraid to face the world and all its critics. Such a span of time helped him to realize that he couldn't stay hidden forever.

He bravely walked into Assisi to the cries and jeers of "*Coocho, coosa de pazzo, pazzo,*" which means "fool and madman."[24] He was God's fool, presenting himself to the world just as he was. When Pietro heard the commotion over his son, he ran into the street like a mad animal. He dragged Francis into their house and chained him inside a closet for several days, hoping it would bring him to his senses.

Trial before the Bishop

Madre Pica realized this method was of no use and gave her beloved son his freedom. Released, Francis left his childhood home for good, but that was not the end of it. Padre Bernardone decided his son must renounce his inheritance in a court of law, lest he squander more family property (it was always a matter of money with Pietro di Bernardone). Since the church was involved, the civil authorities would have to yield to a church court. Dutifully, Monsignor Guido, the Bishop of Assisi, summoned Francis to his palace for a trial. The townspeople gathered with titillating curiosity when Francis arrived splendidly dressed. The bishop gave the judgment:

> Francis, Your Father is greatly humiliated by your behavior. If you wish to serve God, you must first return your Father his money. God does not want you to use this kind of money for sacred things. As for San Damiano, trust in the Lord, my son, and act manfully, fearing nothing, for will not the Lord help you and provide you with all that is necessary to repair the church?

Francis was enthralled; this wisdom had not occurred to him. He said, "My Lord, I will cheerfully give back not only the money but also the clothes I have received, to my father."[25]

Francis stood up from his kneeling position, disappeared into a side room, and reappeared moments later with all of the garments he had been wearing, folded neatly in his hands. He was completely naked. Everyone was stunned.

He went straight to Pietro and laid these possessions at his feet, saying, "Please listen, all of you. Up to now I have called Pietro di Bernardone my father. Now I return to him his money and all the clothes I have received from him so that hereafter I shall not say, Father Pietro Bernardone, but Our Father Who art in Heaven, and I shall go naked to meet the Lord."[26]

Pietro scooped up the clothes into his arms and turned away in disgust, leaving his son standing alone in his unseemly condition. Bishop Guido responded differently. He stretched out his cope (a long, loose vestment worn by priests and bishops on ceremonial occasions), wrapped it around Francis, and led him away to his private room. The bishop seemed to know that this young man had acted under divine inspiration. From that moment, he comforted and helped Francis. He would be a friend for life, advising Brother Francis with tender charity.

Francis's behavior was a spectacle, but it was his way. His act of stripping was a form of public penance.[27] He was stripping himself of the signs of wealth and the pride of youth. From now on, he would take the side of the outcast, the poor, and the disinherited. He was given a peasant hermit's robe. He had never worn anything like that before. Now Francis called himself the *novellas pazzo sue mundo*, the "new, crazy man in the world," because he was rejecting the ways of the world and would seem very odd to others. In the spring of 1206, he left Assisi, not knowing where he would go or what he would do. In his wanderings, he stopped in Gubbio to nurse lepers alongside Benedictine monks. The sight of lepers had always repulsed Francis, as it did most people, but things were different now. God's Spirit was remaking his life and values. Truly, we must love the leper and the outcast, for did not our Lord and Savior wish for our sakes to be considered a leper himself? Was not the Son of Man called the "Suffering Servant" (Lk 17:25)?

Repairing San Damiano

When Francis left the lepers, he began to repair the crumbling walls of San Damiano and two other churches. There was a spirit of happiness in his efforts as he labored. In the morning, he begged for stones in nearby towns, singing praises to God:

Stones for San Damiano, peace and good.
Pace y bene, peace and good,
the Lord give you peace, the Lord give you peace.[28]

In the afternoon, he repaired walls, working until dark, and then he begged for his supper. Passersby mocked the poor, little mason who worked so hard, who had learned the skill needed while assisting the rebuilding of

Assisi's walls after a war. Others stopped to watch, and still others joined in the work at his cheery invitation to help him. One particular day, working on the roof of San Damiano, Francis shouted out to his collaborators and those who happened to be walking by, "Come and help me build the monastery of San Damiano, because holy virgins of Christ will dwell here who will glorify our Heavenly Father by their holy manner of life."[29] It was an inspired prophetic statement, and I will explain its fulfillment to you later. The Holy Spirit puts His desires into our hearts, whether we realize it or not.

Sermon at La Portiuncula

Another momentous day, Francis was walking in a forest of oak trees when he came upon an old, ruined chapel that measured only twenty-three by twelve feet.[30] It was used by foresters and belonged to the Benedictines; it was called *La Portiuncula,* which means "of the little portion." Francis was delighted. It was perfect, modest, and small. He would repair it and live next to it as a hermit. When it was finished, a priest from nearby Mount Sabasio came to deliver an early Mass for the faithful country folk. The Gospel text read that morning were the words of Jesus admonishing his apostles to go out into the world to preach the Good News of eternal life:

> As you go, proclaim this message: "The kingdom of heaven has come near." Heal the sick, raise the dead, cleanse those who have leprosy, drive out demons. Freely you have received, freely give. Do not get any gold or silver or copper to take with you in your belts; no bag for the journey or extra shirt or sandals or a staff, for the worker is worth his keep. (Mt 10:7–10)

Francis began to physically shake; it seemed as if Christ was speaking directly to him. When the Mass was over, he begged the priest to explain Jesus's discourse, line by line.

After hearing the priest's explanation, Francis was ecstatic, saying, "This is what I want; this is what I desire to follow with all my heart!"[31]

He gave away his walking stick, his cloak, and sandals. He made himself a plain tunic of coarse material, the deep rich color of the earth. To spell out the meaning of his mission, he cut the garment into the form of a cross. He was not to be a hermit but an evangelist. He was not to be silent but a preacher, proclaiming that the Kingdom of God had come to the kingdom of earth. The blind would see, the lame walk, and the poor would have Good News preached to them (Lk 7:22). Barefoot with a cord for a belt, Francis returned to Assisi and began to preach in the public square of the need for forgiveness, turning from sin, and living righteously before God. He expressed himself so passionately that many people followed him, marveling that Francis spoke a language so different from the sermons they heard on Sunday mornings. Instead of a vengeful deity, he spoke of a good and loving God.

Conditions of the Medieval Church

It grieves me to say this, but history does record that the church in the twelfth and thirteenth century was in a disgraceful place. Pope Innocent III was a godly man, and one of the greatest men to sit on Peter's chair, but he had to issue papal bull after papal bull (decree) against a variety of scandalous abuses.[32] There was unheard of depravity inside the church: luxury and lust, heresies and hypocrisy, political upheavals and corruption. However, there are always the faithful. With all its excesses, the church still had the power of the "keys of the kingdom" (Mt 16:19) to open the gates of paradise and confront sin. Francis preached the great need for repentance of sin and proclaimed peace and joy to those who love Christ. His ordinary words taught that God hates sin but loves the sinner and gives to the repentant heart holy joy.

To Francis's great surprise, men came asking to join him in his radical way of life. The first was a wealthy nobleman of Assisi, dear Brother Bernard di Quintavelle, who was also a doctor of law, both civil and canon, from the University of Bologna.[33] Sylvester joined them next, then a knight, dearest Brother Giles, and the fourth, a priest. They each sold all their possessions and gave the money to the poor. The people of Assisi had never seen such generosity. Soon there were twelve Brothers, singing through the hills and towns of Umbria, dressed like paupers, preaching two by two, just like the first apostles. Was it possible to own nothing and live happily on the earth?

The men greeted all they met on the road with the ancient salutation, "Good People, the Lord give thee peace."[34] When the Brothers returned from their forays in the world, Francis would wash their feet and feed them. They were first called the Penitents of Assisi and then simply the *Friars Minorias*, that is, "Brothers Minor" or "Little Brothers."[35] Fame of them spread across Italia because they were not cloistered, they worked with their hands, and they gave things away, for was it not Christ who said, "Give to the one who asks you" (Mt 5.42)?

Journey to Rome

One day, Francis was told that he needed papal permission to establish a religious order. It never occurred to him that he was starting a "religious order." He always believed himself to be under the authority of Christ's Holy church. You must remember there was only one Christian church in the West. We were not Protestant and Catholic, nor Baptist, Methodist, or Lutheran. These groups would come years later. In 1209, Francis and his disciples walked to Rome to ask the Supreme Pontiff himself to bless their way of service to Christ. The Brothers naively thought they could simply request an audience with the Lord Pope and be led before him. Providentially, Bishop Guido of Assisi just happened to be in Rome. He would once again be the instrument of intercession on Francis's behalf. Guido's good friend, Cardinal John of Savena, made it possible for the Brothers to have an audience with the Pope and plead their case.[36] Kneeling before the Curia (the papal court at the Vatican), Frances made his request for a new order that wanted to preach the Gospel in the open air, refuse property, and beg for food. Pope Innocent III was thoughtful:

> My dear son, your plan of life appears to me too severe. I see indeed that your fervor is great. But I must consider those who will come after you, lest your way of life be beyond their strength." Francis persisted, so the Pope offered, "Go and pray God to reveal to you how far what

> you want coincides with his will and when you have an answer return to me.[37]

Francis had his answer the next morning. As the pope looked down on the little poor beggars before him, a recent dream came clearly into his mind, a dream that had filled him with disquiet.[38] Dreams and visions in our time were taken seriously, often seen as God's way of communicating his holy will to us. In his dream, Innocent III saw himself seated with his tiara on his head, which turned into St. John's Lateran Basilica, the Mother Church of all Christendom. It began tilting to one side and was about to fall, when, most fortunately, a little monk, who looked like a beggar, leaned against the church and kept it from collapsing with his shoulder.[39] To the pope's amazement, the beggar in the dream was now kneeling before him. Francis began to speak in the most unusual manner, by telling a parable. This was never done in the Curia because a parable was a teaching method, and who dared to teach the pontiff? Standing up (another daring move), Francis began:

> An extremely rich king had married in the desert a very beautiful and very poor woman. She gave him many children, but she remained in the desert. When her sons were grown, they complained that they had nothing. She told them: "Do not be fearful for you are children of the king; go to his court and he will give you what you need." Then they went to the palace of the king, who was astonished by their beauty. "Whose sons are you?" he asked. "The sons of the poor woman who lives in the desert," they said. "Have no fear, you are my sons. Those who are nothing to me are nourished at my table, all the more reason why I shall take care of you."
>
> Francis added: "There is no danger that the sons and heirs of the eternal king will die of hunger, for the king in the parable was Christ, who would provide for everything; and it was he, Francis, who had given birth to them.[40]

The Holy Father was deeply moved, and a recess was ordered. The Cardinal of Savena addressed the Court, "These men only want us to allow them to live after the gospel. If we now declare that this is impossible, then we declare that the gospel cannot be followed and thus insult Christ, who is the origin of the gospel."[41]

Innocent III had no words with which to counter this persuasive argument. He gave the Lesser Brothers his verbal consent to their request and blessed them with admiration, saying he would follow their progress. Before leaving Rome, Cardinal John gave each Brother the monastic tonsure, which was the outer sign of the papal permission they had received to preach the Word of God. The newborn Franciscan Order joyfully preached its way back to Assisi and into its destiny.

New Life

It was so good to hear the Brothers singing in the streets of Assisi again. Night after night, I listened at my window for their approach as they begged for food, singing:

We adore you, Lord Jesus Christ,
and we bless you, in all the churches of the world.
For you, by your holy Cross, you have redeemed,
redeemed the world, redeemed the world.[42]

Oh, how I longed to be with them; to be free to follow wholly after God, to sit among them and hear inspired preaching of the Word of God. They said Brother Francis preached like no other. But I was not in a position to seek him out. I was just sixteen years and a female. I could not come and go as I pleased. Then, one happy day, Francis was invited to preach at the Cathedral of San Rufino, my parish church. I could not go to him, but God was bringing him to me. Madre was as deeply moved by his words, as I was. Oh, it was true: Francis's preaching was rare, not learned or eloquent, but simple and right. Francis knew God and spoke of him in such pleasant ways that my desire for the things of the Lord grew so intense that I hardly knew what to do with my thoughts and feelings. I wanted something wonderful to happen to me, but I didn't know what. I needed counsel. I would speak to Francis himself. Two of my cousins, Sylvester and Rufino, were now Friars Minor with Francis. Secret meetings were arranged with *El Poverello*, "the Little Poor Man."[43] Two other cousins, Pacifica and Bona di Guelfuccio, would act as my chaperone for our many clandestine meetings.

I told Brother Francis of my desire to know God better. He spoke of desiring eternal beauty rather than earthly things and of the joy in renouncing property, position, comfort, and worldly duties. But with even more glowing terms, he spoke of his Beloved, Christ the Cornerstone, Christ the Lamb of God, Christ the Vine, Christ the Way, Christ the Light of the World.[44] For two years, we met many times, always with Pacifica or Bona and some Brothers. My parents would have feared these meetings if they had known about them. I wanted to be free like the Little Brothers, to cast off the things of the world and walk the streets, singing of the goodness of the Lord. I wanted to preach like them of Christ and beg for my daily bread. I looked at my fellow Assisians and saw that so many were anxious, acquiring and building up little perishable kingdoms that consumed all their energy. Still, they were unhappy. I pleaded with Francis to let me join his community of Brothers. But it was not possible, for I was a woman. There were many nunneries, Benedictine and Cistercian, dotting the countryside that I could join. But Francis knew instinctively, as I did, that they were not right for me. I wanted to embrace "evangelical poverty" as he did, because without property for which to care and protect, there would be more time for God. I knew in my heart if I emptied myself of everything, there would be space for God to fill with himself.

How was it possible for me to join in the vision of Francis? He would help me, acting on my behalf. Like a biblical figure in ancient Jewish culture, Francis took the role of the friend of the bridegroom and acted as a mediator for a wedding. Since the time of Christ and for centuries before, a bride and groom-to-be did not meet from the day of the betrothal till the evening of the wedding. The friend of the bridegroom attended to all the details of the engagement. Such a friend meant nothing to the bride apart from his relationship to the groom. The bride meant nothing to the man save that she would soon be his friend's wife. Do not be mistaken; I loved Francis deeply, but there was never any romance between us because we each loved Jesus more.

Palm Sunday 1212

As the friend of my Bridegroom, Francis arranged my betrothal and looked after every detail. Finally, all was ready. The appointed day was Palm Sunday in the year of our Lord 1212. With the knowledge and blessing of Bishop Guido, I would leave the world to follow Jesus Christ as a spiritual daughter of Father Francis. That morning, I dressed for Sunday worship with much care, in my best robes and jewels to attend services with my beloved family for the last time. In the evening, while my parents were entertaining according to their tradition on this holy day, it was my moment to escape from the palace and the world. You must understand that only by a secret departure could I evade my family's opposition. Ever since I was twelve, my father had been looking for a productive marriage for me. Only a year before, Padre presented a man to me that he desired me to marry. I had to tell Madre, alone, that I had no intention whatsoever of marrying this suitor or any other. I think Madre knew in her heart that I had already given myself to God, and Christ Jesus would be my only love.

There was only one way for me to leave the great house: through the jib door. This was a special door used only for the passage of a coffin, known as the "door of the dead."[45] It was right for me to leave this way for I was now eighteen years old and chose to be dead to my life of position and wealth, since I had already sold all my inheritance and given the money to the poor. Pacifica joined me in the street; all was well. We hurried in silence for the closest city gate. It usually was locked, but Francis and the bishop had secretly attended to this obstacle. Safe outside the city wall, we headed for the woods. In the distance, we could hear the Lesser Brothers reciting the midnight prayers. They were waiting with burning torches to escort us to the Chapel of La Portiuncula. There, beneath the light held by the Brothers, I took the vows of poverty, chastity, and obedience. It was not a hard thing to do; it was pure, unspeakable joy. I was not sacrificing my life; I was embracing it. I was not running away from living; I was giving myself to the Creator of life. I wanted the whole world to know that I belonged only to my Lord Jesus Christ.

It was a bishop's responsibility to confer the habit and cut the hair of a postulate, but as someone ordained by the Lord, Francis quietly handed me my new habit—a rough robe made of undyed wool.[46]

In a simple ceremony used by thousands before us, Francis began, "What do you seek here?"

I renounced the world and all of its vanities, and gave myself totally to God. As the Brothers sang praises to God, I took off my slippers, silver belt, and fine jewelry. Pacifica assisted me with my outer garments, and I laid them at the foot of the altar as an offering to God. Father Francis, though only a deacon, cut my hair with shears, dropping it to the dirt floor. I put on the guimpe (a white cloth covering the neck and shoulders) and cap that Pacifica had brought for me. This was the proper headdress that all married women wore to cover their hair as a symbol of faithfulness to their husbands. Then Brother Francis placed a black veil upon my head as the symbol of affirming my total devotion to the Lord. We were now one, Brothers and Sister together in a common consecration to the Lord.

The Consecrated Life

My life was sealed and set upon its course. As I prayed before the altar, named in remembrance of Mary, the mother of Jesus, I thought of her. The Holy Spirit quickened to my memory her prophetic words in response to Elizabeth's proclamation that she was carrying the divine Son of God. Those magnificent words stirred my heart: "My soul glorifies the Lord and my spirit rejoices in God my Savior, for he has been mindful of the humble state of his servant" (Lk 1:46). I did not know what my life would be like from that moment on: where I would live, what I would eat, what I would do. But Francis said he and the Brothers would assist me in whatever way the Lord would lead. Life would be an adventure. That night, as arranged by Francis and the bishop, I stayed with Benedictine nuns a few miles away at the monastery of San Paulo delle Abbadesse Bastia.[47]

As we all feared, my family was shaken by my disappearance and began searching the countryside for me. A day later, my uncle Monaldo appeared at the monastery. I ran into the chapel to pray. He and his men burst into the room, shouting and cursing. Monaldo was my father's oldest brother and the head of the family; he demanded I return at once to my home. I grasped the altar cloth with both my hands and proclaimed my life choice. He brushed aside what I had to say and refused to believe that my decision was final. So I removed my veil and gimp, exposing the evidence that I had received the tonsure (cutting or shaving some or all of the hair on the top of the scalp as a sign of humility and religious devotion to God).

When the entire company saw that my hair was really gone, they accepted the fact that my life was now firmly fixed upon its path.

To my surprise, two weeks later, my younger sister, Catherine, ran away from home to join me in the consecrated life. Now our family was possessed with rage, for she at age fifteen was already betrothed to a nobleman of Assisi. Men came this time with strong-armed tactics. They captured her and beat her unmercifully, thinking this would sway her from her decision. I was not present but heard her crying out in great pain. I ran into the room where they were struggling and said forcefully that they were interfering with the will of God. Suddenly, as if struck by the powerful presence of the Holy Spirit and not my pleas, the men stopped. Feeling great pain and weakness in their bodies, they went sheepishly to their horses and rode back to Assisi, never to bother us again.

San Damiano Given to the Poor Ladies

The nuns in the monastery naturally feared further disturbances; we had to seek refuge elsewhere. Besides, we were not called to follow their lifestyle under the Rule of Benedict. Happily, through the petitions of Brother Francis and the empathy of the Bishop of Assisi, we were allowed to live on the grounds of San Damiano. It was a place for me and those who would join us. Imagine: The first church repaired with Francis's own hands, where he received the call of the Lord to rebuild God's church, was to be the home of the Poor Ladies. We lived in the little house and garden beside the church. For the next forty-two years, I would not leave its walls, save but twice.

Our family was beside themselves with disappointment. Little could we imagine that in the months that followed, another sister, Beatrice, two cousins, and several excellent noblewomen would join our simple way of life; after my father's death, my dear mother also joined our simple way of life. Unbeknown to us, we would become the second of three great Orders of Franciscans serving God throughout the world. The Brothers Minor never forgot us, for through Francis, they were our spiritual mentors. They begged food for us when we could not, distributed the altar clothes we made for the poor churches, and brought the sick to us that we might nurse and pray for them. We would live by the rule written for us by our blessed Father Francis. It began with a very simple statement that was more like a promise:

> Since, by divine inspiration, you have made yourselves daughters and handmaids of the Most High Sovereign King, the Heavenly Father, and have espoused yourselves to the Holy Spirit, choosing to live according to the perfection of the Holy Gospel, I am resolved and promise for myself and for my brothers the same loving care and special solicitude for you all as I have for them.[48]

The Poor Ladies enclosed community at San Damiano was a companion home to the Little Brothers of La Portiuncula. Our daily lives were very simple, full lives, busy with purpose and meaning. Every day was organized around prayer. At seven regular times, we would remember the life of Christ and the different hours of his Passion by reading appropriate psalms, hymns, and scripture passages, praying the Divine Hours.[49] These divisions of the day and night were set to remind us that all twenty-four hours of the day are consecrated to God, the one who sustains us with every breath we take.

Oh, how glorious it is to contemplate the Word of God, the written Word, where we meet the Living Word. I do not believe it is possible to really know God until you spend time alone with him in prayer and meditation, listening to the voice of the Holy Trinity. I do not believe that anything of good and eternal value transpires in this earthly life unless it has first been asked in prayer. God is good and desires to give nothing but blessing, health, and peace to every creature. We do not have the material and spiritual things we need because we do not ask for them. God desires to do more for us than we can ask because we refuse to recognize the depth and width of his promises. Ours was the privilege of a double portion of worship in ministry unto the Lord through intercessory prayer. That is prayer for others, prayer for the world, and special prayer for the poor, who do not have all that they need.

Life inside San Damiano

We would live a life of penance,[50] voluntarily fasting three times a week to remember we were born with a fallen nature. There were periods of silence, to recognize in the quietness that God is ever-present with us, and his voice is the sweetest one of all. We would live the cloistered life so we might come apart to be with the Lord in prayer and ministry unto the Lord. We would sleep upon mats on the floor in one large room and grow our own fruits and vegetables. We would spin, making vestments and altar clothes for the poor churches. Our work would never be a business, but only a free service to bless others.

We would remain barefoot to remember that where God's Spirit dwells, there is Holy Ground. Our convent would be different; other monasteries required new candidates to bring a dowry with them for its support. All our ladies gave away their worldly wealth before entering, just as the Lesser Brothers did. We wanted to show that it was possible that one could live literally according to the Gospel. We would do exactly what Jesus said to the rich young ruler: "If you want to be perfect, go, sell your possessions and give to the poor, and you will have treasure in heaven. Then come, follow me" (Mt 19:21). Every woman who came to the community of San Damiano came with nothing. It wasn't hard for us to do, but it was hard to convince the hierarchy of the church that we could live this way as pilgrims in the world.

We wanted everyone to understand that our life of poverty was not only of a material nature but also a spiritual one. We were not abasing ourselves in an effort to earn God's favor. Through our dedication to Lady Poverty, we would learn a spiritual dependence upon Christ our Savior. We would wait upon the Lord, turning to him for all of our necessities. We would not be ashamed to live in the humility of poverty, since for our sake, Jesus Christ made himself poor in this world. Having emptied himself, Jesus purchased for you and for me a royal inheritance, even the Kingdom of Heaven, which is the greatest of spiritual treasures. Neither Francis nor I ever intended to begin a religious order. We simply wanted to imitate the life of our Lord Jesus as closely and, *Si*, as radically as we possibly could, and to our surprise and delight, others of the same desire joined our company.

Healings and Miracles

As we grew in the grace and knowledge of Jesus Christ, we began to see more manifestations of the Holy Spirit around and among us. God was accomplishing something new in the world, and it was exhilarating. There were healings and miracles similar to those described in the Gospels of the Holy Scriptures. I remember the first wonder-filled physical healing we saw within the community. Five of our Sisters suddenly came down with the same illness. All were burning with fevers and lay in their sickbeds, shivering. I besought God to raise them up and finished the prayer by anointing each one with oil on their foreheads with the sign of the Cross. Within a few minutes, all five had their fevers break, and all were well again.[51] Glory to God.

Another time, Sister Benvenuta had suffered for twelve long years with a sore under her arm that was called a fistula. Many of those twelve years had been in the convent with us. When it grew so sore that no one could touch her, she asked for special prayer. When the prayer was over, with the sign of the Cross, in the name of the Father, Son, and Holy Spirit, the bleeding began to stop. Days later, she was completely cured.[52] Not long after, Francis sent to us Brother Stephano of the Friars Minor, who was afflicted with terrible seizures and a kind of madness.[53] I prayed for him in Jesus's name, anointing his forehead with oil with the sign of the Cross. The dear Brother slept for a time in my prayer place, and when he woke, he ate heartily and departed in good health, never to be afflicted with symptoms again.

In the years that followed, people of the towns and countryside brought their sick to us. Some we nursed in the infirmary until they were well. Others were brought just for prayer. I remember a deaf man who received back his hearing. One little boy, carried in his father's arms, was stricken with a coating over his eyes so that he could not see. After a prayer in Jesus's name, the malady dissolved, and he could see. I can still see the little one skipping away, hand in hand with his happy padre. I did not think I possessed a special gift of healing. God is the Healer; it is the prayer of faith that the Holy Spirit honors, not the person who prays. We were also privileged to witness other kinds of miracles. Let me just share one of them with you.

Fire at La Portiuncula

I rarely saw Francis since he was often away preaching the Gospel, but when he was in Umbria, I longed for his counsel and bade him come preach to us. One particular year, I asked him to take a meal with me, something we had never done. When he agreed to the meal, he decided that it should take place at La Portiuncula. Since I had not left San Damiano, he believed it would strengthen me to once again be at the place where I had taken my vows. It was a most gracious gesture. When the appointed day arrived, twelve Brothers came to escort a Sister and me to the church. Francis had the meal laid upon the ground, as was his custom.[54] We sat in a circle, two Sisters and thirteen Brothers.

The first dish was offered, but we never started to eat. Father Francis began to talk of God's goodness with such wonder that the presence of God descended upon us and filled the whole room. We rejoiced together, praising God and lifting our eyes and hands toward the heavens. Time seemed to stand still, but after what might have been a half-hour, we heard strange noises outside, several horses and people shouting.

Abruptly, the door flew open, and men came running into the room, shouting, "Where is the fire? Are you all right?"

They seemed more puzzled than frightened. More and more people gathered outside the door. Seeing us sitting peacefully on the floor startled them as well. These were residents of Assisi and Bettona and the surrounding farms, so they told us their story.

From as far away as the walls of their cities, they could see what seemed to be a great blaze around the whole church of the Little Portion. From many different places, people thought La Portiuncula and its forests were on fire, and the people came running to aid in a rescue. Now, they looked down at the meager bit of food arranged upon the floor and saw the Friars Minor and the Poor Sisters sitting in their places. The people marveled and understood that what they had seen was a divine fire, not a physical one.[55] As they went away chattering together, they were amazed and comforted by what they had just witnessed, and so were we. I don't think we ate one morsel of the food that day. God had fed us to overflowing with his very presence.

Evangelical Poverty Spreads

To our great surprise, we began to receive requests for our written rule and for Sisters to begin other communities as Abbesses in other parts of Italia and beyond. It was absolutely incredible to think that the hidden life of twelve Poor Ladies inside the walls of San Damiano would be known by half the entire world. This was not our doing. As we grew in numbers, so did the Brothers Minor at an amazing rate.

Francis decided that twice a year, on Pentecost and then in September, all the Brothers from across Europe should gather together at La Portiuncula. The purpose was twofold: to reawaken the spirit of the Brotherhood and to decide where next to preach the Gospel. By the fifth year of the gatherings, no less than five thousand Franciscan beggars came to hear El Poverello. This great gathering became known as the Chapter of the Mats,[56] since the only way such a crowd could be accommodated was to have each monk make his own mat from the rushes along the river and sleep beneath the stars and Sister Moon, praised in the *Canticle of the Sun*. It was a glorious meeting that told the world that evangelical poverty was truly possible. One could take the words of Christ seriously and imitate Jesus in his way of life: "The blind receive sight, the lame walk, those who have leprosy are cleansed, the deaf hear, the dead are raised, and the good news is preached to the poor" (Mt 11:5). The church of Jesus Christ was being renewed at its lowest level, where the common people lived their daily lives.

The Brothers came far distances to be encouraged by the teaching of their Father Francis. When all present had received his blessing, they spread out through the world as pilgrims. The chapters became more important, and churchmen started to come, even bishops and cardinals. Soon, the Brotherhood was too large, and it had to be divided into provinces and chapters.

At this time, Francis felt a renewed call to the missionary journey. The East beckoned him, so in 1212, he left the Brotherhood in capable hands and headed for Syria, but he was shipwrecked off the coast of Yugoslavia and returned home.[57] The next year, he successfully preached through Spain, in an attempt to go to Morocco, but illness stopped his progress. Finally, in 1219, with the blessing of Pope Honorius, Francis was able to join the soldiers in Egypt on the Fifth Crusade, taking some Brothers with him.[58] At an extraordinary meeting in Damietta with Malik-al-Kamil,[59] the Sultan of Egypt, he tried in vain to convert the Muslim but won instead the right of safe passage to Jerusalem for the Brothers Minor.

Fighting for the Privilege of Poverty

Unfortunately, while Father Francis was away in the Holy Land, great changes had taken place among the Little Brothers. When he arrived home, he was grieved to find several new buildings, including a refractory and a library, and fine gold pieces decorated the rooms. He walked into the new refractory and thought it was a feast day but learned this was their daily fare. He tried to persuade them to return to Lady Poverty as their spiritual ideal, but it was too late. At the same time, His Holiness Pope Gregory IX was urging me to accept the right to own property, just like the Brothers Minor.[60] I was not sure how I could resist his plea. Our order was based on complete poverty, the right to own nothing ourselves. What could I do? My answer came in an unsolicited letter from Father Frances, which began:

> I, little Brother Francis, wish to follow the life and the poverty of our most high Lord Jesus Christ, and I desire to persevere until death. … I beg you, Poor Lady, and advise you to live always in this most holy life and in poverty. Beware of departing in any way from it because of the advice or teaching of anyone whatsoever.[61]

This was the encouragement I needed. Even after Francis died, more than one pope asked me to relax our rule to include the ownership of property. One argued that we should be like the other orders and not an exception in Christ's Holy Church. All my life, I needed to stand firm in faith to my original call from God. The church had granted me the right not to own property under the rule we lived by for several years. Therefore, I saw no reason why it was acceptable to God at one time, but not at another.

I wrote to His Holiness Honorius III in the humblest of terms, but concluded my final argument with a distinct plea: "Lord Pope, absolve me of my sins, but let me follow the way of Jesus Christ in all things!"[62]

Almighty God did not desert me; the Lord Pontiff relented at that time. I prayed and waited many years at San Damiano for an official bull from Rome approving the rule that I wrote. I based it on the ideal of Lady Poverty, which meant we would not own property, individually or collectively.

God was faithful, as always, for a leather-bound bull from the Lord Pontiff finally arrived at San Damiano; it came while I was extremely ill. One sentence was all I needed to hear from the parchment: "We confirm by our Apostolic authority the form of life that blessed Francis gave you and which you have humbly requested."[63] With this in hand, I could face Sister Death in peace, knowing my Sisters would remain free to imitate Christ in our chosen way of life.

Please do not think that Father Francis and I naively believed all people should follow our way of life. Evangelical poverty is a special calling and spiritual gift from God, who with any call always provides the ability to carry out his bidding. Still, the Franciscan movement with its spiritual idealism appealed to all segments of society, from poor families to royalty of the highest rank. Many people felt spiritually obligated to their responsibilities as family members or their positions in society, and therefore, they could not forsake all to join the monastic beggars. However, by relaxing some of the rules, laypeople could join the Third Order of St. Francis, the Brothers and Sisters of Penance. This idea was something new to the world. There had been secular people attached to cloisters who followed rules of daily life, but never had the goal of Christian perfection itself, coupled by a special rule, been proposed. A parent at home, husband and wife, merchant and peasant, master and servant, could remain at their posts, but all were to practice the same spirit of detachment from the world. They could live in an attitude of penance, with loyalty to the Body of Christ, the Ekklesia. It is to God's glory that centuries later, the Brothers and Sisters of Penance still thrive today.

The Stigmata

After Francis gave up the entire leadership of the Brothers Minor, he became one Brother among thousands. He had always desired a life of contemplation and prayer. Now there was time. In 1222, just two years before his death, he walked to a hermitage in the Apennines Mountains with Brothers Leo, Angelo, and Rufino.[64] He wanted to fast for forty days, so he made himself a hut on the ledge of a deep ravine on the Mountain of La Verna. Before him was a vista of God's majestic handiwork. He asked that only Brother Leo visit him, and only once a day. Weeks later, on September 14 (the Feast of the Exaltation of the Cross),[65] after a night of prayer, Francis was kneeling in prayer and sensed the Spirit of the Lord all around him. He told me later that he asked God for two graces. He wanted to feel in both his heart and also in his body the pain that Christ Jesus had suffered upon the Cross.[66] Suddenly, Francis saw a seraph with six wings swooping down from the sky. Two wings covered the seraph's head, two reached to his feet, and two were spread in flight. The image bore the likeness of a crucified man, his hands and feet nailed to a cross.[67] When the vision faded, Francis felt strange pains in his hands, feet, and side. The marks on his body resembled in place and color the wounds made by the nails and the lance that pierced Christ Jesus, just like he had seen them in the vision.

Blessed Francis did all within his power to conceal these marks, not wishing this manifestation to be seen by his Brothers and Sisters, but he could not always hide them. When Brother Giles first told me of these wounds, I could only weep for joy. I had not heard of such a physical occurrence before, but I believed it to be true. I could only praise God for choosing to answer Francis's prayer in such a magnificent visitation of himself. I do not propose to understand God's ways, but I rejoice in everything he does.

Brother Leo nursed the wounds and kept them bound most of the time. I made slippers for Francis's feet. Finally, he was persuaded that such a manifestation of God must not be kept a secret. No less than fifty people documented their eyewitness testimony of observing the stigmata wounds on Francis's body. He would not remain the only person in history to experience this extraordinary phenomenon. I truly believe the inner life can be externalized in the physical world. By faith, we know that our all-powerful God does reveal himself in mysterious ways, as he chooses.

Francis and Nature

If I were to simply say why I believe God selected Francis as his chosen instrument, I would have to say it was because Francis understood two things. First, the greatest thing anyone can do is love God with all their heart, with all their soul, and with all their being: the very first commandment. Then, because you love the Creator, you must also love all of his creation, every living thing. How can you love God without loving the things he has made, especially those created in his own image? It is true that Francis dearly loved nature, but not because it pleased him. He enjoyed the natural world because it so marvelously praised God. He saw in living creatures object lessons of God's love. The raven and the sparrow "do not sow or reap or store away in barns, and yet your heavenly Father feeds them" (Mt 6:26).

I have often been asked if Francis really preached to the birds. I heard this story too, so I asked Brother Giles one day, "Did Francis really preach a sermon to the birds on the road to Cannara?"

With a sheepish grin, he said, "*Si*, Sister Clare. He did indeed, but he did it for a lark."

You may ask, "What does one preach to larks and canaries?" That is easy to answer. He might say:

> My little sisters, dear birds, you owe much to God, your Creator, and you ought to sing His praises at all times and in all places, because He has given you liberty to fly about. He has given you fountains and rivers to quench your thirst, mountains and valleys in which to play and trees in which to build your nests. Beware my little sisters of ingratitude, and study always to give praise to God![68]

When Francis preached to the birds, it was not so much for their instruction, but for his own. Like King David, Francis saw that "the heavens declare the glory of God; the skies proclaim the work of his hands"

(Ps 19:1). Since all creation tumbled from the touch of God's hand, there was a kinship with creation, but do not be confused. Francis was not a pantheist who said God was in the tree, the grass, or the water of the stream. We must never confuse the creation with the Creator.

Illness Births Italy's Finest Poem

Toward the end of Father Francis's life, he lost his sight. After weeks of fasting on Mount La Verna, Brother Leo had him carried down the mountain on a donkey. Francis wished to preach and wanted to leave the hermitage for the towns of Italia, but he only got as far as San Damiano. I had to persuade him to stay and be nursed until he was stronger. The Brothers built a little hut for him in the garden of our cloister, where he stayed for fifty days.[69] In the hut, Francis's eyes pained him so badly that he could not endure the sunshine by day or the light of a fire by night. He cried out to God for help to patiently bear his affliction. Long days turned into weeks, and then the answer came, a joyous tiding from the Holy Spirit: "Sing amid your pain and infirmity, for the Kingdom of Heaven, an everlasting treasure beyond your dreams, is already yours."[70]

From Francis's heart came forth a song to the Lord of Creation. His suffering had released the song with its great secret. The whole world must lift God up in praise—the world that brings both pain and joy, even Brother Sun, in whom Francis once delighted, but which now brought pain to his eyes. In ecstatic thankfulness for the created heavens and earth, the Little Poor Man wrote a poem called *Canticle of the Sun*:

Most high, Omnipotent, Good Lord,
To you alone belong praise and Glory, honor and blessing.
No man is worthy to breathe your Name.
Be praised, my Lord for all your creatures.
In the first place for the blessed Brother Sun
Who gives us the day and lightens us through you.
He is beautiful and radiant with his great splendor;
Giving witness of you, most Omnipotent One.
Be Praised, my Lord, for Sister Moon and the stars
Formed by you so bright, precious, and beautiful.

Be praised, my Lord, for Brother Wind
And the airy skies, so cloudy and serene;
For every weather, be praised, for it is life-giving.
Be praised, my Lord, for Sister Water
So necessary yet so humble, precious, and chaste.
Be praised, my Lord, for Brother Fire,
Who lights up the night,
He is beautiful and carefree, robust and fierce.
Be praised my Lord, for our sister, Mother Earth,
Who nourishes and watches us
While bringing forth abundant fruits with flowers and herbs.
Praise and bless the Lord.
Render him thanks.
Serve him with great humility. Amen.[71]

A few months later, Francis realized he was dying and added the final verse:

Be praised, my Lord, for our Sister Bodily Death,
From whom no living man can escape.
Woe to those who die in mortal sin.
Blessed are those, whom are found in Your most Holy will,
For the second death will not harm them.
Praise and bless my Lord and thank Him,
And serve Him with great humility![72]

Sister Death

On October 3, 1226, Sister Bodily Death came to Francis, in the forty-fifth year of his life. All Italia, and most of Europe, knew El Poverello was dying. News spread like the wind, and Brothers Minor began walking towards Assisi just to be closer to him. His last request was to be laid upon the ground and stripped of his clothing, in the same manner as Jesus was at the time of his death. His last two days at beloved Portiuncula were spent praying and listening to the Word of God being read. Francis called his Brothers around him to give them his last exhortation:

> Up to this moment gentle Brothers we have done nothing. Eye has not seen and ear has not heard all that God has prepared for those who love him. I have done what was mine to do, may Christ teach you what you are to do.[73]

The next morning, Sunday, October 4, 1226, the Brothers carried our Blessed Father Francis's body in a processional to San Georgio's Cathedral, stopping first at San Damiano so we, his Poor Ladies, could see him one last time.[74] The grille gate was lifted, and the Brothers held up, as long as we wished, the bier on which Francis's body lay. Our loss was comforted by the sure knowledge that we would be together again for all eternity in the heavenly Kingdom. The people of Assisi came to pray and join in the march. The town that had once mocked him, yelling, "Pazzo e Coocho," now wept openly over the one who had touched their lives as an instrument of peace, peace in their world and peace in their hearts.

How I missed his wise council, but his words were always with me. It is important to do daily tasks when one is grieving great loss, to enhance healing for the sake of others and oneself. So both Brothers and Sisters Minor continued our lives as we did when El Poverello was with us, imitating the life of Jesus, as we had been taught. The hardships of the Middle Ages remained, and we would face them, along with our fellow citizens. In the year 1240, Frederick II came fighting across Umbria, heading for Rome with twenty thousand soldiers and horseman at his command. Assisi was in his way, and we heard the news of his mercenary troops pillaging, slaughtering, and burning. The residents shuddered in fear, even terror.

Miraculous Divine Protection

On a sunny September day, my Sisters were at prayer at San Damiano during *Terce* (9 a.m.). I was in my bed taken, with a fever. My daughters ran up the stairs to tell me horsemen and pike blades were seen in the orchards outside the convent. Another Sister appeared with frightening news; men had scaled the walls and were in the garden. I bade my daughters, "Take me down to the refectory and bring me the Sacrament box." Downstairs, I took the ivory box containing the Host and stood in the open doorway.

There before us were faces of five men wearing red turbans and gold suits of armor. These were Saracens, the feared infidels.

I prayed, "O, God look upon these servants of yours, for I cannot protect them. Save the city as well, Lord."[75]

God's voice spoke to me, saying, "Do not fear; I will always protect you."[76]

I opened the simple box, exposing the Blessed Sacrament for the men to see and held it out, saying nothing. These Saracens were all Muslim believers. What would they know of the Host and of our God? What was their intent?

Unexpectedly, the men drew back in surprise; eyes full of fear, they stood still as statues for a moment, then ran to the walls, climbed over, fell into the olive trees, and scurried away.

A scripture came clearly to my mind that Moses said to the children of Israel at the Red Sea: "Do not be afraid. Stand firm and you will see the deliverance the LORD will bring you today" (Ex 14:13). We did not hear any more clanging of swords or cries of battle. Assisi was saved that day, as were we. Our God is able and answers the prayers of his people. Never doubt this, beloved friends.

How good our God is! How excellently he blesses us, beyond our wildest imaginations. When I look back over my life, I can only marvel in thankfulness for the multitude of things he has done for me. Some would argue, "You lived sparsely with little food and comforts when you didn't need to do so. You could have married a wealthy knight and had many children. You spent many years with sickness confined to a bed." I ask what is physical suffering compared to having an intimate relationship with the Lord of the universe?

God provided abundant human relationships for me. God honored me by bringing three of my Lord Pontiffs to visit me at San Damiano on several occasions. They came asking for prayer and even counsel, which was my privilege to give. Each one became a close friend. Over the years, five popes acknowledged our way of life and cared about the comfort of Francis and their spiritual daughters, my Poor Ladies. God gave me fellow disciples, the Brothers Minor and my Sisters, my true daughters-in-the-Lord, as well as many friends, both met and unmet. These are the true joys of life, all gifts from God. What are material things compared to relationships? They are nothing, dear ones; nothing.

Dear brothers and sisters-in-the-Lord, God is worthy of all our love and all our life. All parts of our body and all aspects of our being are his and should bring praise and glory to his Holy name. Our love for God is not meant to be a private love affair. It must embrace his entire Creation and all souls that live in it. Be courageous, holy and loving children of the Light. May Christ draw you ever nearer. Remember me, *Chiara*, a servant of Christ, a little plant of our Blessed Father Francis, and Mother of the Poor Ladies. I admonish and bless you:

In your rising, gaze upon Christ,
in your waking hours, consider Christ,
in your praying, contemplate Christ,
and desire always to imitate Him.[77]

Your servant,
Chiara

Conclusion

In Mother Clare's generation, her mentor, Father Francis, through no conscious effort, desire, or power of his own, became one of the most influential, loved, and admired persons in the world. Eight centuries later, he is still a household name. Garden statues of St. Francis holding a bird or with animals huddled around him can be found throughout many countries, recalling his love of God expressed in nature. He did far more that preach a sermon to a flock of birds. Instead, he taught the Western world to value the things made by God rather than the things made by man. He made his fellow man think anew about what was good and right and true. He and all his followers, both then and to this day, simply want their lives to show that God is good and absolute, that he is Almighty God, and as such, he loves all living things, especially those created in his image.

St. Clare of Assisi was equally revered as St. Francis in her lifetime, but her fame has faded over the centuries. She would not care about this but prefer that only the name of Jesus be lifted up and worshipped unreservedly. It would surprise her to know that in the twenty-first century, there are Poor Clare convents around the world. They still follow the rule she wrote herself while wearing the same barefoot habit and embracing the Privilege of Poverty. Lady Chiara's life choices demonstrate forever what a person can do who passionately follows Jesus Christ as closely as possible, abandoning worldly comforts and giving themselves to a life of prayer and the nurturing of others. The Catholic Church has not forgotten St. Clare's shining light, and she remains connected to the legacy of the rejuvenating Franciscan movement in the medieval church, whose followers continue to this day.

It has been noted that any business or organization that keeps growing over a period of time will add more rules to its traditions, thereby making its structure cumbersome and forgetting its original purpose. The church is not exempt from this phenomenon. The Spirit of the Lord in the book of Revelation wrote to the church in Ephesus saying, that while he saw their hard work and perseverance, "Yet I hold this against you: You have forsaken the love you had at first" (Rev 2:4). The holy lifestyle of Francis and Clare brought the Christians of their day back to a desire to follow after their first love, Jesus Christ, and his simple way of true living. By the fifteenth century, one-third of the population of Europe was living in monasteries. Many joined the monastic life because the church taught the surest way to heaven was by taking Holy Vows. As the years passed, the life inside these religious communities varied greatly; many rules and practices made the established church powerful and wealthy, while the peasant masses remained poor. It was again time for a return of the church to its first love!

One monk in the little town of Wittenberg, Germany, seeking peace with God, would protest against the cumbersome rules in which he found himself. In the next chapter, we will meet an ex-nun who became the perfect helpmeet to this outspoken man. Like Francis, he would seek to reform the wayward practices of the church of Rome and return believers' hearts back to their first love. The marriage of Katharina Von Bora to the Reverend Doctor Martin Luther would make the happiest twenty years of their lives, in spite of the chaos and attacks of the world around them.

Discussion Questions

1. What enabled Lady Clare to give up her wealth and position in society to live a lifestyle at poverty level?
   What does her example teach us about living for Christ?
2. Mother Clare was admired for the fact that she never asked any of her sisters to do anything that she would not do herself, even insisting at times that she would do the most strenuous or menial task alone. How does that characteristic of humility manifest itself in your life?
3. Mother Clare never asked or expected others to follow her austere lifestyle. What was it about her that drew so many to her for friendship and counsel?
4. What strikes you about the results of Mother Clare's life of persistent prayer?

Mother of the Reformation

Introducing Katharina Luther

In1983, the Christian church celebrated the five hundredth anniversary of the birth of Martin Luther, the Reformation's greatest reformer. A lowly Augustinian monk confronted the greatest power on earth of his day, the Roman Catholic Church, by simply posting ninety-five theses requesting debate on the door of the University Church, Wittenberg. Luther ignited an explosion that continues to this day, planting the tree of Protestantism that counts scores of branches, numbering more than 800 million Christian members.[1]

While Martin Luther's contribution to Western civilization is well acknowledged, few know he had a wife. Katharina Von Bora was born in 1499 to an impoverished family of the lower nobility. At the death of her mother and subsequent remarriage of her father, she was sent to a nunnery at the age of nine and took her vows as a novice at sixteen, as there was little else for her to do. Views favoring a Reformation in the church crept through the walls of her convent, and on the eve of Easter Sunday 1523, Katharina and eight other nuns escaped to Wittenberg by a plan arranged by none other than Dr. Luther himself. He quickly arranged marriages for all these former Sisters except one, Katharina, often called Katie. After two years, at her suggestion, he proposed marriage.

When Katharina married Martin in June of 1525, the Western world was shocked with outrage and ridicule at the breaking of their holy vows. Undaunted, Katie proved herself up to the challenge of helpmeet to her famous, genius husband. Possessing many talents, Mrs. Luther was a highly proficient homemaker, realtor, farmer, and outstanding practical nurse.[2] In the first eight years of their marriage, the Luthers were blessed with six children, three boys and three girls. Descendants of the youngest child, Margaretta, live today in Mohra, Germany, in the same area as the Luthers.[3]

During Dr. Luther's marriage and last twenty years on earth, he faced a price on this head, blame for starting the Peasant Wars, and unending demands for his time and attention from paupers to kings. Yet he declared those years were the happiest of his life. Marriage and family were joys he never expected. Martin and Katie's converted monastery home became the first Christian parsonage, which established the precedent for Protestants of a married clergy for the next five hundred years.

An Open Letter from Katharina Luther

Guten tag, new friends,

A very good day to you in grace and peace in the wonderful name of our Lord and Savior, Jesus Christ. I am truly surprised that you would ask me, an ordinary woman, to write to you of our controversial lives. It was my dear husband who seemed to always have a goose-quill pen in his hand, scratching out a letter, not me. Herr Doctor must have written a hundred thousand letters, if he wrote one. I had no time to write to friends, only to him, when he was called away from us. Please know, as I address you in this letter, that I am nothing more than a runaway nun whom God took pity upon and chose to become the wife of a truly great man, the Reverend Doctor Martin Luther. That is all I am, just a runaway nun. My story is really his story, for I believe my life began and ended with his, and I am not ashamed to say so. Were it not for my celebrated husband, no one would know my name or the names of my children.

Is life not strange and full of paradox? God chooses the smallest and simplest things to confound the wise. Why else would he take a lowly monk from a little village in Saxony to confront the strongest power of our day, the Holy Roman See? I will guess that I first learned about Martin Luther the same way you did. We each read about him in print, you from a history book and I from a newspaper. I was living in the convent of Marienthron in the town of Nimptsch, a half-day walk south of Grimma, in the eastern part of Germany.[4] It was a Cistercian Order for ladies of noble birth. We were not among the strictest nunneries, but we were still cloistered away behind stone barricades. We were not to know what was happening in the outside world (or should I say the real world?). Yet through the walls seeped news of great changes taking place. Long-held practices and even church doctrines were being questioned.

Debate in Leipzig

Papers that mysteriously appeared in my convent were discreetly passed from one nun to the next. One article in the summer of 1519 described a famous debate that took place in Leipzig between two rival university professors, a Doctor Johann Eck and a Doctor Martin Luther of Wittenberg. Dr. Eck was recognized as the supreme theologian of the day as well as the champion of the papacy in Rome. He and the pope had labeled Friar Luther the "Son of Iniquity!"[5] The paper reporting the debate was clearly one-sided. You be the judge. It described Johann Eck (and I thought it a good name for him, Eck!) this way: "He is a square set fellow with voice more rough than clear. His eyes, mouth and whole face remind one more of a butcher or a bulldog rather than a theologian."[6] Concerning Martin Luther, there was a detailed description:

> Martin is of middle height, in the vigor of manhood and has a clear, penetrating voice. He is learned and has the Scripture at his fingers' ends. He knows Greek and Hebrew sufficiently to judge of the interpretations. A perfect forest of words and ideas stand at his command. He is affable and friendly, in no sense dour or arrogant. He is equal to anything. In company he is vivacious, jocose,

always cheerful, no matter how hard his adversaries press him.[7]

The article rightly identified the fact that the content of the debate was not its published subject, on the merits of indulgences. Instead, the real issue at stake was the source for spiritual truth. What was the highest authority in the Christian church, or more importantly, the Christian faith? The Vatican's official position claimed that the pope was the oracle of God and spoke for him. Luther asked, "Which one?" There had been (as we say in German when counting from one) *eins, zwei*, and *drei* popes, all at once. Frustrated from the laughter and taunts from the spectators, Professor Eck cunningly switched his position to say church councils were the correct source for spiritual authority. He pointed proudly to the Council of Nicaea, which met in AD 325 and produced the noble Nicene Creed.

Luther quickly asked the celebrated antagonist of the great accomplishment of the Council of Basil, which met for eighteen years and wrote nothing. Having lost yet another debate round, Eck resorted to the sly tactic of changing the subject completely from the issues under discussion to Friar Luther himself.

Eck faced Martin and flattered him, saying, "You sir, are an orator among orators. You beguile us with your eloquence of clever speech. There is none greater than you in disputation for you can speak for over an hour on any subject you wish."

Dr. Luther would not be outdone by such a simple ploy. He immediately retorted, "Ah, but you, sir, are a far greater orator than I. For you, sir, can speak for over an hour without any subject at all!"

The article concluded with Dr. Eck, exhausted after eleven long days of debate, proclaiming Luther a heretic equal to John Wycliffe and John Hus, because he made shocking statements that were insolent to the church. Dr. Luther declared that he would "accept neither pope nor council for they often err and contradict one another, and only that which is supported by Holy Scripture can be true revelation from God."[8] People throughout Europe admired Dr. Luther because he accurately put to pen what so many people were thinking but were afraid to say. He soon became the champion of the common person.

In the following months, a stream of banned articles, tracts, and pamphlets continued to flow through the cracking walls of my cloister. Dr. Luther became our secret hero and the popular topic of gossip among the nuns. He wrote on many subjects and often attacked the abuses of the papacy in Rome. The pope, in response, excommunicated Friar Luther from the church. We were so concerned for him. Without the church, to whom could you confess your sins and receive absolution for them? How could you receive the elements of the Eucharist, if barred from attending Mass? Without the church, how could you go to heaven? Dr. Luther did not worry about this but declared instead that it was easily fixed. He gathered together with fellow professors and students, who built a bonfire on the Main Street of Wittenberg by the old Elster Gate. With dramatic ceremonial flair, he tossed the Papal Bull *Exsurge Domine*,[9] that declared him a heretic, onto the flames, to the shock and delight of the crowd. If that was not enough, he took a copy of the Roman Catholic Church Canon Law, tossed it onto the fire, and declared the Roman Catholic Church excommunicated from Christianity.[10] It was not so, but he had made his point.

Freedom in the Christian Life

Dr. Luther wrote often about the freedom there was in the Christian life, which intrigued my fellow nuns the most. There was little freedom in our regulated days. News came that a dozen monks from the nearby Franciscan Monastery of the Holy Cross in Grimma had left their monastic life for good to marry.[11] The men became convinced that the celibacy demanded from the Vatican was just a human imposition. Apparently, Luther had written on the subject in three different treatises, arguing for a better understanding of marriage, declaring it to be equal to that of celibacy. In fact, he reasoned that there was no scriptural basis for a life of celibacy to gain favor with God. In *Concerning Married Life*, the bachelor friar wrote that whether a person married or remain single was a question of individual choice, and neither state should ever be said to be more holy than the other. Please understand that the good doctor never told anyone to break a holy vow in favor of marriage. Instead, when Dr. Luther first heard that monks and nuns were leaving their cloisters and marrying, he snapped, "Good heavens, they won't give me a wife!"[12] I laugh now, knowing what God had planned for him.

Monastic life had been my experience since I had been sent to the nunnery in my ninth year. My gentle mother passed from this life when I was almost six springs old, leaving Father to grieve for her and raise three brothers and me. Father was considered lower nobility. He owned lands, yet money was a struggle. Giving me to a religious order was not just considered a holy parental sacrifice to God; it also eased the family finances. Besides, I don't think my stepmother liked me. She said I was willful, and I did not care for her much, either. I want you to know that cloisters served more than just the mystics of our day. Society did not provide orphanages, old folk's homes, or any kind of institutions to help the homeless, mentally ill, or poverty-stricken. If a family had a member they did not particularly want, you could buy their entrance into a monastery or find sanctuary there as an outcast yourself. Many within the cloistered walls had no place to go, so it was not uncommon for children to take their novice vows as they became of age. Such was the case for me when I took the veil at only sixteen years.[13] I was not opposed to this step because I did love God and embraced the teachings of the church the way they had been taught to me. But Dr. Luther's writing made sense, and upon contemplation, a number of Sisters decided with me that we wanted to be wives and mothers. We would need husbands, and for that we realized we would not find them inside the nunnery. We confided in Sister Magdalena, my aunt by birth, who secretly appealed to Dr. Luther, petitioning him to aid us in obtaining our freedom.[14]

Midnight Escape to a New Life

Months passed after the correspondence, and then a directive came. We were to be in the back courtyard by the delivery gate at nine o'clock on the eve of Easter Sunday, April 4, 1523.[15] There were no other instructions. The hour was perfect, for it was a regular sleep time. The cloister would rise two hours later to ready itself for the Easter midnight Mass. At the appointed time, our racing hearts gathered in silence, anticipating our escape, though we did not know what we would face. We heard the sound of a clamoring wagon pull up to the gate. It was Leonard Koppe;

a merchant from Torgau, accompanied by his good friend, Wolfgang Tommitsch.[16] They had often delivered barrels of herring and kegs of wine to the convent. The co-conspirators unloaded a delivery of kegs in their noisy manner and then signaled for us to come. They helped us onto the wagon, which was full of empty herring barrels, and threw a heavy canvas over their live cargo and strapped it down tightly. We jostled about over rough roads throughout the night, and oh my, the smell was unforgettable. We did not complain because we had to cross the border, and this ruse was necessary. It was against the law in Duke George's territory to break a holy vow or assist someone in breaking one.[17] The penalty was death; no other, just death.

As morning dispelled the darkness, we arrived safely in Torgau, which was a town favorable to the Reformation. After a quick bath and change of clothes prepared for us, we celebrated Easter Mass, truly free women in body and spirit. We were apprehensive about our future but ecstatically happy. After that night, I can tell you true, I never wanted to eat a herring again. At breakfast, we learned of our final destination: Wittenberg. We would meet the great doctor himself. At dusk on Easter Tuesday, we pulled into the courtyard of the Black Cloister of the university town.

We were astonished to see the figure that briskly came through the door heading toward us. Dr. Luther hailed Master Koppe with a hardy embrace, first congratulating and then thanking him for his brave deed. Turning his attention to the teamster's cargo, Dr. Luther greeted us, smiling broadly, and dismissed our gushes of praise and gratitude. He was light-hearted and cheery, yet there was a serious air about him. A few directions about our immediate comforts, a gesture to a worker to assist us, and he was off to a meeting; he was always off to a meeting.

In the weeks and months that followed, I saw him little, mostly in the pulpit at the City Church, the people's church in the heart of the town square. The good doctor took the responsibility for his "wagonload of vestal virgins"[18] very seriously. Three of our numbers were received back by their families. The rest had to be found husbands or positions. I was placed in domestic service of Philip Reichenbach, a city magistrate and personal friend of Dr. Luther. It was a lovely home that I managed, assisted by a cook, gardener, groomsmen, and more household servants. It was work I greatly enjoyed, and the town was even more exciting. Living in a university environment meant there were lots of intelligent young men about, and there was an atmosphere of culture and learning. I joined the local thespian club and acted in its modest productions. There were student parties and academic events at the Castle Church that brought a constant flow of visitors into our little Elbe River town. But more outstanding than the activity was the constant buzz of theological discussion, and the Reverend Doctor Martin Luther was the hub of the wheel around which the community turned. I had to learn more about him. It was not difficult to do, for everything about his life was as open for viewing as he was himself.

Martin's Childhood

Martin was born around the midnight hour of November 10, 1483, in a middle class home in the mining town of Eisleben, in the German state of Thuringia.[19] The next morning, Hans Luther wrapped his firstborn in a little blanket and walked half a block up the hill to St. Peter and St. Paul's Church to have him baptized. The ritual was done quickly, lest the child die suddenly and "miss the right to enter heaven." In a side chapel before a gold-leaf altar, depicting baby Jesus, his mother Mary and her mother, Anne, the newborn baby was given the Christian name, Martin. According to custom, the name was chosen in honor of the saint whose holy feast was celebrated that day. With the holy water poured over his head three times, each in the name of a member of the Holy Trinity, this promising son was received into God's holy church.

Martin's father, Hans, was a son without an inheritance, who had left his father's farm to work in the copper mines. He was a clever man, and with hard work and "the help of St. Anne," the patroness of miners, he progressed from laborer to smelter to foundry owner. Martin described his mother, Margaretta, as a woman of prayer, but like the rest of the peasantry, she believed flying fairies, elves, gnomes, sprites, and witches inhabited the woods around her home.[20] The Luthers expected their firstborn to become a successful jurist-advocate, make a prosperous marriage, and support them in their old age, a worthy dream in their time.

Before the year was over, the little family moved to Mansfeld; there, on March 12, 1488, when Martin was five years old, he began his public education.[21] Two years later, Father Hans was doing well and could afford the tuition at Mansfeld Latin School for his bright son. The object at this school was to learn a spoken knowledge of Latin, because it was useful, as it was the language of the church, law, diplomacy, scholarship, and travel.[22] Only boys attended school because girls had too many domestic skills to learn at home. Students learned by recitation and drill, punctuated by applications of the rod. Speaking German was not allowed in class. Poor performance or lapses into German meant wearing a donkey mask while sitting on a stool in the corner, until it could be passed on to a worse offender. Other infringements were recorded by a mark on your slate. At the end of the week, each mark was punished with a firm whip across your backside, and then your slate was wiped clean. Martin said he was beaten for things without ever knowing why, which irritated him immensely. Years later, he wrote to parents that corporal punishment should always be tempered with an apple nearby.[23]

At fourteen, Luther transferred to Cathedral School in the town of Magdenberg, which was called a "miniature Rome."[24] After only a year, he transferred to Eisenach, where he and the other students would sing for their supper in the streets outside the grand houses of the town. Martin tutored the sons of Frau Cotta and so impressed her that she invited him to live with their family. Dr. Luther said his three years living there were among the happiest of his life, for it was among the Cottas that he experienced unconditional love from no effort of his own.

Then in 1501, when only seventeen, Martin matriculated at Erfurt University to dutifully study law, in preparation for civil service, according to his father's explicit wishes. Erfurt was considered one of the finest universities in all the German lands. Martin was an excellent student, good in disputation and quite popular; yet he was unhappy. There were many tranquil moments, contrasted with illnesses and accidents. Students carried swords as part of their uniforms. The seniors teased the new students each year, saying they must carry swords to protect themselves from their teachers. But one day, Martin fell on his sword, slicing into a main artery in his leg.[25]

He almost died. During the yearlong, painful recovery, spiritual questions consumed his thoughts. The church taught the surest way of salvation was to renounce the world, the flesh, and the devil by living in a religious order.

Searching for Life's Meaning

At twenty-one years, Martin completed his master's degree. Now, armed with the entire expensive set of law books, *Corpus Juries*, purchased for him by his proud father, he began the final courses to become a lawyer. Everything looked serene on the outside, but inside Martin's heart and mind, a battle raged. What was the purpose of his life? Aware of his own sinful nature and therefore fearing separation from the Holy God of the universe, Martin went home to ask his father about entering religious orders. Hans Luther was not amused by such a foolish idea. More disturbed now than ever, Martin walked back to the university.

In Stotternheim, not far from Erfurt, he was caught in a fierce thunderstorm.[26] Taking refuge under a tree from the pelting rain, a violent bolt of lightning struck within inches of him, hurling him to the ground. He said of that moment of terror, "There was God the all terrible, Christ the inexorable and all the leering fiends springing from their lurking places … that they might seize me and bolt me into hell."[27] He cried out, "St. Anne save me, and if I live, I will become a monk."[28] He lived. Such a vow had to be fulfilled without question. Remember, please, that all of Christendom in Europe was one church, the Roman church, and it completely influenced all sixteenth-century thought. Doing good works and total dedication to the church (not Jesus Christ, mind you, but the church) was the way to receive forgiveness from sin. Monasticism was the way par-excellence to heaven. Martin Luther's purpose in becoming a monk was to save his soul from hell and eternal separation from God.

Two weeks later, at a party arranged for his friends, Martin gave away his cloak, a prized lute, and his set of law books, thereby announcing his intention to become a religious.

"No, Martin," they pleaded with him. "This is not for you. Do not throw your life away. You are too smart for this."

The next morning, July 17, 1505, unswayed and empty-handed, with no particular inner joy, Martin walked to the nearest monastery in the town to simply knock on the back gate and ask for admittance. This was all one needed to do. It was a strict Augustinian reformed order, founded in Italy in 1287 and named after the great monk, St. Augustine.[29] A message was sent to Martin's father, who was shocked and utterly outraged. A month later, before brilliant, stained glass windows, Martin presented himself as a novice, in an obedient attempt to follow the dictates of the church. He lay prostrate on the floor before the high altar, with outstretched hands in the form of a cross, upon the burial vault of Johann Zachariae. This was a tremendously historic moment! Zachariae was one of the principal accusers and chief judges of the Council of Constance, who a hundred years before had condemned Johann Hus to death at the stake for his reformed theology.[30]

When fire was put to the timber, Hus made this prophetic statement: "You may do this to me now, but in one hundred years there will come a man whom you cannot do this to for teaching these same truths of God."[31]

Luther posted his Ninety-Five Theses 102 years later. Of the many thousands of monasteries in Europe Martin could have entered, he took his vows in this one. No one can tell me that God is not in control of human history.

Ideal "Monkery"

When Martin took his vows, there was an altar directly facing him with a special vault in its center, which housed the monastery's sacred relics. They believed that viewing these items on special holy days took years off of one's time in purgatory. Much later, I heard Herr Doctor bellow, "What lies there are about relics! One claims to have a feather from the Angel Gabriel's wing, and the Bishop of Manze has a flame from the burning bush of Moses, and how is it that eighteen apostles' skeletons are buried in Germany when Christ had only twelve disciples?"[32]

Inside the cloister, Luther devoted himself to hours of prayer, days of fasting, and endless intense study. He would do his chores and then ask the others if he could do theirs as well. He became very popular, but then he was trying to earn God's favor. There were no private cells; the brothers slept in one room on grass mats in long rows, head to another's feet, so they would not talk to each other. In a study cell, more than once, Martin was found unconscious on the floor from self-flagellation. He whipped himself because the church said it would bring his body into submission to his soul and eradicate any sexual urges (Martin said it didn't work). All these efforts were motivated by one desire: to be the best Catholic possible, so God would accept him. He recalled years later, "If ever a monk was to earn the right to heaven through his monkery, I was that monk."[33]

In the year of the Lord 1507, after intense study, Friar Luther was ordained a priest in the Erfurt Cathedral, St. Mary's Church. It was to be a joy-filled occasion. His father rode into town with an escort company of twenty horsemen and presented the monastery with a handsome contribution. Hans's presence was an attempt at reconciliation with his firstborn son. He had recently lost two of his other sons to a plague, which had swept through his town.

When Martin took his place before the altar to preside over his first Mass, all went well until he came to the words, "We offer unto Thee, the living, the true, eternal God."[34] At that moment, he became terror-stricken and asked, "With what tongue shall I address such majesty? Who am I, that I should lift up mine eyes or raise my hands to the divine Majesty?"[35] His thoughts kept running: "For I am but dust and ashes and full of sin, and I am speaking to the living, eternal and true God."[36]

He wanted to run as fast and as far away as possible. He feared while holding the elements of the Eucharist, he would drop a morsel of the body of Christ. This may be hard for some to understand because they think of Jesus only as good friend and forget that he is also the Holy Judge of the universe. Jesus is our beloved Savior, indeed, but he must also be the Almighty Lord of all.

The next three years, Friar Martin agonized to understand one thing: our relationship to God. He spent hours in the monastery library, reading its only Bible. It was chained to the wall, for fear someone might steal it. Unaware of God's providential hand, Luther's life was being carefully guided toward its destiny. Since God has said, "You will seek me and find me when you seek me with all your heart" (Jer 29:13), several events now fell into place. First came an opportunity to visit the Eternal City, Rome. Martin was elected to represent the Erfurt monastery's views on a proposed change in the strict rules of the Augustinian Order before General Egidio at the Vatican.[37] He would walk the 850 miles to Rome with a brother monk.

Visiting Rome

At the first sight of the city, after the cold and arduous journey of forty days, Friar Luther fell to the ground in thanksgiving. He was not interested in the Rome of the Renaissance, nor of antiquity, but of the saints. He was a pilgrim, expecting a spiritual encounter with God. He celebrated Mass at the sacred shrines, visited the catacombs, viewed holy relics, but was deeply disillusioned to find irreverence and immorality rampant among the clergy.

Doubts overtook him when he reached the top of the Santa Scala, the Sacred Stairs of Pilate. Having climbed them according to custom, on hands and knees, repeating a Paternoster ("Our Father") and kissing each step one by one, Martin was told that doing this would free a soul from purgatory. These steps were haunting to him. How was it that these same stairs walked by Christ in Jerusalem were now in Rome? They had been dismantled and transported by boat to the Eternal City. This fact was too simple. The church had a better answer: Angels picked them up and carried them to Rome. Martin crawled up the stairs, nonetheless; perhaps he could free his grandfather from purgatory. But when he reached the top, he muttered, "Who knows whether it is true?"[38]

Finding Peace with God

The answer to the disillusioned friar's quest came not in Rome, but in little Wittenberg, where Luther's Father Confessor, Johann Von Staupitz, had him transferred.[39] Staupitz further pressed Martin to stop studying scholasticism altogether and study only Holy Scripture. He would now study for a degree of doctor of theology while teaching. One ordinary day in 1514, during his regular Bible reading time, alone in the tower of the Augustinian cloister in Wittenberg, he said, "The meaning of Romans 1:16, 17 burst forth like a blaze of light. All at once, I began to understand the justice of God being that the 'just' live by faith, which is a gift of God. The whole Scripture revealed a different countenance to me."[40]

Here was the answer to our relationship to God, and here was peace: "I felt such relief and easement as if I were reborn and had entered through open gates into Paradise itself!"[41]

With this new vision of the living Christ, God's justice that had seemed so harsh and unforgiving was now gracious and loving. In Psalm 22, he realized that God's own Son had felt rejected as Martin had felt. Christ's death and resurrection had purchased for him and all people forgiveness and life eternal. Beloved ones, these amazing divine gifts are simply received by faith and cannot be earned or deserved.

Professor Luther enthusiastically shared his spiritual discovery with his students. He explained his newly developed "Theology of the Cross,"[42] when he ascended the pulpit several times a week to preach to the common folk at City Church. People stood captivated, listening to the humble preacher during his hour-long sermons. We did not have seats in our sanctuary buildings. Standing for an entire service did have one advantage: You were less likely to fall asleep. Luther's sermons were not boring but filled with new concepts of divine love and grace.

These powerful truths might well have remained confined to scholarly lectures and inspiring sermons, were it not for one more papal extravagance in Rome. Pope Leo X needed money to finish building the great cathedral of St. Peter. Its walls were completed but not its grand dome. Desperate for money, the pontiff authorized one of the biggest fundraising campaigns for the basilica with the creation of St. Peter's Indulgence. For twenty silver coins, one could buy a document that insured its owner against spending years in purgatory for any and all of their sins. The same indulgence was also good for the immediate release of a soul already in purgatory.

St. Peter's Indulgence

In October of 1517, the papal salesman, Johann Tetzel, paraded into the neighboring town of Brandenberg, accompanied with colorful banners and beating drums to wring the hearts of the townsfolk to buy St. Peter's Indulgences.[43] Groans rose in the town square as he evoked the pitiful wailing of dead parents, pleading for their release from purgatory. When Luther heard of this carnival atmosphere and Tetzel's motto, "As the coin in the coffer rings, a soul from purgatory springs," he vowed. "I will knock a hole in Tetzel's drum!"[44]

Incidentally, in August 1519, when my husband learned that Tetzel was dying, neglected and full of misery, he wrote to him a kind letter, forgiving him. Such was the heart of Martin Luther.[45] So on the eve of All Saints

Day, October 31, Dr. Luther walked the length of Wittenberg's main street to nail ninety-five different theses for debate on the wooden door of the University Church as an invitation to examine the doctrine of indulgences.

He also sent copies to six different universities, inviting them to debate. In Latin, the paper read, "Out of love and zeal for the elucidation of Truth, on the following theses I invite debate ... in the Name of our Lord Jesus Christ."[46] It was signed, "The Reverend Father Martin Luther, Master of Arts and Sacred Theology, presiding."[47]

Unbeknown to Luther, a local printer took the theses documents from the door that served as the university's announcement board, translated them, and then duplicated them. Within four weeks, by means of the newly invented printing press, the theses were circulating throughout Europe, as if they had been carried by the wind. A contemporary noted their spread through Christendom was "as if the angels themselves were messengers."[48]

The furor they created shocked everyone. Luther's candor and logic captivated the common peasant, because what he put to pen made sense. For example, thesis number 82 read, "If the Pope has the power to free suffering souls from purgatory, why does he not for the sake of Christian love empty it out altogether all at once!"[49] The sales of indulgences suddenly dropped.

The statements that hung on the church door resulted in a series of spirited debates. No one came to debate these particular theses, but Dr. Luther was summoned to defend himself in Heidelberg, Augsburg, Leipzig, and Worms. Whereas a hundred years earlier, the "heretic" Johann Hus had attacked abuses in church practice, Luther was now attacking church doctrine. Dr. Luther's fame spread. Students walked across nations to hear him lecture. Church councils planned strategies to quiet him, cardinals planned festivals to upstage him, and young and old priests rallied to support him.[50] Luther's name became a household word in all walks of life.

Kidnapped, Alone, and Hidden Away

The church hierarchy now wanted their self-appointed antagonist dead. For all his remaining years, Martin's life was in danger. At one point, before we were married, his prince, Frederick the Wise, the Duke of Saxony, had Luther mock-kidnapped and hidden in the Thuringian Forest, high inside the Wartburg Castle.[51] Donning a disguise, Martin became *Junker Jorg* (Squire or Knight George), grew a beard, and lived virtually alone. For ten lonely months, he stayed in a single room next to the stables. Castle life was cold and unromantic. Life in the days of knights and fair maidens was not glamorous like a romance novel reads. It was far more coarse and rough. Certain parts of the castles were elegant and beautiful, but other customs prevailed. At dinner, a toss over the shoulder would dispose of a chicken bone quite nicely. After drinking too much beer, a remote corner of the room might be as far as a banquet guest might venture to alleviate his problem. A few years of this behavior required the castle to be aired out, which allowed Martin to stay there incognito. Living alone was not easy for a gregarious man. After weeks of illness, insomnia, loneliness, headaches, and depression, Luther found the best medicine for these ailments was hard work. He determined to translate the New Testament from Latin into the German tongue, since it had not yet been done, and he wanted even a plowboy to be able to read the Word of God for himself. Dr. Luther accomplished this enormous endeavor in only twelve weeks' time! When it was published, it served to unify the many German dialects into one common language.

While Dr. Luther was hidden away, the infant Reformation churches were having serious problems. Statuary and church property were being vandalized. Rioters plundered and burned churches in the name of reform. These things were enough to give Luther the excuse he needed to leave the castle, even though his lord duke told him he could not do so.

Dr. Luther called his time on the Wartburg mountaintop "my Patmos," saying, "I didn't want to be hiding behind fortress walls, but in the thick of spiritual battle."[52] On March 5, 1522, Herr Doctor slipped back into Wittenberg to quell disturbances, restore order in the congregations, influence labor laws, and inspire reforms. It would continue to be his home for the next twenty-four years.

I cannot wait any longer in this correspondence to answer the two questions I am asked the most about my celebrated husband. The first query was usually, "What was Martin Luther really like?" or, "What was it like living with such an important man?"

In one honest word, my friends, that word would be difficult. It was hard living with a short-tempered, sharp-tongued man who was always putting both boots in his mouth and later needing to apologize profusely for what he had said. But it was even harder living with the kind-hearted, naive gentleman all the beggars in Saxony knew well. My husband could not turn away anyone who knocked on our door, asking for help. If he could find no money or food at hand, he would pick up an object like a candlestick and say, "Sell this and buy food." Many of my household belongings disappeared exactly that way.

Courtship and Marriage

The second question I am often asked is, "How did a nun and a monk come to marry at all?" I was once engaged to marry Jerome Baumgartner, someone I believed I loved deeply. He was a handsome Wittenberg University student from the city of Nürenberg, who courted me in the best of fashion. At our final parting, Jerome promised he would convince his family of our love and return to marry me. When a year passed without a word, I prevailed upon the kindness of Dr. Luther to inquire as to the silence. I was quietly informed that the Nürenberger had married someone else. Herr Doctor wasted not a moment selecting a fellow professor, Dr. Glatz, for me to marry. I found him totally unacceptable, as he was far too old to be anyone's husband. My position was delicate in this matter, for I was twenty-six and verging on the upper limits of marital eligibility![53] This was true for females. It was embarrassing but necessary for me to take action and speak to the good offices of Dr. Amsdorf of Magdenberg. I asked him to please inform Dr. Luther that I could not accept Dr. Glatz, but I was not unreasonable. I would be pleased to take Amsdorf himself or Luther to be my husband.

How I would have loved to see Martin's face when this suggestion was related to him. Friends had urged him to marry many times. Even when told his own marriage would support his teaching on the state of marriage, he would lose his composure, citing a litany of arguments as to why he could not marry. He expected the sentence of death as a heretic any day. He said he "was not a sexless stone, nor at all hostile to marriage, but had poor health with much work to do, so there was no time for a wife!"[54]

However, at a visit with his parents, Martin related my proposal as a joke to his father, who seized the idea as a realistic possibility. Papa Hans wanted his son to pass on the family name. Dr. Luther believed that the commandment to honor one's father and mother was intended to be for a lifetime. The will of God could be determined through obedience to one's parents. After much prayer and analysis, Luther decided to marry, before his sure martyrdom, for three reasons: first, to please his father; second, to spite the devil (that is, to "make the angels laugh and the devil weep");[55] and third, to seal his witness of his belief in the freedom in the Christian life.[56]

On June 10, 1525, after making this decision, Luther proposed to me. We were publicly betrothed three days later, because, he argued, "the gifts of God must be taken on the wing; because, by delay Esau forfeited his birthright, and Hannibal lost Rome."[57] The wedding ceremony was two weeks later. There were many famous guests in attendance, but none more tenderly honored than Martin's parents.

It was such a blessed day. Dr. Luther, accompanied by the music of pipers, led the wedding party through the streets as our guests joined along the way. Religious wedding ceremonies were not held inside the church building proper, but outside by the main portal. Afterward, there was a banquet in the cloister, followed by a dance at the town hall, and in the evening another banquet. At eleven, all the guests took their leave, on pain of being sent home by the magistrates.

The night we were married, Martin sat me down, went to his knees, took my hands, and delivered a speech he had rehearsed. He began with a confession that he was not in love with me, but he cherished me as his wife. Furthermore, I was not to worry because he would be a faithful husband. He believed we would come to love each other in time, for that would be the heavenly Father's will. End of speech.

He was so serious and yet childlike in his approach to this unfamiliar territory of life, that I think it made me love him even more. I must explain that love was not a prerequisite to marriage. Parents usually arranged marriages for the welfare of their children. Dr. Luther wrote a great deal on the subject and suggested that no one be forced to marry without his or her personal consent; otherwise, there was little chance for happiness. We thought, as did the Chinese, that love was better if it began as a small flickering flame that grew over time into a raging fire, rather than beginning with great flames of desire that could die out over time.

Marriage for a forty-one-year-old monk was quite a shock. Martin confessed he had some odd thoughts that first year of marriage. While sitting at table, he would suddenly share his amazement that years before he was one, and now he was two. He mused about waking up in the morning to find a pair of pigtails lying across his pillow that never appeared there before. Dear friends, I celebrated my honeymoon, not with a romantic holiday, but with a thorough housecleaning. The straw in Dr. Luther's bed had not been changed in a year and had turned sour. My new husband explained that he worked so hard and was so weary when he tumbled into bed that he never noticed anything was amiss. If ever a man needed a wife, the Rev. Dr. Martin Luther was that man.

Family Life

I do not know when Dr. Luther fell in love with me. I was too busy to notice; there was so much work to do. Herr Doctor called me his "Morning Star of Wittenberg," because I rose at four o'clock to begin my daily duties.[58] Martin and the children slept till six, at which time the entire family studied the Catechism and sang hymns, accompanied by father on his lute. To provide two meals a day, I kept cows, pigs, ducks, geese, pigeons, and bees. I made all our cheese and brewed our own beer, which Martin bragged was the finest beer in all the German provinces and beyond. Over the years, we acquired a vineyard, orchard, fishpond, and a farm, some two days' travel away in Zulsdorf. Martin's Prince-Elector doubled my husband's salary and frequently sent cloth, game, and wine for special occasions. These provisions were much needed, for the Lord God blessed us with six vivacious children, to which he added thirteen more orphaned nephews and nieces and orphans of friends. Yah, tis true. Not all at once, I'm glad to say. There were also student boarders, and if that wasn't enough, there was a constant stream of resident houseguests, from widows to royalty.

The old Augustinian monastery, called the Black Cloister, was given to us as a wedding gift by the duke, since Martin was the only one still living there. It served as an orphanage, old folks' home, halfway house, hospital, asylum, and hotel. We did have forty rooms. So be glad if you only have one guestroom. Seriously, the Luther *Haus* numbered at least twenty to twenty-five at the daily main meal, which was served at ten o'clock, and the other meal was served at five o'clock.[59] While Luther had to divide himself between husband, father, reformer, professor, pastor, author, and famous defender of the faith, I had to juggle being wife, mother, farmer, brewer, cook, nurse, gardener, and comforter to all the beggars of Wittenberg. I was the *Doctorissa*, who was to prove herself worthy of her celebrated husband and entertain guests on a meager salary of two hundred guilders a year.

Daily life for us was one of hard toil and not just because we had to grow our own food, or make our own clothes, but other factors could suddenly be upon us. The night we were married, after all the wedding guests had departed, there was a loud banging on the door. It was Pastor Andreas Karlstadt, fleeing from the Peasant Wars.[60] We never knew when a needy refugee would knock on our door for a place to stay. Then, twice in our twenty years of marriage in Wittenberg, the Black Plague came through our river port town.

Herr Doctor's grave face displayed his deep concern the first time he came with the news, "The plague is here. Many are fleeing to the country. The Elector has ordered the university to remove to Jena. Do you want to take the children and go?"[61]

I had only one question: "What are you going to do?"

Pastor Bugenhagen and my husband had already decided to stay; he said, "We must comfort the grieving and care for the dying. It is what Christ would have us do."[62]

Hearing those words, my decision was made: "Then I will stay. My place is with you."

We stayed and lost many good friends. While the plague raged on, so did the Peasant War. By the end of the revolt, one hundred thirty thousand peasants had been killed.[63] Of this number, ten thousand were executed.[64] My husband was nauseated by all the bloodshed, as were we all. But one must do what one can, so our home became a hospital. Though I was expecting our second child, the Lord gave me strength to nurse the infirmed who stayed with us. In God's good providence, no one in our household became infected by the plague that year. That was miraculous, and not just during that one plague, but also through the next time the epidemic came through our town as well.

Papa Luther

To the surprise of a great many friends, Luther took to the new roles of husband and father quite readily. After a year of marriage, Martin wrote to a friend, "My Katie is in all things so obliging and pleasing to me that I would not exchange my poverty for all the riches of Croesus, nor would I surrender my Katharina for France or Venice."[65] When we were apart from each other, his letters told me of his love. One began, "To my beloved wife, Katharina, Mrs. Dr. Luther, Rich Lady of Zulsdorf, Mistress of the pig market, and whatsoever other titles may befit thy grace."[66] The letter continued, "The greatest gift of grace a man can have is a pious, God-fearing, home-loving wife, who he can trust with all his goods, body and life itself, as well as having her the mother of his children. Kate, you have a good man who loves you. Thank God and let someone else be Empress!"

Many fathers love their children dearly, as they should, but none could love his more than Papa Martin. Yet they did greatly try his patience. Once at his desk, rocking a cradle with one foot in an attempt to do his work and assist with the children, he stopped in anguish, looked down at the babe, and said, "Child, what have you done that I should love you so? What? You have disturbed the whole household with your bawling."[67]

Another evening, we were entertaining important guests, and the children were screeching while at play. Following a pensive silence from the conversation, the good doctor looked heavenward and lamented, "Christ said we must become as little children to enter the Kingdom of Heaven. Dear God, this is too much! Must we all become such idiots?"[68]

Martin believed that being a parent taught men and women how God loves them. By being a parent, we can experience in part our heavenly Father's love. Likewise, there is much to be learned from children themselves. On this topic, Luther wrote:

> In all simplicity and without any disputing, children believe that God is gracious and that there is eternal life. … Children live with all sincerity in faith, without interference of reason, it is as Ambrose says: "There is a lack of reason but not of faith. It is a shame that childlike faith is lost with age."[69]

Daughter Magdalena's Death

Luther's children gave their father exceeding joy. Papa played with them, sang to them, and wrote letters to them when apart. It was for them that he created the Small Catechism, as well as dramatic plays, poems, stories, and songs.[70] In the Larger Catechism written for adults, pastors, and teachers, Herr Doctor shared his strong belief that with the blessings of children comes the responsibility to teach them to love and reverence God. We must spare no diligence, effort, or cost in raising and educating our children. I have to tell you that the deepest heartache of Martin Luther's life was not excommunication, vicious gossip, having a price on his head, or being blamed for starting the Peasant Wars. It was the loss of his cherished daughter, Magdalena.

Our dearly loved third child lay upon her deathbed when only fourteen. She was such a special child to everyone who knew her. She had a gentle countenance that made the picture of a charming, well-mannered child. I can see again Martin kneeling beside her feverish face, saying, "*Magdalenchen*, my little girl, would you like to stay with your father here or go to your Father in heaven?"[71]

With a look of complete trust she answered, "*Yah*, dear Father, whatever God wills."[72]

Next came that holy moment of transition from this life to the next. Father held daughter in his arms in a timeless stillness. When he finally laid her back on the pillow, he cried out, "Darling *Lenchen*, how well off you are. You will rise again and shine as a star. *Nein*, as the sun!"[73] After a stone silence, he turned to those of us grief-stricken and speechless in the room and said, "How strange it is to know that she is at peace and all is well for her, and yet to feel such sorrow."[74]

The sparkle in Martin's eyes was never quite as bright after her passing. One grieves and cries within and without at great loss. I know. Yet, in Christ, we keep living (perhaps at times only out of a sense of duty), for we know that the Lord God will sustain us with his healing love.

The School for Character

Whatever Dr. Martin Luther did seemed to turn into history, and his marriage was no exception. With much thought, Martin said, "Children are gifts from God and pledges of a loving marriage."[75] He called marriage and family life "the School for Character."[76] There was a reason for his choice of words. Herr Doctor said, "The mere differences between male and female is enough fuel in marriage for battle!"[77] He also decided that women have three shortcomings: they are nosey; vain; and given to superstition. To that I answered, "That's all right, at least we only have three!"

When writing to friends, my husband referred to me as "my rib" and at other times, "my lord."[78] Sometimes in my absence, he would change my name from Kate to "*Kette,*" which is the German word for "chain." I can say there were times when circumstances demanded I take the upper hand. I recall the time of preparation before the Augsburg Conference, which produced the great confession by the same name. Not able to attend the gathering in person, the doctor was so irritable from worry that he fussed and complained about the house before leaving for Coburg; no one could tolerate him.[79] I wondered what I could do to change his mood. Inspiration came to me. I prepared my husband's favorite meal and then disappeared just before he came to table. As he sat impatiently, I donned my black mourning dress and made him wait. He never started a meal until I was in my proper place at table. Distraught, I entered the room, weeping into my handkerchief.

Herr Doctor asked sympathetically, "Oh, dear Katie, who died?"

"God," I mumbled.

"Who?" he questioned.

"God," I repeated.

Confused, he queried, "God? Did you say God?" I nodded my head. "God is not dead, Kate," he snapped.

"He's not?" I asked with a shocked look on my face.

"*Nein*, Kate, God cannot die. What made you think God was dead?"

"Because, dearest, the way you have been acting lately, I thought surely God was dead."

The room went so quiet you could have heard a flea sneeze. He thought for a moment and then suddenly roared with laughter. He appreciated the gesture, and from that moment, faith in the Providence of God returned to his heart. He was a good and humble man who loved a playful joke.

Incidentally, I have often been asked where I hid the infamous chalice. If you know not of what I speak, I must tell you. The vow of poverty my generous husband had taken as a monk never quite left him. He would not take a penny for anything he wrote, because he thought it would be sinful to make money from teaching God's Word. He never worried about money, for he said, "As soon as one bill is paid, another comes."[80] To give gifts to friends, he would find something and pass it on, so to speak. There was one small, exquisite chalice I especially liked. He wrote to a friend, "I am sending you a fine chalice as a wedding present."[81] He never asked me where it was, but I watched him search for it for three days before he gave up and wrote a postscript to the letter: "P.S. I cannot send you the present. Katie hid it."[82] The chalice stayed in its hiding place all the while, a deep pocket in my mourning dress, whether I wore the garment or left it in the wardrobe.

Martin's advice to this young couple was a far greater present when he wrote to the bride, "My dear, make your husband glad to cross his threshold at night."[83] The letter continued, advising the groom, "Make your wife sorry to have you leave. The dearest life is to live with a godly, willing, obedient wife in peace and unity. Union of the flesh does nothing. There must be union of manners and mind."

The Augustinian monk of Erfurt may have started out naive about marriage, but he did not stay that way. He loved his family time the best and stated that the last twenty years of his life were his happiest. Marriage is to be of a lifelong duration with the wife of a man's youth, as the scripture teaches. One should not change a spouse like changing a winter coat. Forgive me if I offend. I have been criticized for expressing my strong opinions out loud.

Power of the Pen

It can never be said that Herr Dr. Luther was naive about the world's ways. Why men need to amass power might have eluded his understanding, but he did realize that his fame was used to political advantage by others. Johann Tetzel and his cohorts crowed after the distribution of the Ninety-Five Theses that Luther would be burned at the stake as a heretic within three weeks.[84] Yet three years passed before the bull of excommunication was issued. In those turbulent years, Luther's pen waxed prolific, and his popularity grew steadily. At the same time, his books and his effigy were burned many times over.

In one year alone, the good doctor wrote three Reformation manifestos.[85] There was *The Freedom of the Christian*, which encouraged a personal relationship with God instead of reliance on good deeds or rituals; *On the Babylonian Captivity of the Church* rejected the sacramental system of the day, citing from scripture that Jesus Christ instituted none of them, save Baptism and the Lord's Supper. In the *Address to the Christian Nobility of the German Nation*, Dr. Luther urged the abolition of both indulgences and the veneration of saints. He declared that heretics should be refuted with argument, not fire.

By the year 1523, Luther's pamphlets sold over a million copies, which up to that time no one had done. Between 1516 and 1546, he averaged a treatise every two weeks; writing enough to fill 102 large volumes of the famous Weimar Edition, making him the most prolific writer in history, and all this with a goose-quill pen![86] By the way, you should read these books. They are particularly sound theologically; truth remains relevant for all time. Just because a book is old does not mean it is out of date. It may even be better for its age because it has stood the test of time. Dr. Luther's writings eventually changed our world; his opinions were dangerous to the power structures that ruled the masses of Europe. German magistrates wishing to be less attached to the authority of papal Rome were happy to use any opportunity to exercise their own rule over the domain of the church. So when Pope Leo X demanded that the Holy Roman Emperor ban Luther for heresy, Frederick the Wise, the Duke of Saxony, appealed to Emperor Charles V that he, as a Christian statesman, should first grant the little friar a public trial.[87]

The Diet of Worms

In response to Frederick's plea, the twenty-one-year-old emperor summoned Luther to the Diet at Worms. This was a governing body of seven noblemen who made laws and judgments, not the kind of diet when you eat little to get skinny. It was in Worms, a town in Germany pronounced *Vorms,* not worms—you know the little things you put on a hook on the pole to catch the fish, worms? It doesn't sound like the wiggly things, because in German, a "W" is pronounced as an English "V." On April 17, 1521, at six o'clock in the evening, Friar Martin Luther was led into the courtroom of the palace, crowded with the emperor's notables. The arrogant Charles V fancied himself a knight-errant leading a united Christendom in glorious crusade against the enemies of the faith. He proclaimed himself "God's Standard Bearer."[88]

Not lowering himself to address such an insignificant person, the emperor leaned over to the imperial herald, Casper Strum, and said, "He looks harmless to me. Let us see if he dares to defy me."[89]

Luther had been intentionally led to believe he was coming to debate theology before the Diet, so he was visibly shaken when the chief inquisitor only asked him two questions.

Pointing to a table full of books, he asked, "Are these your books?"

Martin recognized the titles and replied, "The books are mine, and I have written more."[90]

The second question queried if he was ready to revoke the heresies they contain or, in essence, would he prefer to be burned at the stake? My goodness, that was a harder question. Martin declared he would need more time to give an answer. Anxious to discuss other matters, the emperor agreed to a one-day delay.

The following evening, again at six o'clock, Dr. Luther was taken to the same torch-lit room packed with princes, clergy, noblemen, gentry, and doctors of law and theology. He began with a prepared speech: "To condemn some of my books would be to condemn simple Christian morality … to condemn others would be to deny the essential doctrines of Christian faith … in others, I do apologize for the vehemence of my attack, yet I cannot deny that Rome and its canon law has enslaved Christians both body, and soul."[91]

The chief inquisitor became visibly agitated as Friar Martin argued at length in a manner of a confident protagonist debating at a university. Jeers of derision, taunts, and sneers railed throughout the room against him. In response, his voice grew louder and his stance stronger.

Finally, the inquisitor yelled, "Do you or do you not repudiate your books and the errors which they contain? Give us an answer without horns!"[92]

Luther's counter ended with a ringing defiance: "Since your Majesty, and lordships desire a simple reply, I will answer without horns and without teeth. Unless I am proved wrong by Holy Scripture and plain reason, my conscience is captive to the Word of God. … I cannot and therefore, I will not recant anything, for to go against conscience is neither right nor safe."[93] Then realizing what he had said, he mumbled a prayer ending, "God help me, Amen." He had made his stand because he could do no other. He was dismissed.

Pressed hard with a crisis in Italy, a war in Spain against France, and a strong Turkish threat, Emperor Charles rendered his opinion the next morning to dismiss the matter.

He began, "I am descended from a long line of Christian Emperors." He droned on about his credentials and self-importance. Finally he concluded, "A single friar who goes counter to all Christianity for a thousand years must be wrong. I will have no more to do with him."[94]

With that, the trial was over. Are we not intolerant with anyone who dares to be different? The official edict outlawing Martin Luther was not issued until May 26, thirty-eight days later. It read, "We declare Martin Luther to be an avowed heretic, no longer a member of God's Church."

Now he could be hunted down and killed like a common deer by anyone. However, God had other plans, and what man, no matter how great, can thwart the plans of the Most High? Charles fought four wars, plotted and counter-plotted between the church and the state, with much money changing hands, but it was impossible for him to stop the growing tide of the Reformation. There are those who say my husband was just a man in the right place at the right time. I agree, because God can use anyone he pleases if that man or that woman be willing to stand for him. I believe my husband's contribution to the church was to re-establish the proper source for all spiritual truth: that of Holy Scripture as God's revelation of himself to humankind.

The Theology of the Cross

The authority of scripture was not the heart of Dr. Luther's theological teaching. *Nein*, not at all. Dr. Luther was known for his love of the Bible. By age thirty, he had memorized all of the New Testament, word for word.[95] He went on to memorize the book of Psalms and other portions of the Old Testament. He studied through the Bible twice a year, because he loved it for its message. After all his years of intense study, he concluded that it is the very God-breathed Word. Furthermore, it only has one main message, only one. This is the heart of Luther's theological understanding; he called it the theology of the Cross. The Bible's one main message is Jesus Christ, the Living Word. The Old Testament points forward, preparing the way for the Anointed One who would come and die upon the Cross. The New Testament points back to Jesus Christ and his work upon the Cross, explaining its meaning to us. All of human history revolves around the Messiah and his mission on earth, the Cross. It is the Cross of Christ that explains the Advent of Christmas, and the Cross of Christ that enables the glory of Easter.

My dear husband's message to the entire world was that it is by God's grace that we are saved through the means of faith: "For it is by grace you have been saved, through faith—and this not from yourselves, it is the gift of God—not by works, so that no one can boast" (Eph 2:8, 9).

Oh, please let me warn you, faith does not just mean belief. If it were just mere intellectual assent, then your faith would save you. Your faith would be a good work, something you do to gain favor with God. If that were all faith is, it would diminish God's gift. The faith of which my husband spoke he called saving faith. This is quite different from ordinary faith. I have heard some claim, "It doesn't matter what you believe as long as you truly believe it." This statement exonerates faith for faith's sake. The consequence of your faith is not related to how much faith you possess. Instead, it depends upon what the object of your faith can do for you. The object of Christian faith is the Lord Jesus Christ. It is by his grace that we are saved: *Sola Gratia* (grace alone). It does matter what we believe in. Saving faith is the channel through which humankind can receive the gift of salvation: *Sola Fida* (faith alone).

Dr. Luther declared that faith is "an unceasing focused looking at

Christ Jesus," who is the only giver of eternal life: *Solo Christo* (Christ alone). Christians can know personally the object of their faith and stand with the apostle Paul and the saints through the ages and say, "I know whom I have believed" (2Ti 1:12). May Jesus Christ be your confession. May Jesus Christ be your stand.

Soli Deo Gloria, Glory to God Alone! Amen

Katharina, Mrs. Dr. Martin Luther

Conclusion

Occasionally, time can aid in the revelation of truth and even heal old wounds. It is rather striking to note that when Dr. Martin Luther was alive, the pope declared him a heretic and enemy of the church. Yet, five centuries later, another pontiff of the same Roman Catholic Church declared the year 1983 "the Luther Year," in remembrance of Martin's five-hundredth birthday anniversary.[96] At the time, Pope John Paul II also proclaimed Dr. Luther to be a "great scholar and theological genius!"[97] This was done in remembrance of the fact that the early Protestant movement caused the Counter-Reformation within the Roman Catholic Church, which embraced many welcomed changes that strengthened its structure, faith, and practice.

Time can also erode the tenets of the faith when it is void of diligent observance and conscientious effort. Unfortunately, there is once again a great struggle within Christianity today that twentieth-century theologians called "the Battle for the Bible."[98] The question being asked today is once again, "How much authority does Holy Scripture have?" This is the same issue that was intensely scrutinized at the Leipzig debate and the Diet at Worms. What Martin Luther said to his century, he would say again to ours: The Bible is the very Word of God.

Luther viewed Holy Scripture in the same manner as the apostle Paul and Jesus, who also spoke of the Torah as the very Word of God. He quoted it to validate what he was teaching about the Kingdom of God. Christ often prefaced his teaching with the words, "Has it not been written?" and "Has it not been said?" Old Testament scripture was Christ's supreme authority, and it must be ours as well. Some critics say the creation of the modern "historical critical method,"[99] by which the Bible is investigated and analyzed, demythologizes the scriptures and retains only the Gospel message. This is the same as saying, "I choose to believe this part, but not that part."

Not taking all of scripture is very dangerous. It is like peeling an onion layer, by layer. You must keep peeling and peeling, and soon you have a pile of skins on the floor, tears in your eyes, and no onion in hand. Christians must be very careful not put their reason or opinion above Holy Scripture, by deciding what they think is God-breathed revelation and what is not. If we give ourselves this option, we would place reason as our authority instead of God's own revelation. The Reformers taught *Sola Scriptura* (scripture alone) as the answer to the question of the identity of spiritual truth, for all peoples, in all times.

Few Christians are equipped by God to be a theological genius like Martin Luther. Nevertheless, we are all called to a role for service in the Body of Christ. The apostle Paul's metaphor found in 1 Corinthians chapter 12 perfectly demonstrates that each separate part of a body is of equal importance to the whole. Whether a foot, an eye, or a hand, all are necessary to accomplish their designed task for the benefit of the functioning of the whole body. We can admire the lesser-known Katharina Von Bora Luther for fulfilling her God-given roles as a dedicated wife and mother. Without her faithful service in these roles, the good doctor would not have been able to complete all he was called to do. Katie could not do what he did, and neither could he have accomplished what she did, but both separately and together redirected several key beliefs and practices of the Christian church.

Their simple wedding turned into the symbol of the Reformation's liberation. Similarly, their home, complete with children, established the model for a Protestant parsonage and the Christian family for the centuries that followed them. Whatever our role in the Body of Christ, may we go about our task with total commitment, contentment, and inner joy.

As we continue to travel down the path of church history, we will find in the eighteenth century another indomitable mother who looked to the ways of her family with fortitude and disciplined care. We will see how Mrs. Susanna Wesley fulfilled her assigned place in the Body of Christ, somewhat confined within the walls of a rectory in the swampland village of Epworth, England. Her incisive teaching, disciplined methods, and exemplarily life will expand far beyond her children, parish, and country to a worldwide spiritual movement respectfully credited to her by her famous sons, John and Charles.

Discussion Questions

1. Katie Luther saw her roles as wife and mother as God-given, which she embraced wholeheartedly. How do you see your roles in God's plan for your life?
2. How did God use Katie Luther's skills and talents for the advancement of the Kingdom of God?
   How are you using the gifts, talents and graces that God has given you? What things would you like to do in the future for the glory of God and the benefit of others?
3. Martin and Katharina Luther were greatly criticized for breaking their vows of celibacy to marry, thereby making the statement that celibacy is no better than marriage and vice versa in God's view. How should we handle personal criticism by others?
   How should we relate to married and single persons in the church?
4. The Luther's stood up against extreme opposition for what they believed about the Bible and Christ. What are some constructive ways to withstand people's opposition to your faith without compromising what you believe?

The Mother of Methodism

Introducing Susanna Wesley

On his deathbed in 1735, eyes fixed on his sons John and Charles, the Rev. Samuel Wesley spoke a prophetic pronouncement he had held for many years: "The Christian faith will surely revive in this kingdom; you shall see it, though I shall not."[1] He believed with his whole heart a spiritual revival was coming to England, never knowing that his very own sons would be the catalyst for its fulfillment. Their mother, Susanna Annesley Wesley, would live to see her husband's prophecy come to pass while living at the Methodist Headquarters in London.

Historians have credited the Wesley family's formation of the religious awakening of their day as having "saved England from the terrors of a French Revolution."[2] The eighteenth-century spiritual awakening began within the confines of a rector's home in an insignificant township of Epworth, Lincolnshire. John Wesley, the founder of the worldwide Methodist movement, told his friend Adam Clarke, "If I were to write my own life story I should have to begin it before I was born."[3] Confined to stringent roles for women in English society and limited to life within the walls of the rectory, Mrs. Susanna Wesley focused her attention on the raising of her children. Reflecting back on those years, John Wesley wrote in his journal,

> Take her for all and in all, I do not believe that any human being ever brought into the world, and carried through it a larger portion of original goodness than my dear Mother. Everyone who knew her loved her, for she seemed to be made to be happy herself, and to make everyone happy within her

> little sphere. It is from her that I have inherited that alertness of mind without which it would have been impossible for me to have undertaken half of what I have performed. God never blessed a human creature with a more cheerful disposition, generous spirit, sweeter temper, or a tenderer heart.[4]

Susanna was born on January 20, 1669, the twenty-fifth child of the Rev. Dr. and Mrs. Samuel Annesley. She lived in London until her marriage to the Rev. Samuel Wesley in 1689. In the following span of twenty-one years, she gave birth to nineteen children, ten of whom lived to maturity. The Wesleys' last pastorate was in Epworth, where they would reside for thirty-nine years. During those laborious years, Susanna's methodical and disciplined lifestyle set the practices that would establish and guide the revival movement that spread across the British Isles, to America, and around the world.

The "kitchen meetings" Mrs. Wesley led and named Our Society became the forerunner of the classes and societies of the Methodist movement. Susanna can be credited with the early development and promotion of the concepts of lay leadership, small groups, a worldwide parish, the home school, the emancipation of women, and Christian unity through the formative ideas of the doctrine of Christian Perfection.[5] These can be seen in the daily life of this indomitable woman of faith, who has been afforded the title "the Mother of Methodism." Her life's purpose, "to save the souls of her children," transferred to her son John's famous charge to his preachers, "You have nothing to do but to save souls!"[6]

An Open Letter from Mrs. Susanna Wesley

Dear Brothers and Sisters in Christ,

I greet you with heartfelt joy in the wondrous name of Jesus, our Lord. I do not take lightly this opportunity as a common, eighteenth-century woman to address future generations in this letter. I had to be mindful of the urgings of Methodist leaders for me to record my family's story. I only agreed to do this when they told me I could expand my personal story to that of all my children. Please know I am not an author, for I have not received training in the art of composition. However, I wrote a prayer daily in my journal and reflections on the scripture passage I was studying. As time allowed, I did send letters to family and friends. Written correspondence was practically an art form of English society in our day, because literacy among the masses was so rare. To the upper classes, writing letters was deemed a pleasurable pastime; something one did at leisure as a recreation. Letters were difficult and expensive to deliver since there was no national mail system, well-marked maps, or even numbers on homes. Paper was very costly, so one took care in what was written, for once a thought be put to pen, it could never be revoked. Therefore, I will relate my concerns and observations upon living the Christian life, this blessed life that you and I share in common, irrespective of any years or distance between us.

Eighteenth-Century British Society

To understand the era in which my family lived, let me describe some of the conditions of our society. Wages were terribly meager for a six-day workweek, each day lasting from dawn to dusk. There was no relief for the poor. Workers had no rights or breaks, and they could be dismissed for the slightest provocation without a reference. Travel was time-consuming, with only an occasional inn at the end of a long day's coach ride over a system of badly neglected dirt roads. I hardly know what can be said in support of the administration of British justice. There were above 150 different crimes for which a person could be hanged, ranging from premeditated murder to the cutting down of a tree.[7] Punishment for crime was administered publicly, with stocks, whipping, or the clipping of ears, nose, fingers, or toes. We had no cures for common diseases. Infant mortality was 50 percent. I was born only a few years after the lethal Black Plague swept across Europe to our little island country for the second time. The Great Fire of London in 1666 turned out to be an unexpected blessing that stopped the Plague from returning. Rodents ran freely in our streets and homes, and the poor lived with lice in their beds, clothing, and hair. Most homes had no inside running water or inside bathrooms, and while soap had been invented, people did not buy it because it was too expensive.

In spite of these many difficulties, my friends, great strides were being made in our world. There were major advancements in chemistry, biology, and physics that transferred things being made by hand to newly invented machines. There were the first chemical table, the first experiments with electricity and photography, and the first biological classification systems, which resulted in improving distilling, smelting, and spinning. British literature sparkled with master storytellers and poets like Alexander Pope, John Milton, Jonathan Swift, Samuel Johnson, Daniel Defoe, John Dryden, John Bunyan, Joseph Addison, and Richard Steele.[8] Johnson and Defoe were personal friends of my father, and they stayed in our home as frequent guests. Another friend of my father was the brilliant architect Sir Christopher Wren, who was overseeing the construction of St. Paul's Cathedral, which would dominate the skyline of London. These advancements, along with eminent artists and musicians, prompted the aristocracy to declare that Englishmen had created a Golden Age. Imagine never having heard the strains of Handel's *Messiah* or reading the saga of *Robinson Crusoe* or the rhyming verse of Milton's *Paradise Lost.*

Nevertheless, the masses of commoners were genuinely poor. The majority lived on a diet of almost entirely oats, rye, and barley. If you did not find work, you did not eat, so the streets were strewn with robbers and beggars as well as the destitute and insane. Dying from starvation, suicide, or murder was a common occurrence of everyday life, hardly a Golden Age at all. Jesus did say that the poor would always be with us, but not because it should be so. He knew that men and women would turn their backs on God and on one another.

My Resolute Clergy Father

In the seventeen and eighteen hundreds, there was a great chasm between the nobility and the commoners, with only a small segment of the population in between the two. My dear father, the Reverend Doctor Samuel Annesley, a man of sterling character and well loved, fit into the middle category. Raised in a Puritan clergy family, he could not remember a time when he did not love the Lord Jesus Christ. Upon graduating from Oxford University in 1644, he was ordained to pastor Puritan churches. We were quite comfortable living in a brick home in Spital Yard, Bishopsgate, London. However, the Church of England was in terrible spiritual decay and functioned as a structural support to Britain's economic and social class system. It preached that a man's station in life reflected his state of grace before God. Kings ruled by divine right as God's vicar, and power flowed down through the aristocracy and the Anglican church hierarchy. Having a state church meant there was no line between politics and religion. Monarchs and Parliament together dictated faith and its practice.

My parents' life abruptly changed in 1662, when Parliament passed the Act of Uniformity that was intended to eradicate all traces of Puritanism and dissent from Britain. It required all ministers to conform to the official rules and beliefs of the Church of England. Overnight on August 25, 1662, above two thousand ministers lost their positions and were literally turned out of their rectories, along with their shocked wives and children.[9] Labeled nonconformists and dissenters, they were forbidden to preach, vote, or assemble privately, and their children were barred from attending public schools and universities. This event, called the Great Ejection, meant utter poverty for most of these families. It was for this cause that John Bunyan suffered years in prison, but thankfully, they were not wasted years. While incarcerated, to make use of his time, Bunyan wrote daily. The resulting manuscript, the best-selling book entitled *The Pilgrim's Progress*, was the one good thing that came out of the inhumane Parliamentary act.

My father lost his income of seven hundred pounds a year; nevertheless, our mother shielded us from any worry and taught us our lessons at home. My dear mother was the greatest woman I ever knew. No one worked with more diligence or with a happier countenance than she. As a child, my favorite place was my father's library, where he allowed me much use of his good books. He was not averse to spending his time teaching me the subjects of Latin, logic, and theology or whatever else I asked of him. When King James II finally relaxed the harsh laws against the dissenters, my father leased a meetinghouse in London on Bishopsgate Street and developed another influential congregation.

Once again, prominent divines of his majesty's kingdom entered our threshold, men like Richard Baxter and John Owen, esteemed as the prince of Puritans, and Thomas Manton, whose *Works* occupy twenty-two volumes.[10] (How could I have ever known my son John's writings would fill forty volumes by the end of his life?[11]) A din of lively debate on politics and theology reverberated through the walls of our house, and it was my delight to participate. I have to laugh when I remember William Fitchett teasing me when I was still a child, calling me "a theologian in short skirts."[12]

Seminary students were regularly received in our home. I met Mr. Samuel Wesley on the happy occasion of my sister Elizabeth's wedding to the respected publisher John Dunton. That fateful day, Samuel was nineteen years of age, and I had not yet reached my thirteenth year. While some perceived Samuel as brash and impudent, we had much in common that gave us a comfortable understanding of one another. Samuel's father, John Wesley of Whitechurch (yes, he had the same name as my famous son), was educated at Oxford and became an active dissenter and gifted preacher.

Like my father, he had been rejected from his living under the Act of Uniformity and was arrested many times and imprisoned four times for preaching in violation of another Parliamentary act of 1665.[13] Woefully, during his last incarceration, he fell ill after sleeping on the cold ground and died at the age of forty-two, a martyr for the dissenting cause.[14] His wife lived out her years as a penniless widow in a room in London, supported solely by her two sons, Samuel and Matthew. Though Samuel and I admired our fathers for their sacrifices for their beliefs, we each separately came to the conclusion that their dissenting positions were wrong. Samuel joined the Church of England when but sixteen years, and I did whilst I was not fully thirteen, much to the chagrin of my parents.

Love and Marriage

It is fair to say that Samuel Wesley and I were infatuated with each other from the beginning. However, we did not form an attachment until Samuel graduated from Oxford University six years later, earning a degree of bachelor of arts in theology. He had borrowed, struggled, and tutored others to stay at his studies. After being ordained, on the promise of living as a curate at St. Botolph, Aldersgate, in London, we were married on November 12, 1688.[15]

The curacy living of twenty-eight pounds a year did not prove sufficient, so Samuel became a chaplain on a naval vessel on the Irish Sea. In February 1690, I moved to my parents' home to give birth to our first child. Regrettably, my husband was in a constant state of debt throughout his lifetime, which put a strain on his decision-making. Each parish paid little more than the former, but each move accrued more debts and borrowing.

At Samuel's third parish at South Ormsby, Lincolnshire, the rectory was composed of reeds and clay, with no electricity or furniture. Six more children were born to us there, and Samuel published two scholarly books while attending to his parish duties.[16] Like all eighteenth-century British husbands, Samuel was the lord of the manor and the undisputed king of his castle. In personal letters, I addressed him as "my Master," and the children were instructed to address their father as "Honored Sir." Samuel's poetic prowess honored me with a poem expressing his appreciation of my role as his helpmeet:

She graced my humble roof, and blessed my life,
Blest me by far greater name than wife [friend].
Yet still I bore undisputed sway,
Nor was't her task, but pleasure, to obey:
Scarce thought, much less could act, what I denied,
In our low house there was no room for pride:
She studied my convenience day and night,
Nor did I for her care ungrateful prove.
What'er she ask'd I gave, without reproach or grudge
For still she reason ask'd and I was judge;
All my commands, requests at her fair hands,
And her requests to me were all commands.
Her house her pleasure was, and she was mine;
Or when by pity call'd, or charity.[17]

As a pastor's wife, attending to the needs of my family was the focus of my life. Daily life was difficult and strenuous. Yet we always lived in hope, though we had more than our share of illness, troubles, and tragedies. When we left South Ormsby for a new parish, we left behind three young children buried in the churchyard cemetery.

St. Andrew's Parish

Our next home, where we would spend four consecutive decades, was in the capital of a river island. Its name, Epworth, means "Farm on the rising ground."[18] St. Andrew's Parish offered a large two-story rectory made of timber, plaster, and straw thatch. Though the stipend for St. Andrew's Church was larger, it still was not enough to properly feed and clothe our ever-growing family or arrest our accumulating debts. There were increased taxes to pay, numerous repairs to make, furniture to purchase, and more mouths to feed. Finding money for our sons' education was done with much sacrifice and heavy borrowing. It was necessary for us to tend the glebe lands (fields owned by the parish) and raise our own poultry, pigs, sheep, and cows, skills neither Samuel nor I learned in London. Farming was a hoped-for supplement to our income, and raising animals was to be a source for food and money, but their price and upkeep caused more debts than it lessened. Unfortunately, other forces at work seriously affected our plight.

It is not surprising that Samuel was disliked by the uneducated fernlanders because of his royalist sympathies to the Crown and his High Church beliefs and standards. The established Church of England assigning a theological and literary scholar as vicar to an illiterate farming community made little sense, if any. Rev. Wesley preached an uncompromising view of Christianity in faith and practice. Regrettably, some local ruffians expressed their fierce disapproval with malice.

One day, rocks were thrown at our children, and on another, the hinges were removed from the doors of our home.[19] Tragically, our horses were hamstrung (cutting the tendons right above the hoof) and our cow's udders stabbed so we could have no milk.[20] Twice our fields were set ablaze. All these things were meant to scare or hurt us financially, in the hope we would leave town. Some even cruelly attempted to cut off the leg of the household dog, but the mastiff, thinking otherwise, would not let them.[21]

What prompted such intense behavior towards a quiet clergy family that never responded in kind is difficult to comprehend. However, some of our misfortunes could have been avoided with a little more common sense and wisdom on our part.

Religion versus Politics

I advise preachers to not use the pulpit to attempt to sway their parishioners' political votes. I remember the election of 1705 as being particularly volatile. Samuel urged the vote for a Colonel Whichcott. Yet after learning the colonel had taken monies from dissenters for his campaign, he vehemently denounced his support of him from the pulpit the following Sunday. It caused a grievous response from some townspeople, who gathered underneath our second-story bedroom window, where I was confined to my bed, having given birth that very day.

Unbeknown to them, Samuel was away in London, and our children were huddled together in the next bedroom, trembling in fear of what the noisy crowd might do. I slept very little that night, as the revelers beat drums, clattered pots and pans together, sang drinking songs, and occasionally shot off pistols.[22] I remember one bullet crashing through a windowpane, striking the bedpost above my head. A midwife had taken our newborn infant down the street to her home to escape the racket. My only concern was the safety of my family.

I was startled awake in the early morning by wailing screams of the maid, who thrust the now cold, dead baby into my bed. Apparently exhausted, the nurse in a deep sleep had overlaid the child, smothering it. All I could do was compose myself as best I could and arrange for the baby to be buried that day.

Life at Epworth was never easy. I called my remaining charges to my bedside and admonished them, "We Christians are not spared the hardships of life. The rain falls equally on the just and the unjust. But we have an Advocate and sure Hope in Jesus Christ, nonetheless."

We know God is on the throne of heaven, sustaining the universe, and therefore, we can trust that all is well, according to his divine purposes. This is not fatalism but true Christian faith.

One never knows what a day may bring. One Sunday, parishioners arriving for morning worship watched their rector being arrested on St. Andrew's steps for a debt of thirty pounds. The officers were willing to give my husband a few hours to raise the money, but his vengeful enemies would not agree. As Samuel was being led away to the debtors' prison at

Lincoln Castle, he was heard to say, "I am grieved to leave my little lambs in the midst of so many wolves."[23]

A week later, Samuel wrote to me his resilient resolve: "I'm getting acquainted with my brother jailbirds as fast as I can; and shall write to London next post, to the Society for Propagating Christian Knowledge, who, I hope, will send me some books to distribute among them."[24] He also wrote immediately to the archbishop that he hoped to do more good in this, his new parish, than he had in his old one.

Debtor Prisons

We were left for four months with only ten shillings with which to feed and clothe the family, Samuel included. Inmates inside debtor prisons had to supply their own food, or it could be purchased or brought to them by friends. Some prisons that allowed no visitors had tall wooden fences with an occasional bucket on a pulley that could be hoisted over the fence with food, hopefully to the right person. I was so concerned for Samuel's welfare. What was he eating? I sent to him the only thing I thought he might sell: my wedding rings. However, being the gentleman he was, he returned them to me forthwith. Instead of selling them, he wrote to the Archbishop of York, the Right Rev. John Sharp, pleading for his intervention and financial mercy, something Samuel had done several times before.

With no advanced warning, the archbishop called at our front door. His Honor took a chair in the parlor, as if he had arrived for high tea in the West End of London. He wished to greet all the children, and after eating a plate of biscuits and jam, directly inquired if we were truly in want of bread. I then realized the purpose of his visit. He had come to see if Samuel's descriptions of our plight were accurate.

I confessed to him, "We never actually wanted for bread, but we had so much care to get it, and to pay for it after, that it made it most unpleasant for me."[25]

I did want him to know that acquiring bread under such terms is the next degree of wretchedness to having none at all![26] He said nothing in response, but after his leave-taking, a generous bag of money was found that had been tactfully placed behind the tea tray.

Before Samuel's release from prison, his friends strongly suggested that he seek a more agreeable congregation elsewhere for his services. Such a change would have pleased the rector immensely. He was always strategizing to be assigned to another place, but the timing to leave now would be misinterpreted.

He wrote to Archbishop Sharp, "My friends advise me to leave Epworth. I confess I am not of that mind, because I may yet do good, and it is like a coward to desert my post because Satan fires his darts thick upon me."[27]

Forgive a digression, but I am astonished that some Christian leaders have decided that Satan no longer exists. Throughout church history, it has taught of the existence of Lucifer, the fallen archangel, who coveted the position of Christ and attempted to usurp his authority. But great thinkers have determined that Satan is just a metaphor for evil. My dears, I can think of no greater lie for Satan to invent himself than that he does not exist, for if he does not exist, you would have to reason that there was no evil as well. If there is no evil, then there must not be sin, and if there is no sin, Jesus Christ need not have come to earth to die upon the Cross. How preposterous to acquiesce to such illogical and wishful thinking. Forgive me if I offend, but never stray from the straightforward teachings of Holy Writ, for they are the God-breathed truths, "once for all entrusted to God's holy people" (Jude 3).

Fire, Fire!

Sadly, I have not related all our misfortune, nor do I wish to do so. However, I would be remiss if I did not explain the effects of the final burning of the Epworth Rectory. Four times, locals attempted to set fire to our home. The third time, half the house was destroyed, but the last time, after a harrowing escape, we watched our home with all its contents burn to the ground in fifteen minutes. The great loss was not the furniture or our clothing but my father's irreplaceable books, manuscripts, and papers he had bequeathed to me.

Naturally, I remember that dreadful day very well. It was February 9, 1709, midwinter and midnight. My daughter Hetty, then eleven years old, awoke first, giving an alarm. Embers falling from the eaves of the corn chamber had set her bed quilt alight.[28] Simultaneously, someone in the street (most likely the same persons who had set the fire) yelled out, "Fire! Fire!" They did not wish us to perish, just suffer. Samuel, working in his study, opened his door to find flames in the hallway. He shouted, waking all.

I was ill that night, being eight months with child. I ran to my bedroom chest to save the few shillings we had, but Samuel, observing me, yelled, "Nay, nay, run for your life!"[29]

The maid snatched up the baby in the nursery and led the other children down the staircase, which now showed flames. We all gathered at the front door, but it was locked, and the door key was upstairs. Samuel flew up the stairs to fetch the key while the children scrambled for the kitchen back door. Our little ones climbed upon a table and jumped out of a window since intense flames blocked the door. I was in no condition to climb or jump, so I searched my way through the dense smoke to the back door, which was now open. Thrice I attempted the flames before the open door and was thrice held back, overwhelmed with heat. So I prayed to the Lord to preserve my life for the sake of my children, if it was his will. Mercifully, in the fourth attempt through the doorway, the flames warmed my legs, hands, and face, but little else. Much later, I realized Isaiah 43:2 applied to me: "When you walk through the fire, you will not be burned; the flames will not set you ablaze."

In the confusion, one child had not awakened, John Benjamin Wesley, little Jacky, then but six years old. As Samuel was fleeing through the front door himself, he heard fright-filled screams of a child up in the nursery. He attempted the stairs to rescue him, but the steps had burned through and could not sustain his body. Utterly thwarted, Samuel knelt down in the dense smoke and commended the soul of the child to God, helpless to do otherwise.

Outside, he was ushered by friends to find the rest of his family collected safe in the side garden. In the bedchamber, Jacky, aware the flames were blocking the path for any rescue, had the presence of mind to push a chest of drawers in front of a window and climb upon it. A passerby saw his silhouette against the light of the flames behind him and yelled for a ladder.

Another shouted, "Nay, there's no time!"

Suddenly, a neighbor came running across the street, sscreaming, "I will fix myself on the wall; set a light man upon my shoulders."[30]

They created a human ladder. Their first attempt failed, but the second time, Jacky was snatched out of the window by his shirt collar, just as the whole of the roof fell inward. Had the roof fallen outward, all might surely have been crushed.

When Jacky was brought to us in the garden, the very sight of him brought Zechariah 3:2 vividly to my mind. Here was "a brand plucked from the burning."[31] I knew at that very moment God had saved this child for a special providence, and I resolved to be particularly careful to teach him the principles of true Christianity.

Samuel was also overwhelmed with intense emotion. He called out, "Come neighbors, gather round, let us kneel down in thanksgiving, God has given me all my children. Let the house go; I am rich enough."[32]

My master's heart was fixed aright on what was truly valuable. The following year, the house was rebuilt of brick in classic Queen Ann style, at a cost of four hundred pounds.[33] Thereafter, we would never be solvent, nor would we have as much as before this fire.

Marital Misunderstanding

Living on the edge of poverty can cause great stress, even to a loving family. Every evening before bedtime, all the family and any houseguests gathered in our parlor and knelt in a circle for prayer. We began with spoken thanksgivings and then prayed for those in authority over us, as Holy Scripture commands believers to do. One evening, Samuel ended with his usual prayer for King William III of Orange. After all the children were kissed good night and safely upstairs, Samuel chided me for not saying, "Amen," to his prayer for the king.

I explained to him that my conscience would not allow me to say it because I did not believe William was the rightful heir to the throne. Mine was not the official Tory party view. Samuel's mind strained to accept how this could be possible. After days of discussion, he acknowledged our polarized positions, saying, "If we must have two kings, we must have two beds!"[34]

He left a fortnight later for London to conduct church business, as it was the time for convocation. At our parting, my lord declared that he fully expected I would come to reason and join his position during his absence.

I did not fully realize why this matter was so important to him. Apparently, an Englishman's political affiliation was the chief characteristic of his identity in the 1700s. Every gentleman had firm opinions and associated with persons most like-minded to himself. A wife, having no voting privileges or social identity apart from her husband, would naturally acquire his opinions.

But, my friends, there was more at stake in Samuel's mind than what this might do to his public leadership image in the family and parish. Apparently, he learned that several clergymen, labeled nonjurors, were expelled from their livings because of their refusal to recognize William of Orange as their sovereign. My husband was simply afraid this would happen to him if anyone learned that his wife was also a nonjuror. Furthermore, his long-held hope that the King himself would give him a better preferment (as Queen Mary had done in giving him St. Andrew's) would be dashed if it was known his wife had refused to say, "Amen," to a prayer for the king.

About six months later, Good Queen Ann ascended the throne, which was perfect timing for our marital unity. Queen Ann was a Stuart, and we both agreed on the Stuarts. Less than a year after our reunion, we were blessed with a special gift: baby John Benjamin Wesley. Incidentally, Matthew Wesley, Samuel's apothecary brother, repeatedly pointed out to his sibling the cause for our costly and ever-growing family. But Samuel refused to admit that he was in any way responsible.[35] There must be some moments of humor in life, or it would be very dull, indeed. Whether he was teasing with his well-known wit or not (blaming God's providential intervention for the large number of his children), I can say I believe the roles of wife and mother are the greatest callings a woman can desire.

School in the Home

On the matter of the religious training of children, it will not surprise you that I have strong opinions. I believe that the parent works in concert with God in the salvation of the soul of a child.[36] This becomes evident when we understand Christianity to be the doing of God's will rather than our own. How can adults in later life acquiesce to the will of their heavenly Father, if they do not first learn at an early age to acquiesce to the will of their earthly parents, who also seek these benefits? Therefore, the subjecting of the will must be done at once, for by neglecting timely correction, they will contract a stubbornness that is rarely conquered afterward.[37] This is not to break the spirit of the child, mind you, but rather the innate defiant will. Self-will is the root of all sin and misery; it is that one grand impediment to our temporal and eternal happiness.

I believe there are two ways children learn: by precept and by example. I will give you a case in point of my meaning. First, precept: The Bible is God's Holy Word. It is God's revelation of himself to humankind. By studying this God-breathed Word, we can come to a saving knowledge of Jesus Christ, the Living Word. That is precept. Secondly, example: We read God's Holy Word, discuss it, and memorize it to seal it in the heart, joining together with believers to share its application to our lives. That is example. Which do you think teaches more, precept or example? Any child would say, example, for did not our Savior live a perfect life of example in all things?

If you are able to send your children to a public school, you are most fortunate. We were unable to do so. There were a few public schools, but our children could read and spell better than the poorly educated teachers. It became obvious that I was the one who must teach our children. Six hours of each day were set aside for instruction, the hours 9 a.m. to 12 p.m. and 2 p.m. to 5 p.m.[38] It was equally apparent that a strict schedule for each day was required. I cannot conceive of any other way to manage. When my son John was beginning the organization of Christian societies and classes throughout the British Isles, he also put his mind to establishing Charity Schools for the education of the very poor.

Manual of Discipline and Education

John besought me repeatedly to write down what he titled for me *A Manual for Discipline and Education*, describing my methods for teaching children.[39] To please him, I acquiesced in a letter penned on July 24, 1732:

Dear Son,

According to your desire, I have collected the principle rules I observed in educating my family. As to the writing down of them I am much adverse, for I cannot see how anyone else would want to read them. The children were always put into a regular method of living in such things, as they were capable of, from their birth. ... In order to form the minds of children, the first thing to be done is to conquer their will and bring them to an obedient temper. To inform the understanding is a work of time and must proceed by slow degree with children, as they are able to bear it. It is incredible what can be taught to a child in a quarter of a year with rigorous application.

The children of our family were taught as soon as they could speak, the Lord's Prayer, which they were made to say at rising and at bedtime constantly; to which, as they grew bigger, were added a short prayer for their parents, and some portion of Scripture as their memories could bear. None were taught to read until the age of five, and on that birthday they learned the alphabet. There was no such thing as loud talking or playing during lesson hours.

There were by-laws (that is, expectations) observed among us:

1. It had been observed that cowardice and fear of punishment often led children to lying. To prevent this, a law was made that whoever was charged with a fault of which they were guilty, if they would confess it and promised to amend, should not be beaten.
2. No child should be chided twice for the same offense.
3. Promises made are strictly observed.
4. If performance was not well, the intention should be kindly accepted.

5. That no girl be taught to work till she can read well; the putting of children to learn sewing before they can read perfectly is the very reason why so few women can read fit to be heard.[40]

There were many other enumerated expectations than these, but my principle intention was the salvation of the souls of my children. What could be of greater import? My second goal was the formation of each child's character; that they might be kind-hearted, with a love for God, followed by a love for their fellow human beings. Third, I wanted to impart a love of learning that would blossom through all their years into happiness and productivity. "My world was a simple one, but I was content to occupy but a small space if God be glorified in it."[41]

Something More

One day in the year of our Lord 1710, very unpredictably, my life was to change when Samuel was away on church business. My eldest daughter, Emilia, recommended I read an obscure book overlooked in the library. It was an account of some Danish missionaries sent out under the auspices of King Frederick to the far country of Tranquebar.[42] I think I was never more affected by any book, save Holy Scripture. I spent a good deal of a week of evenings praising God for inspiring them with ardent zeal for the Lord's service. For days, I could think or speak of little else. I wanted my life to have some higher purpose, so I earnestly prayed for God to use me, but I knew not how with my limited opportunities.

Then a clear insight came to me. Though I was neither a man nor a minister, if my heart were sincerely devoted to God and his glory, I might do somewhat more than I was doing. I decided to pray more and speak with those to whom I conversed with more warmth and affection.[43] There was only one place to begin: my Jerusalem, my family. I would spend one hour each day alone with one of my children, discussing their lives or whatever subject they wished. John's day was Thursday, and Charles's was Saturday, and two girls shared Sunday. This time meant so much to John that when he left for Charter House School, he asked me to write to him one hour each Thursday, as he would do the same to me. This practice we continued all our lives whenever apart. I cannot commend this practice to you more highly. Nothing was more effective than this in the rearing of my children. Do spend time with your children and grandchildren, for they desire your guiding attention more than they can express.

Church in the Home

We also resolved to sing praises to God on Sunday evenings with the family because the curate, who was hired to preach in Samuel's absence, had ceased Evensong. Imagine a church not providing worship on Sunday evenings. Inconceivable. To compensate for this oversight, we read aloud the best sermons we could find in the rector's study, sang hymns, and offered prayers in our kitchen. First, servants asked to sit with the family, and then neighbors attended, and soon parishioners were included. We named this gathering Our Society.

Soon, the evening attendance at these meetings numbered above two hundred, attempting to hear in the house and out in the garden, with the speaker standing by the open kitchen door. Even so, many went away from want of room to stand. The curate, Mr. Inman, became, one would have to say, rather jealous, since more were attending these evening gatherings than his morning services. He sent off an irate letter to Samuel, demanding these "unseemly" meetings conducted by a woman be stopped. Samuel's response was a letter to me requesting a full explanation. I obliged his request with arguments penned on February 6, 1711:

> As I am a woman, so I am also mistress of a large family. And though the superior charge of the souls lies upon you; yet, in your absence, I cannot but look upon every soul you leave under my care as a talent committed to me under a trust, by the great Lord. … If I am unfaithful to him or you in neglecting to improve these talents, how shall I answer to him?[44]

I went on to explain in detail how these meetings innocently evolved in lieu of lack of instructional preaching at services and the positive use of available time on Sunday evenings. I freely admit another argument I penned was an emotional plea: "There are good effects of these meetings. Our Society has wonderfully conciliated the minds of people towards us that we now live in the greatest amenity imaginable. Some families who seldom went to church now go constantly."[45]

I can't remember how many letters we exchanged on the subject, but my last correspondence was a single sentence request: "My Lord, if you do, after all, think fit to dissolve this assembly, do not tell me you desire me to do so, for that will not satisfy my conscience; but send me your firm and positive command, in such full and expressed terms as may absolve me of all guilt and punishment for neglecting this opportunity of doing good, when you and I shall appear before the great and awful tribunal of our Lord Jesus Christ!"[46]

Could a mere, mortal husband dare resist such an appeal? Our kitchen meetings continued until Samuel returned to the parish, and Sunday Evensong was reinstated, this time with a congenial friendship with our parishioners.

Clergy and Laity

I want to share an incident that happened while I was living at the Foundry in London. The Foundry was an old cannon factory that lay with its roof blown off from an explosion. John had purchased and converted it into the headquarters of the Methodist Societies. While he was away on one of his endless journeys, a layman, Thomas Maxfield, ventured to preach in the chapel. Laymen were never permitted to preach, but all the ordained preachers were traveling on their circuits. The news of this event reached John, and he hastened home to rectify the transgression.

I kept watch for him that I might engage him on the subject at the earliest moment, before any action could be taken. I had rehearsed my argument in my thoughts: *Dear son, you cannot expect me of favoring readily anything like this. I implore you, nonetheless, to take care with what you do with that young man, for he may be as called by God to preach as you are. I beg of you two things. Examine what have been the fruit of his labor, and hear Mr. Maxfield preach yourself.*[47]

John agreed, and after hearing him preach, he said, "Let the young man do what seems right to him. It is the Lord. Who am I that I should withstand God?"[48]

Such was Rev. John Benjamin Wesley, a gifted leader and yet a humble man, always ready to follow the promptings of the Spirit of God. To be firm in one's conviction and theology does not mean that you cannot be open to embrace new ways. Within the year, Thomas Maxfield and seven other laymen were formally consecrated to preach God's Holy Word. They were the beginning of a force of seven hundred lay preachers who served the Methodist movement during John's lifetime, without which the societies would not have been properly led or replenished spiritually. Dear friends, are we not all called to the priesthood? Is it not all our tasks to speak of God's grace to all we meet and give to them of whatever means, skills, and abilities we have in Jesus's good name?

Mothers and Daughters

I am certainly proud of my girls. Martha was a constant houseguest of Dr. Samuel Johnson, the literary genius of our day. She entered into the political and philosophical discussions around his table as an equal with the intellectuals of Britain who came to dine. Hetty wrote articles for *Gentlemen's Quarterly* and other eminent publications. Emilia founded and administered a girl's school in Gainsborough.[49] Yet it grieves me to share the sad truth that all but one of my daughters suffered a miserable marriage for want of a better dowry, education, clothes, means to travel, and introductions into society circles. Mary, my daughter who married for love, had grown up crippled from an accident in infancy, never imagining that any man would want to marry her. But a bright young man began to work at the rectory, transcribing for my husband. When he graduated from Oxford, he became Samuel's curate.

It was a hope-filled day in 1734 when Mary married John Whitelamb. The Lord Chancellor appointed the newlywed cleric to the parish of Wroot, where their happy life together seemed certain. But alas, Mary died in childbirth a fortnight before her first wedding anniversary, and the poor infant also died. I can tell you there are worse pains for a mother to bear than poverty, illness, or fire, when one must helplessly observe the sufferings of one's own children and be able to do nothing. I can say it is often more difficult to be a mother of adult children than when they are small. I suffered many days in a sickbed, put there from worry. I might have better spent my time in some useful work that could have relieved someone else's pain and suffering. Still, all our remaining girls embraced for themselves the Methodist movement as it swept across the British Isles, and they each served in the societies wholeheartedly.

My Three Sons

Oblige me to tell you of my three sons. You probably know of John and Charles, who were opposite in both temperament and manner, yet totally dedicated to each other's welfare. John was the energetic, talented organizer with a brilliant, analytical mind. Charles was the creative, congenial personality with a compassionate heart. He composed more than sixty-five hundred hymns, only seventy-seven of which were included in the official Methodist Hymnal. Tis a great pity they kept so few! Charles wrote for me a three-line verse of his regard for music. It is a favorite poem of mine that I happily share with you:

For the common things of every day,
God gave man speech in the common way.
For the deeper things men think and feel,
God gave the poet words to reveal.
For heights and depths no words can reach,
God gave man music the soul's own speech.[50]

Perhaps you have heard of my first-born child, Samuel Jr.? People often said he was my favorite child. He probably was; you see, I knew him the longest. Samuel Jr. was sincerely generous and lived frugally so he could be so. When he received his first wages as a teacher at Westminster Abbey School, he determined to send half his earnings home to his poor parents, a practice he continued all his life. After his father died, he continued to distribute half of his monthly income to the rest of the needy women of our family. His lovely wife was equally benevolent, never once complaining of her husband's great generosity. I wonder how many couples have maintained such a sacrificially kind practice?

Possessing Assurance of Salvation

It is with heartfelt regret that I must tell you something about which I am not proud, yet my conscience will not allow me to remain silent on the matter: I did not possess for myself the assurance of my own salvation until I was in my seventieth year. I resided in the converted living quarters of the foundry that stood beside the meeting room of the Methodist Societies in London. I witnessed daily the remarkable accomplishments and spiritual zeal of the people who worshipped there. They are called, simply, Methodists.

I studied the writings and sermons of their leaders. When I was reading one of John's papers, I realized I had scarcely heard mentioned "having the knowledge of forgiveness of sins" in this life, or of "God's Spirit bearing witness with our spirit," and abiding there. Much less did I imagine that this was the common privilege of all true believers. Therefore, I never had asked God for assurance of forgiveness of sin for myself, because I did not realize it was something I could possess.

One ordinary Sunday, I was kneeling at the altar rail and offered the Communion cup by my son-in-law, the Rev. Westley Hall. I heard familiar words from his lips that I had heard throughout my life: "The blood of the Lord Jesus Christ, which was given for thee." This time, those words struck through my heart with new meaning, and I knew that God, for Jesus Christ's sake, had forgiven me all my sins.[51] I grasped at once I was God's very own child, totally forgiven, and of that, I had complete confidence. A new joy pervaded my being. I felt different: peaceful, happier, stronger, and more alive.

Do you know of what I speak? John said this was the Holy Spirit bearing witness with my spirit, empowering me for greater awareness of and service to Christ. Upon reflection, I believe my case was rather like those in the first-century church of Ephesus. I had not been faithful to the talents committed to my trust and had lost my first love. When I had forgotten God, he had not forgotten me by telling me with an inner witness that Christ died for me. My husband's deathbed exhortation to Charles was, "The inner witness, son, the inner witness, that is the proof, the strongest proof of Christianity."[52] My friends, it is possible to know all about God and, yet, not know God. The Holy Spirit must give us the assurance that we belong to him.

God's Providential Leading

Looking back to that experience, it was then that I understood both John and Charles's confusing behavior from years before. In 1738, they had returned to England a year after their missionary endeavors in Georgia in America. All the family became alarmed when at the age of thirty-five, John suddenly announced he was now a new Christian. I confess to you that I was deeply worried that he had taken leave of his senses. How preposterous such a claim appeared to me. The Rev. John Wesley, Oxford Fellow in Theology, missionary to the American Indians, ordained Anglican priest, *not* a Christian? When Charles wrote me that he, too, had a similar salvation conversion, just three days prior to John, reason required that I not react without discussing the theological basis for their claim.

I wrote to John a specific request: "Pray tell me the Scriptural foundation for your claim of salvation by faith alone?"

I need not have asked, for John put to pen innumerable arguments for his new faith, citing from Ephesians, Romans, and the book of Acts. The crowning text that gave me pause was Ephesians 2:8, 9: "For it is by grace you have been saved, through faith—and this is not from yourselves, it is the gift of God— not by works, so that no one can boast."

John wrote of his own spiritual awakening, beginning with his frustration in America:

> All the time I was at Savannah in all my preaching, I was thus beating the air. Being ignorant of the righteousness of Christ, which by a living faith in him bringeth salvation to every one that believeth, I sought to establish my own righteousness, and so labored in the fire all my days. I was now, properly under the Law; I knew that the Law of God was spiritual; I consented to it that it was good. Yea, I delighted in it. But I was still under the Law, not under Grace, the state most that are called Christians are content to live and die in. For I was only striving with, not freed from sin. Neither had I the witness of the Spirit with my spirit. And indeed could not, for I sought it not by faith, but as it were, by the works of the Law.[53]

The sojourn in the colony of Georgia arranged by Governor Oglethorpe profoundly influenced John to question his personal faith as the result of several experiences. The first incident occurred while voyaging outbound across the Atlantic Ocean to England. Caught in a fierce gale, John described his intense fear at sea in a journal entry dated July 25, 1736:

> At noon our third storm began. At four it was more violent than any before. The waves of the sea were mighty and raged horribly. They "rose up to heaven above, and clave down to hell beneath." The winds roared round about us, and (what I never heard before) whistled as distinctly as if it had been a human voice, but shook and jarred with so unequal, grating a motion, that one could not but with great difficulty keep one's hold of anything … every ten minutes came a shock against the stern or side, which one would think should dash the planks in pieces. … At seven in the morning I went to the Moravians. … In the midst of the psalm wherewith their service began, the sea broke over, split the mainsail in pieces, covered the ship, and poured in between the decks, as if the great deep had already swallowed us up. A terrible screaming began among the English. The Germans calmly sung on.[54]

While the English passengers, clinging to their bunks, wailed in fear that they were about to die, a band of Moravian believers sat on the deck, men, women, and small children, singing praise to God in a scheduled Sunday service.

When the wind and sea finally calmed, John sought them out individually, asking, "Was you not afraid?"

The reply: "I thank God, no."

John was struck not only by the answer, but also by the amazement at his very question. He asked again, "Were not your women and children afraid?"

The second mild reply, "No, our women and children are not afraid to die."[55]

Here was a trust in God, even down to their youngest child, the likes of which the Rev. John Wesley had never seen. He realized there was something greatly amiss in his own faith. God's providential hand caused him to befriend the Rev. Peter Boehler, a leader of the Moravians, by whom he and Charles were challenged to examine their own understanding of the means of salvation.

Transforming Conversion

One evening, John announced to Charles and Peter Boehler that, in his doubt, he had decided to leave off preaching altogether because he had no real faith. Boehler objected, arguing for John to take a step of faith, "Preach faith until you have it, and then because you have it, you will preach faith!"[56] John reluctantly agreed but expected nothing. All his life, he had been taught the virtues of a pious life and was devoted to the disciplines of the Christian religion. Even at Oxford, he had led the Holy Club that his brother Charles had begun. This group of students, never numbering more than twenty-five, met regularly three times a week. They discussed scripture passages, spent an hour in prayer, and queried each other on the quality of the holiness of their life, asking, "How is it with your soul?" From these discussions, they decided to make practical application to their study by visiting the poor in debtor's prisons. They preached to the prisoners of God's love and brought them food and medicine, purchased out of their own purses. In addition, they fasted twice a week and memorized scripture, which brought ridicule from their fellow Oxfordians, who nicknamed them Enthusiasts, Bible Moths, and Methodists.[57] Oh, what a band of remarkable souls they were. Out of their ranks came outstanding leaders of the spiritual awakening they were to ignite, transforming their generation. Yet the Holy Club's quest for religious devotion did not satisfy the spiritual longing in both John's and Charles's hearts. In later years, John referred to the Holy Club's endeavors as nothing more than "works righteousness," in a useless attempt to earn God's favor.

Providentially, a short time after returning to England from the Americas, John was invited to attend a Moravian meeting one evening in London. He remembered being depressed in mind and spirit, but felt obliged to attend since he had promised a friend. His journal entry records the date as May 24, 1738:

> I went very unwillingly to a society in Aldersgate Street, where one was reading Luther's Preface to the Epistle to the Romans. About a quarter before nine, while he was describing the change, which God works in the heart through faith in Christ, I felt my heart strangely warmed. I felt I did trust in Christ, Christ alone for salvation; and an assurance was given me that he had taken away my sins, even mine, and saved me from the law of sin and death. [58]

What instinctively followed is most noteworthy. I do not want you to miss it, for John continued, "I began to pray with all my might for those who had in a more special manner despitefully used me and persecuted me. I then testified openly to all present, what I now first felt in my heart."[59]

That which began as an experience of personal salvation now found immediate expression in a desire to pray for others that erupted into personal witness. John shared his newfound faith, as he called it, with those present. Then he prevailed upon them to walk with him to a house nearby, where his brother Charles lay in a sickbed.

Bursting into the bedchamber with friends in tow, John exclaimed, "I believe!"

All were elated to learn that Charles had experienced a similar awakening just three days prior! There was great rejoicing in the room. The Holy Spirit had been graciously working within these two blood brothers for his sovereign purposes. Charles and John sensed they were on the precipice of a new move of God in the world. All celebrated in the manner of the angels when Christ was born; they sang praises to God with a song Charles had scribbled within minutes of his conversion. The paper was still within reach on his bedside table.

Spreading the Good News

The message of that song is most plain. It is a song of salvation, an evangelistic call to believe in Christ and be forgiven. Once we are bound to Christ, his concerns will be our concerns, and his purposes our purposes. A grateful Christian will care about the lost and call out, urging men and women to receive the free gift of salvation. When the disciples of Jesus were filled with the Holy Spirit on the Day of Pentecost, my dear friends, there was a definite purpose for that supernatural event. Jesus promised he would send the Spirit so that "you will be my witnesses" (Ac 1:8). The wonderful thing about Pentecost was not the rushing, mighty wind, or the tongues like as a fire, but the disciples being filled with the Holy Spirit that they might witness of Christ to unbelievers. Jesus Christ has commissioned every believer to make disciples in the world. We must be about our heavenly Father's business until Jesus returns, for God has transferred Christ's mission to us.

For this reason, John Wesley, at age thirty-seven, began to travel and preach anywhere people could assemble. His message of the new birth offended many clergymen, which resulted in Anglican pulpits being closed to him. Instead, he rose at 4 a.m. to preach in the open air at an entrance to a coal pit when the miners were heading to work at 5 a.m. He made it his practice to preach three times a day, whether on an open field or a rainy street corner, totaling over forty thousand sermons in his lifetime.[60] He often covered sixty miles a day, and in his itinerant years, he traveled some two hundred fifty thousand miles on horseback, a distance equal to ten circuits along the equator.[61] He organized new converts into bands and classes, small groups of men or women who met regularly to examine each other's spiritual progress. At the close of his life, he had created schools and orphanages, opened medical clinics for the poor, published books, trained leaders, sent preachers to America, and established thriving societies in England, Scotland, Wales, and Ireland.

Speaking the Truth in Love

My son John did not deem himself as a great reformer. He did not spring to his mission like a man who had seen a great vision before his eyes. He simply went about doing good, relieving pain and suffering wherever he found it. His purpose was to aid men and women in their quest to know God. John and Charles were not miracle workers, but I attribute their success to simply speaking the truths of God in a forthright manner. Such was the need of our day, and I am sure it is the same for yours. Is this not the task of us all, to speak the truth of God from a heart of love?

I beseech you to attend to the rigors of the Christian life so that you may be Christ's fruitful disciple. Remember that we now have direct access to God. It is Jesus our Lord who has promised to take us from one degree of glory to another. Oh, what a wondrous thought to be taken from faith to faith, and grace to grace.

Be on your guard against apathy. Christianity is not meant to be like a cloak that one takes off and on, as one is hot or cold. Rather, Christianity is a relationship with the Savior that is life's compelling force. Be good stewards of what God has given you. Stewardship is not just your money; it is your time, your talent, your knowledge, and your whole life as well.

As I write my farewell, I beseech you to rekindle the gift of God that is within you. No one can say, "Jesus Christ is Lord," lest the Holy Spirit bid him to say it. If you call upon the name of the Lord and accept his forgiveness for your sins, God's very own Spirit has come into your spirit and abides there. Stir up your spirit! Ask God to quicken you with his power and give you a new zeal for his work, that he, and he alone, might be glorified through you. Surely there are those who have not yet heard the name that is above every name, Jesus Christ the Lord. You must lift up that Holy name. You are chosen to be a light set upon a hill for all to see, for you are Christ's ambassador. Above all, dear friend, never, never be ashamed of the Gospel of Jesus Christ, for it is the power of God by which men and women are saved. Blessed be Christ, for he is our all-sufficient Savior. May you love him much, for we have been much loved and forgiven. I commend you to God the Father's gracious protection, and may the Holy Spirit be your constant guide for you and your household.

Your faithful friend and servant,

Susanna Wesley

Conclusion

Mrs. Susanna Wesley would have never thought of herself as a pastor or of acting in any capacity as a spiritual leader over men. When her husband was absent from their home, she assumed the responsibility of her family's immediate welfare because it was the needful thing to do.

When there were no longer Evensong services on Sundays at St. Andrew's Church, she organized an alternative in her kitchen because it was simply the right thing to do. When neighbors and parishioners asked to attend these worshipful gatherings, she invited them to join in because it was the next right thing to do. Just like her son John, who never had a vision to evangelize the world, Susanna never had a grand master plan to evangelize her parish. Instead, she wanted to feed her own spirit and those around her, with the Word of God in the quest for a deeper knowledge of him. What she did throughout her adult life were daily and seemingly ordinary tasks of what she saw as responsible duties of a Christian, a wife, and a mother.

None of us can choose all the circumstances in which we find ourselves. We don't decide when or where we are born or who our parents are going to be. We don't create all the events that come our way, but we have the power to choose how we will respond to them. Susanna did not have worldly wealth, power, or prestige, but she had a determination to do the next right thing, according to her Christian beliefs and conscience. It was important to her to always obey God's precepts, because when acting according to his will, one is in tune with him. When we do the next right thing, we not only put ourselves in step with God's plan, but we also find ourselves alongside others who are in step with God and his will. That means we will join with other brothers and sisters in the family of God, who are doing the same right things that we desire to do. When this happens, we function as the dynamic church, the Body of Christ on earth.

So often, the great things in life are just the sum of all the little things that we do in every day. This was true for Susanna. Her right choice when she decided to speak with more warmth and affection with those she came in contact with, and to begin with her family, led to the next right step and the next. We usually do not skip steps in the Christian life. God promises in his Word to lead us from faith to faith, obedience to obedience, grace to grace, and glory to glory. When Jesus told the servants at the wedding feast in Cana in Galilee to fill jars with water, they did not know that by obeying this ordinary task, they would be used in the first powerful miracle that would enable the disciples to believe in the Deity of Jesus Christ. Most of us will never know the great things that can arise from our simple obedience to God when we do the next right thing.

Mrs. Wesley, being a Christian woman of her era, could never imagine that women could be ordained as priests and pastors, and serve the Communion elements to men. About a century after Susanna, another clergymen's wife in England would not see herself in that role, either, but she did examine the question and opened the door for other women to find their place to serve Christ in the public arena. With a similar desire to do the next right thing, Mrs. Catherine Booth was a catalyst for another worldwide movement for the proclamation of the Gospel around the globe.

Discussion Questions

1. As a country clergy wife Susanna found herself isolated from the family, culture and comfort in which she was raised. Have you ever experienced the feeling of being enclosed within the four walls of your home as Susanna described her dilemma?
   How did Susanna adjust to find contentment in her unsatisfactory situation? What things can you suggest to overcome the problems of isolation and boredom?
2. Mrs. Wesley never sought to be a preacher, teacher or a leader of women and men in her daily life. What was the natural progression that made her an effective influencer in her little sphere that grew to bless the outside world? What influence would you like to have in your place and time? (Please, don't be shy!)
3. Susanna was a methodical and self-disciplined person. How did these characteristics affect her life and the lives of her children?
   In what ways do these disciplines enhance the Christian life?
   In what areas would you like to be more organized and disciplined?
4. The most important task in Susanna's purpose in life was the spiritual rearing of her children. She continued to write her spiritual advice to her adult children throughout her lifetime whenever they were apart. How can you *very wisely* spiritually bless and influence your children both when a child and as an adult?
5. Susanna believed her rules for child rearing were effective for her family.
   Do you think those same rules would be effective in today's world?
   If you would modify any of her rules for today, which ones would you change?

The Army Mother

Introducing Catherine Booth

There is little doubt that the marriage partnership of General William Booth and Catherine Mumford Booth was exceedingly happy. The love letters they exchanged throughout their lives rival those of the Barrett Brownings. The many achievements of their corporate goals changed the plight of the poor masses by providing the basic needs of food, shelter, clothing, and employment, in their own country and on every continent. At the same time, they successfully fought to outlaw the white slave trade, raised the age of consent, and invented safety matches that wiped out the phossy jaw disease that killed thousands of children workers. The greatest legacy of their lives was the establishment of a worldwide Christian ministry, the Salvation Army, whose never-changing purpose remains the salvation of souls. Today, the Army works in 128 countries under the leadership of twenty-eight thousand officers with over 1,182,000 soldiers serving in their own corps/churches, operating homeless hostels, addiction programs, hospitals, day-care centers, refugee programs, homes for children and the elderly, disaster relief programs, and prisoner visitation.[1]

General William Booth's gifts of organization, administration, and preaching skills took him 5 million miles throughout the world, preaching sixty thousand sermons in his ninety-two years.[2] Catherine was never ordained or commissioned as an officer, yet with her brilliant mind, she is credited with giving the Army its fervent spirit and sound foundation of biblical doctrines. Her study and knowledge of Holy Scripture shaped a deep passion for emphasizing a life of holiness and service to Christ. Mrs. Booth's analytical skills were evident in her personal example of outstanding writing and preaching, which opened a multitude of leadership opportunities for women in Christian ministry as never before.

Unable to attend the Salvation Army's twenty-fifth anniversary celebration at the London Crystal Palace in 1890, a giant sheet was unfurled for the audience to read the Army mother's farewell charge to her soldiers. She wrote:

> My Dear Children and Friends,
>
> My chair is empty, but my heart is with you. You are my joy and crown. Your battles, sufferings, and victories have been the chief interest of my life these past twenty-five years. They are so still. Go forward! Live holy lives. Be true to the Army. God is your strength. Love and seek the lost: bring them to the Blood. Make the people good; inspire them with the Spirit of Jesus Christ. Love one another; help your comrades in dark hours. I am dying under the Army Flag; it is yours to live and fight under. God is my Salvation and Refuge in the storm. I send you my love and blessings.[3]

An Open Letter from Catherine Booth

Dear Child of God,

I bid you God's grace in the name that is above every name.

When I was first asked to write down the story of my life, I objected vigorously, thinking there were far better subjects to address for the cause of Christ. Then I was reminded of the power there is in sharing one's own experience with the one, true God. Our testimony is a genuine witness for Christ that cannot be denied. Therefore, I will start at the beginning, since that is a very good place to start! Each one of our stories begins with our kinfolk because God has put us into families, intending them to be the heart of human society. We are so greatly influenced by our family's love and care, for are they not the most important relationships in our lives, save that of Christ Jesus?

I did not live all my life in London, England, but hailed from a small village called Ashbourne in Derbyshire. Ironically, I was born in the same year as my husband, 1829. My mother was the best of women. I can still hear Mum's sweet voice singing a hymn as she worked around the house, and not simply because she was happy, but for her passionate love of Jesus. How I love those old hymns. Charles Wesley and Sir Isaac Watts are two of my favorite composers. Their hymns were not only well-written, but their messages went deep into my soul. One day, Mother took me inside Bunhill Cemetery, the dissenters' graveyard across from Wesley Chapel on Broad Street, where we happened upon the grave of Sir Isaac Watts.[4] She told me an old story of how Isaac, while still a wee lad, had got into the habit of speaking in rhymes, driving those around into great irritability. Isaac's father demanded he stop, but little Isaac couldn't break the habit. Insisting he stop, his stern father bent Isaac over his knee to give him a paddling. Between each lick Isaac begged:

O' Father, do some mercy take,
and I will no more verses make![5]

Do you believe it? I did. But you need to know, I was still a wee child myself.

My Family

Like most British people, my dear mother was raised in the Church of England. In the Victorian era, the spiritual life of the establishment was at very low ebb, so religion made little impression on her. When Mum was in her late teen years, a young man fell in love with her and asked her to marry him. Pressured to accept the proposal by his family, Sarah Milward, nonetheless hesitated, sensing something was amiss. She refused his offer saying, that she was not in love with him, so as not to cast doubts upon his character. Gossip swirled around the refusal, and when the young man suddenly died in an asylum, he left a letter blaming her. Devastated by this accusation, Mother became quite ill, taking to her bed for weeks. At my grandfather's request, a Methodist preacher came to her bedside and explained "the plan of God's salvation in all its glorious simplicity,"[6] that she gave her whole heart to Jesus Christ. Her countenance changed overnight from oppressing guilt to peaceful joy. Influenced by Methodist biblical teaching, she gave away her ball gowns, went regularly to church meetings, and became an intensely committed Christian.

A year or so later, Sarah fell in love with Mr. John Mumford, who was also a Methodist lay preacher and carriage-maker by trade. Of their five children, I was the only girl. Three of my brothers never outlived infancy. Life was so hard in the mid-eighteen hundreds that there was only a 27 percent chance that you would reach the age of twelve.[7] Because of my poor health, my childhood years were very quiet and spent at home. When my elder brother was sixteen, he immigrated to America, so the only playmate I remember was a red-haired retriever dog. Dearest Waterford was my special companion, and one day, he jumped through a large glass window to save me from harm. How I sobbed bitterly at his passing when my father had him put down, believing Red (my pet name for him) had turned aggressive from the incident. Still, my mother was always there for me; my comforter, teacher, confidante, spiritual mentor, and friend. She loved God so much that rather than blame God for the loss of her children, heaven was closer because her boys were there with their heavenly Father. I was schooled at home, and the Holy Bible was my first lesson-book. At five, I would read to my mother as she worked nearby, helping me sound out difficult words. She claimed that by my twelfth birthday, I read through those sacred books eight times from cover to cover.[8] As a result, my childhood heroes were Abraham and Sarah, Joseph and Samuel, Jonathan and David, Abigail, Jochebed, Deborah, and Lydia. I am so happy this was so.

Our contented daily life abruptly changed when Papa started drinking. The stronghold it had over him made him abandon his faith in Christ. He stopped all preaching and attending church altogether. What made him turn to alcoholic drink, I do not know, because he had been an ardent temperance worker. Gin, in particular, was the favorite drink of the masses in Victorian England. Every fifth house in the East End of London was a gin shop, and most pubs had special steps built against the bar to enable even the smallest child to reach the counter. There was no law declaring an age limit to drinking intoxicants. It was possible to get drunk for a penny, and for a tuppence, you could get dead drunk.

It is no secret that I believe one of the greatest ills in the world is the abuse of alcohol. I abhor how it destroys people's ethics and morals. It also causes crime and domestic violence, and it traps entire families in poverty. I can only recommend total abstinence for our testimony as Christian believers. How can we justify taking an occasional drink when it may cause another brother to stumble by our example? Did not Christ tell us that in all things to let our yea be yea and our nay, nay? Oh, how Mother and I prayed in earnest for my father. I became the secretary for the Juvenile Temperance Society and worked meticulously arranging meetings, collecting subscriptions, and writing articles for temperance magazines. God was faithful, but not because of my work. Though it took several decades of waiting, I saw with my own eyes my father give up drinking and return to Christ. What I learned through the experience was simple and profound: God does, indeed, answer prayer.

The Joy of Reading Books

Attending school in my day was a privilege. Parents often could not afford either the cost of sending a child to school or the loss of a child worker in the family. When I turned twelve, I was able to matriculate for the first time. I was thrilled to study new subjects I had no knowledge of, particularly geography, biology, mathematics, logic, and English composition.[9] It was like whole new worlds opened up to me. However, within two years, excruciating pain in my back, diagnosed as severe curvature of the spine, forced me to leave the boarding school, never to return. My therapy was to lay prone in a hammock-like apparatus, hour after hour. My one solace was reading books placed on the floor beneath me. I studied the works of men like Adam Clark, John Wesley, Charles Finney, John Fletcher, Joseph Butler, and Johann Moshein, to name but a few.[10] I especially liked Butler's

Anthology and August Neander's *Ecclesiastical History.*[11] I hope, dear friend, you did as well.

Through my readings, I began to query if something central within me was amiss. I always believed in God, from as early as I could remember. Yet I wondered, was I truly converted? Were all my sins actually forgiven? I did not want to be self-deceived. "It seemed to me unreasonable to suppose that I could be saved and yet not know it."[12] Had I experienced the transformation of heart about which I had read in the testimonies of the great Christian leaders? I read and reread the personal experiences of Charles Finney. I could not get them out of my mind. One particular incident touched my heart. He wrote these words:

> There was no light in the room; nevertheless it appeared to me as if it were perfectly light. ... It seemed as if I had met the Lord face to face. ... He said nothing, but looked at me in such a manner as to break me right down to his feet. I wept like a child. I bathed his feet with my tears. But as I turned and was about to take a seat, I received a mighty baptism of the Holy Spirit. Without expecting it ... the Spirit descended upon me in a manner that seemed to go through my body and soul. I could feel the impression like a wave of energy going through and through me. Indeed, they seemed to come in waves and waves of liquid love ... like the very breath of God. ... He seemed to fan me with immense winds. No words can express the wonderful love that was shed abroad in my heart. I wept aloud with joy and love; and bellowed out the unutterable gushings of my heart. These waves came over me, and over me, one after another until I cried out, "I shall die if these waves continue to pass over me ... Lord, I cannot bear any more."[13]

Was it wrong of me to want to know God like that? I also discovered the incredible accounts of the thousands who were won to Christ through this man's preaching. I studied my copy of Rev. Finney's *Lectures on Revivals of Religion,* longing to be used of the Lord in some meaningful way. I did not want to just believe in God; I wanted to believe God. Oh, my friends, there is an entire world of difference. I had to touch the Kingdom of God, and I would not be at peace unless, like Jacob, I wrestled with God until he blessed me. I must confess that faith did not come easy to me. I remember one night, pacing my room until two o'clock in the morning. Exhausted, I childishly placed my Bible under my pillow, praying that somehow by absorption, I might awaken in the morning with the assurance of my salvation.

Assurance of Salvation

It was a silly thing to do, truly naive, yet may I say, I was only sixteen summers old. Then one day, during my regular time of study and prayer, I read familiar words of a hymn by Charles Wesley:

My God I Am Thine,
What a comfort Divine;
What a blessing to know that Jesus is mine![14]

Scores of times I had read and sung those words, but now they came to my innermost soul with a force they had never before possessed. "Until that moment, not all the promises in the Bible could induce me to believe; now not all the devils in hell could persuade me to doubt—assurance of salvation pervaded my being and never left me."[15] My experience was nothing like Charles Finney's. It was terribly undramatic, yet it was just as real to me as his was to him. "Please do not tell someone they are saved. Leave that for the Holy Spirit to do. Our responsibility is to help others to 'the way of faith.' We bring people up close to the broken body of their Lord to show them how willing Jesus is to receive them. When they really do receive him, the Spirit of God will tell them quickly enough that they are saved."[16]

Shortly after this particular spiritual awakening, my family moved to Brixton in London, where Mother and I joined the Methodists. Very soon, I was distressed by the contempt they verbally expressed for the local Reformers. Why Christians criticize one another utterly perplexes me. I could not withhold my tongue on this matter. So when the time came for my quarterly ticket to be renewed at the chapel, it was withheld. This meant I had been thrown out of the church. I was shocked and devastated. I never expected anything of this kind to happen to me. You may not know that a church committee reviewed its membership rolls four times a year. Were you giving to the Lord's work, living morally and ethically in accordance with God's Holy Writ? Were you in good standing in the church community? Apparently, I was not. Consequently, I joined the Reformers, since this group emphasized the teachings of John Wesley. I taught the Senior Girls Bible Class and led a prayer group afterwards. But despite serious effort, these activities did not give me enough satisfaction. I had expected these believers to be enthusiastic about the things of God. Instead, their meetings were void of power, the sermons superficial and, dare I say, often boring. I wanted to be challenged to live the life of a true disciple of Jesus.

Falling in Love

One Sunday in 1851, a pulpit guest preached on the Person and Deity of Jesus Christ in such a lively manner as to bring the congregation to the edge of their seats. That morning, the Rev. William Booth's style was pleasant yet determined. A reporter described him accurately:

> The young man's deportment was striking with his tall stature; erect posture, dark eyes, dark hair and full-flowing beard. When he spoke, his voice was powerful without being loud. One moment he would be softly pleading the mercy of his Lord and the next thumping his fists and speaking in thunderous tones of condemnation. He would argue his themes persuasively, using a vocabulary that common people could understand. He clarified his points with simple dramatic stories, which could easily be recalled as a reminder of the truth he was teaching. Years later many would use him as their model for preaching.[17]

I'm not sure exactly when I fell in love with William Booth. It could have been that morning or a few weeks later, at an afternoon tea in the home of Mr. Edward Rabbits, a wealthy boot-maker and local leader of the Reformers. (Mr. Rabbits was not a rabbit, but that truly was his last name.) The living room was crowded with guests when Mr. Rabbits saw William enter the room.

Clapping his hands together, our host exclaimed to all present, "Attention, everyone, we are fortunate to have a brilliant new man with us. Ladies and gentleman, may I present the Rev. William Booth and pray silence, Rev. Booth will now recite for you the 'Grog Seller's Dream.'"[18]

Astonished by this request, William protested. He was sure the room was not filled with teetotalers who could easily be offended by this odd American temperance poem. However, Mr. Rabbits insisted, "I heard you deliver the poem, and I want my guests to hear it."

Acquiescing, Rev. Booth began with the presence of an accomplished actor. The first two stanzas were acceptable enough, but as lines went on, some guests began to fidget uncomfortably:

The fools have guzzled my brandy, and wine.
Much good it may do them! The cash is mine.
I've a mortgage too on Mr. Tomkinson's lot—
What a scamp he was to become a sot!
Oh, won't his wife have a taking on
When she hears that his farm and his lot are gone!
How she will blubber and sob and sigh!
But business is business, and what care I?[19]

One hundred and seven lines later, the poem ended:

With a stifled sob and a half-formed scream,
The grog seller awoke! It was only a dream.
Solemn and thoughtful his bed he sought,
And long on that midnight vision he thought![20]

Not exactly a poem to which one usually falls in love, but for me, I think it worked.

William Booth's Conversion Journey

I soon learned that the man destined to be called "the Prophet of the Poor"[21] was not to the manor born. Instead, his childhood home was a red brick terrace house in the suburbs of Nottingham. It was one of eight thousand row houses where entire families weaved stockings from dawn to dusk, just to keep food on the table. Will's father, Samuel, called himself a speculative builder, but rather than a private contractor, William said the business was nothing more than a Grab and Get.[22] Parental dreams of sending their first-born son to school to become a gentleman collapsed when a mortgage was called in during Will's thirteenth year. Instead, he was apprenticed to a pawnbroker. He came quickly to hate the trade because daily he witnessed what poverty did to the human spirit. A worse tragedy overcame his family the next year, when Samuel suddenly died. What greatly impressed young William was the eleventh-hour repentance by his father on his deathbed.[23] Mrs. Booth bravely moved to Goose Gate, where the only work she could find was selling pots and pans to keep her family sparsely clothed and fed.

The next year, a Wesleyan couple invited Willful Will[24] to attend church with them. The genuine enthusiasm in those Wesleyan Chapel services touched William's heart, inspiring him to become a follower of the Rev. John Wesley for the rest of his life. That short, little Oxford Don and founder of the Methodists captivated Will's imagination because he dared to preach in the open air to crowds of drunken miners and the like. "You are the sons of God, the heirs of eternal life," John Wesley told his cynical listeners. Beyond this unconventional clerical behavior, Rev. Wesley opened orphanages and factories, visited the sick in debtor prisons, established free medical clinics, and organized free food dispensaries. "There is one God," William proclaimed at a church assembly, "and John Wesley is his prophet!"[25]

William never recalled a particular day when his conversion took place in his sixteenth year of life. His was not a quick decision for Christ, but a hard-fast one. After a long period of conviction over his transgressions, Mr. Booth remembered he experienced great relief when the heavy guilt of sin was lifted from his heart.

Months later, William again publicly announced a life-decision, saying, "God shall have all there is of William Booth."[26]

There is no doubt that he meant it. Soon afterward, William had an additional life-changing experience. A famous American evangelist, James Caughey, held an extraordinary religious campaign at Nottingham's Wesleyan Chapel. Fascinated by what he witnessed, William decided he would use these same revivalism methods as a preacher of the Gospel to bring the lost to salvation. Furthermore, he would study other American evangelists, including the great Charles G. Finney, Rev. Marden, and the good friend of John Wesley, the gifted Rev. John Fletcher.[27]

Not wasting any time, William convinced several friends to use these new methods to reach the poor of Meadow Platts. These young men, still in their teen years, preached under the light of the evening stars, ending with an invitation to make a decision for Christ. An announcement of cottage meetings for group Bible studies immediately followed. The General would write this same format into the Salvation Army's *Orders and Regulations* some thirty years later.

Local clergymen began urging William to study for the ordained ministry. Their interest was not wholly as it appeared, for they were more intent upon steering him away from this unseemly, American revivalism. The Wesleyans officially recognized William as a minister. However, over time, through a mixture of illness and misunderstanding, Will was labeled a Reformer, had his class ticket withheld, and was expelled from his church. Learning of this, the Methodist New Connection offered young Rev. Booth a church in Spaulding. Shortly after that, we met.

Courtship and Marriage

Our courtship began rather suddenly. April 10, 1852, was not only Good Friday, but it was also William's twenty-third birthday. Furthermore, that fateful day was William's last day to work in the pawnbroking business. Now his full-time ministry as an evangelist would begin. A chance meeting with his benefactor, Mr. Rabbits, caused Rev. Booth to attend a Reformer's meeting on Cowper Street, City Road. Providentially, it was also at this meeting that William first escorted me afterward to my home (but whether this was previously arranged by Mr. Rabbits I know not, but highly suspect). That little journey will never be forgotten by either of us. It is true that nothing particular occurred, except, as William later expressed, "it seemed as if God flashed simultaneously into our hearts that affection which afterwards ripened into what has proved to be an exceptional union of heart and purpose of life."[28]

Marriage is truly a serious endeavor and should not be approached lightly. For myself, I had firm guidelines for this matter that I recommended many times to others, which I am pleased to share with you:

1. Never marry anyone who has not accepted full salvation. God's commandment, "Be not unequally yoked," is unmistakable.
2. One should be a total abstainer from all intoxicants.
3. The consent of parents must be obtained. Marriage is a divine institution, and therefore, a couple's suitability should be evident to others.[29]

I had for myself alone other considerations regarding my husband:

1. His religious views must coincide with mine. He must be a sincere Christian.
2. He should be a man of sense. I must respect my husband's character and thoughts.
3. Any idea of lordship and ownership must be lost in love. I had no doubt that by making love the law of marriage, Jesus Christ intended to restore women to the original position God designed them to occupy. Wives are intended to be partners, not possessions![30]

These things being absolutely essential, I did have a distinct preference that my choice should be a minister. William was all these things and more. The Lord, in his loving kindness, gives good gifts to his children exceedingly in abundance to what we can ever hope or think. William and I marveled at how many experiences we had in common. Both of us received our religious training from the Methodists and admired their founder greatly. Having been born the same year, we dedicated our hearts to Christ at the same age and were each ejected from the Methodist

Church for expressing our firm opinions. We even got married the same year, in the same place, and to each other! There was only one difference of opinion that had to be overcome before I could freely marry Mr. Booth, and happily, time was on our side. I have observed that the pit into which couples fall is haste toward marriage. Our engagement lasted three years.

Roles of Men and Women in Church and Society

The issue between William and me had to do with the mental and social equality of women as compared with men. In Victorian society, women took little or no public role in the life of the church or state. There was no universal suffrage or even a national education system. There were no, nor had there ever been, women doctors, scientists, or university professors, and no women members of Parliament. The state recognized a women's legal existence by virtue of a relationship to her nearest male relative; she was a daughter, wife, mother, sister, or niece. Women in the British Isles were comfortable enough if they were middle class; however, if they were among the poor masses, their days were sentenced to endless drudgery of industrial and domestic labor. Upper class women functioned as ornaments of the master's household. Even Florence Nightingale bemoaned "the constant requirements of society of looking merry and saying something lively every morning, noon and night."[31] At the age of thirty-one, she wrote in her diary, "What is to become of me? I see no future but death."[32] With undaunted tenacity, Miss Nightingale created her own meaningful purpose in life, something few women were able to do.

I have discovered in my life that the Gospel of Jesus is a liberating one. Holy Scripture teaches clearly that in Jesus Christ, there is neither male nor female, and the promised outpouring of the Spirit is no less intended for the handmaidens than to the menservants of the Lord (Joel 2:29). In spite of this great truth, the biblical view has been interpreted to mean that women should live in submissive obedience to their husbands on the basis that they were inferior intellectually and morally to men. It seemed to me that such an interpretation, though commonly preached, was certainly not logical and, therefore, not correct.

One morning, I read in a local newspaper of an American husband-and-wife preaching team, Walter and Phoebe Palmer, who were also proprietors of the monthly magazine *Guide to Holiness*. Their revival meetings began the Third Great Awakening in America. Mrs. Palmer promoted holiness, women's ministries, and social reforms. Was she a teacher or a preacher? After examination, it appeared to me that she was the principal figure in their joint ministry. I was not alone in my appraisal, for the Rev. Arthur Augustus Rees of Sunderland denounced from his pulpit Phoebe Palmer's right to preach as a woman, even with the spiritual covering of her husband. It was incredible to me that his congregation, half-composed of women, should sit still and listen to such rubbish! With William's blessing, I published an answer to Mrs. Palmer's critics in a thirty-two-page pamphlet entitled *Female Ministry or Women's Rights to Preach the Gospel.*[33] In it, I put forth my position:

> It is clear that there is no Scriptural reason to deny women a public ministry. Furthermore, what the Bible urges the Holy Spirit has ordained and blessed, and so it must be justified. The Holy Spirit has been given to both sexes. Women prophesied in the early church, and Paul's command, to "keep silent," referred not to preaching but to gossip, interruption and uncalled-for questions. A mistaken application of the passage, "Let your women keep silent in the Churches," has resulted in loss to the church, evil to the world, and dishonor to God.
>
> But if there is only one Gospel, and men and women are equally called to respond to it and be set free, how can women be morally inferior? Moreover, all man-made religions neglect or debase women, but the teachings of Christ recognize her individuality and raise her to the dignity of an independent moral agent. In the Old Testament, we have several instances of Jehovah choosing a woman as the instrument of his blessing, and in the New Testament she is fully restored to her original position.[34]

Called to Preach?

In putting to pen my position, I did not in any way have a conscious reference to myself as a preacher. I did not desire the call to preach the Gospel at all. However, in January 1860 (after we were married), at an extraordinary morning service preached by my husband:

> I was as usual in the minister's pew with my eldest son, who was then four. I felt much depressed in mind and was not expecting anything in particular, but as the testimonies of the people proceeded, I felt the Holy Spirit come upon me. … I felt his presence to the extremities of my hands and feet. I knew I was to testify … but I heard a little voice say, "You have nothing to say." But then that little voice made a mistake and over-reached itself, "You will look like a fool."
>
> "Ah," I said, "This is just the point. I have never yet been willing to be a fool for Jesus Christ. Now I will be one."[35]

Without waiting another moment, I rose and walked down the aisle. My dear husband was just going to conclude.

He asked, "What is the matter, my dear?"

I replied, "I want to say a word."[36]

He was so taken by surprise that he could only mutter that his wife wanted to speak and sat down. For years, he had been trying to persuade me to speak. That very week, he asked me to address a cottage meeting, but I refused. I don't remember exactly what I said standing before the assembly, but I did give my testimony, followed by a confession that I had wronged my Savior by refusing to speak for him in public. Henceforth, I would be obedient to the Holy Vision.[37] William seized the moment and promptly announced that I would preach that evening! I had to oblige, and I chose for my first sermon the title, "Be Filled with the Spirit,"[38] because I would need the Holy Spirit's presence desperately. Oh, how little did I realize how much was involved in my decision to preach. I never imagined the life of publicity and trial awaiting me, for I was never to have another quiet Sunday when I was well enough to stand or speak.

The shocking news that a woman had preached at Bethesda Chapel spread like wildfire across Tyneside, Newcastle, and counties beyond. Requests to preach began to arrive. Once, William fell seriously ill for a fortnight, and I would have to fill in for him. He was confident, but I could hardly eat or sleep for want of my nerves. One evening tent meeting, I was to be the main preacher. As I ascended the podium, a heckler yelled out his objection: "Paul said to the Corinthians it is a shame for women to speak in the church."

"Oh, yes he did," I agreed, "but in the first place, this is not a church. In the second place, I am not a Corinthian. Thirdly," looking straight at the embarrassed wife sitting beside the man, I said, "Paul also said in the same epistle that it was best for the unmarried to remain so for the sake of the Gospel. When all the men who say women should keep silent in the churches stop marrying, I shall gladly stop speaking!"[39]

I am pleased to tell you Rev. Booth, upon hearing my arguments, came in time to heartily agree with them. Years later, when the Salvation Army was marching across the Western world, a reporter yelled a question to the General as he rushed to a meeting: "Why do you allow women to preach instead of men?"

"Why, sir," he shot back, "some of my best men ... are women!"[40]

I did not preach the claims of Christ on the basis of who I was. All my righteousness is as filthy rags. But I proclaim to you in spoken words the message of the Holy Book on the basis of its own authority as the revealed Word of God. The Holy Spirit has written the Bible. Dear friends, it is the only authority upon which anyone can claim the right to preach. I realized after seeing souls receive eternal life when I spoke its truth, why the devil had seduced me to silence. When there was silence, there was no fruit.

Itinerant Ministry Begins

In June of 1855, William and I were each twenty-six years old when we exchanged wedding vows at the Congregational New Chapel in South London. William's sister, Emma, and my father stood as our only witnesses. After the ceremony, we stayed one week at Ryde on the Isle of

Wight for a honeymoon. Then, we took ship for a series of evangelistic campaigns William was to hold in Guernsey. I was so excited when the ship headed south toward that island just off the coast of France. I had never been on a sea voyage before and anticipated a romantic sea crossing, strolling lightheartedly around the promenade deck, arm in arm with my new husband, a fresh breeze blowing through my hair. But as we pulled out of the harbor, the sea began to churn, and dark clouds gathered quickly overhead. The boat began to rise and fall, and rise and fall with ever increasing vigor. Suddenly, I was unable to keep my composure, so to speak. My breakfast ended up off the starboard bow as I leaned across the railing, straining to miss the deck. The only thing to do was put myself to bed for the rest of the voyage.

William found my condition rather amusing, though he was sympathetic. He decided, in one of his mercy visits to my bedside, to cheer me with an old song that he thought appropriate to the occasion. I did not wish to hear a song, but it seemed best to oblige his offering.

"Are you looking at me, darling?" he urged.

"Yes, dear."

Hands clasped formally together, he began swaying rhythmically from side to side, singing to the tune of *My Bonnie Lies Over the Ocean*:

Me breakfast lies over the ocean,
me dinner lies under the sea,

me stomach is in a commotion,
so don't mention supper to me.[41]

Please don't let anyone tell you the British have no sense of humor.

For months, William continued a demanding schedule of preaching as my health worsened. I was plagued with poor health all my life. Some people called me a semi-invalid; others were not half so kind. Seriously, I can scarcely remember a day in my life free from pain. Having good health is a grace-filled gift from God. As William continued his itinerant campaigning, I was sent to Hastings to convalesce by the sea. My heart was profoundly troubled. As a young wife, was I to be a burden to my husband for the rest of my life, if God did not heal me? I agonized over this question in prayer. Once again I read, and read, and read some more. Oh, what a joy good books are. One happy day, I came upon a biography of William Wilberforce, a little Englishman who had been dubbed "the living corpse."[42]

William Wilberforce

This young man, though frail and ill, was a pleasure-seeker, like his peers of the upper class. But when he learned of the slave trade flourishing in the Caribbean Triangle, he became convinced that God wanted him to use his position in Parliament to put an end to that horrid enterprise. The business-trading scheme was extremely simple. Ships along the Thames River were loaded with tons of merchandise like Manchester cloth, coils of beads, and iron bars. Months later, these same ships unloaded goods of tobacco, cotton, sugar, and the most lucrative commodity, rum. The general public was not aware that the original cargo was taken to Africa and traded for slaves, who were transported to the Caribbean under a tight pack, or more benevolent loose pack, allowance of sixteen inches width and six feet length per body.[43]

Wilberforce became so busy doing research, writing books, and delivering speeches that he forgot he was supposed to die. When I read the discourse he gave before the House of Commons, I could envision his gnarled form as he spoke for three and a half hours without notes. I could almost smell the stench in the ship holds, hear the whistle of the lash flogging the slaves, and see the malaise of blood and flesh as sharks attacked bodies tossed overboard. Mr. Wilberforce managed to stay alive until the very day Parliament passed a bill to compensate slave owners for the eight hundred thousand slaves they would free the following year. When this news was brought to his home, Wilberforce turned to the colleagues gathered around his dying sickbed and calmly said, "Well, gentlemen, what evil shall we attack next?"[44]

If this man could withstand the pain in his body for his cause, I could withstand the pain in my body for our cause. Were not the conditions in the slums of London, Leeds, and Liverpool, and the tenant row houses of the Midlands, also life-threatening, like the holds of the slave ships? Those people, too, needed desperately to know that someone cared for them.

They, too, had an Advocate, who is Jesus Christ the Lord. This great truth was our cause. Pain or no pain, I would join my beloved husband in his traveling ministry as long as God gave me breath. It was so good to be by William's side once again.

Connectional Settled Ministry

I had married an evangelist at heart. William had been accepted by the Methodist New Connection as a travelling campaigner at a fixed stipend of two pounds a week, barely enough for daily essentials. We had no settled home, and before long, the strain of shaky trains, temporary housing, and constant preaching services affected William's health and not just mine. Yet William's inspired preaching was effective. His meetings recorded an average of twenty-three new believers a day. But soon the New Connection leaders felt he was going too far, too fast. His methods were unconventional, and worst of all, they were not English but American. Moreover, a Revivalist preacher coming to town like a flood and then departing, leaving the responsibility for the care of new converts to the local clergy, was perceived as arrogant and offensive.

In 1857, the Connection ended Rev. Booth's countrywide travels and confined him to a single circuit in a little town in Yorkshire called Brighouse, a perfect name for how it made William feel. The next year, my husband was given a different appointment, this time at Gateshead. Our settled ministry was worthwhile, but John Wesley's eleventh rule for his preachers echoed in William's mind: "You have nothing to do but save souls … go always not only to those who need you, but to those who need you most!"[45]

While preaching to his thousand-strong congregation of Bethesda Chapel, William's eyes would stray to the miles of slate roof houses beyond the church's stained glass windows. The thought obsessed him: *In how many of those houses is the name of Jesus Christ ever mentioned? Why am I here with this crowded chapel of people who want to hear this message? Why am I not outside, bringing the message of God to those who don't want to hear it?*[46]

We stayed in Gateshead two more years. But when the New Connections Annual Conference met in May of 1861, we knew that William's request to be set apart as a full-time evangelist would be strongly debated. On the last day of the conference, when all the members were anxious to leave, some acknowledged William's special calling and ability. Others argued it would be bad for him and the circuit, and his request was unprecedented.

The president ordered the public gallery cleared for a vote, but when the results were announced, I was standing by the double doors at the head of the gallery stairs. I had vacated my seat according to the conference rules, but when I heard the verdict, my disappointment erupted.

I yelled out, without so much as a thought who might hear me, "No, never!"[47]

Everyone heard me.

Dr. Croft was angry; he called out, "Close those doors. Why aren't they closed?"[48]

I knew at that moment, deep in my spirit, that God's will for us was not the same as what had just transpired on the conference floor. Hearing my voice, William quietly took up his hat and left the chapel to find me. Two months later, he resigned his association papers.

Our hearts were heavy, for we now had no identifiable spiritual home in the Body of Christ. A fellow evangelist exhorted us not to be discouraged, saying, "All Britain is now open to you!"[49]

That pronouncement turned out to be prophetic, though it did not come to pass immediately. Yet we became very busy as itinerant evangelists in Wales, Cornwall, and the Midlands. It was at this time that William had his greatest revival campaign ever. It lasted eighteen months, by the end of which seven thousand Cornishmen and women professed Jesus Christ as Lord and Savior. Requests to preach continued to arrive for both William and myself. I preached so often in the West End of London, it seemed only expedient to remove to London, where my mother could aid in the care of our children.

Our Destiny on a Soapbox

One evening, William was particularly unsettled. He decided to go for a walk, which turned out to be a very long walk, finding himself at Mile End Waste. Half again as long as its name, this infamous alley housed a variety of illicit commerce, from petty dealers, quack doctors, shooting ranges, and more.[50] It was not uncommon in darkest England to find people lying in the gutter, either unconscious or dead, overcome by disease, alcoholism, or starvation. London's three million residents lived together on two thousand miles of streets and alleys, the equivalent of two hundred people per acre, which swelled to two hundred ninety per acre in the East End.[51]

During his walk, William stopped outside the Blind Beggar Tavern to listen to some street evangelists, who invited him to preach after they did. Such a location provided a new challenge. Dutifully, he stepped atop their wooden soapbox. Freedom of speech in England was guaranteed, but the law required you must be six inches off the ground when giving a speech in public. A wooden box, designed as a case for soap bars, met the requirements perfectly. Turned upside down, the box had enough room for two big feet.

Atop the street podium, William began, "There is a heaven in East London for everyone."[52]

A rotten egg was thrown; it whistled past his ear and splattered on the bricks behind him. But thirty minutes later, six destitute men knelt on the ground and gave their lives over to the Lord!

When my husband returned home after midnight, he was exuberant. "Darling," he announced, bursting open the door, "I have found my destiny!"[53]

I wasn't aware that it had been lost. Yet there was earnestness in William's words that night.

He said to me, "I seemed to hear a voice sounding in my ears, 'Where can you go and find such as these and where is there so great a need for your labors?' I offered myself, and you and the children, to this great work. Those people shall be our people, and they shall have our God for their God."[54]

He paused. He was waiting for an answer. I stared silently into the smoldering coals of the fireplace. I knew what this meant; with no church affiliation, our living expenses came from whatever offering our listeners gave. Now we would depend on the generosity of the poverty-stricken East Enders. Ah, but the poor would be generous; they always are.

I heard myself say, "If you feel you ought to stay there, then stay. We have trusted the Lord before for our support; we can trust him again."[55] Those words came from the heart (they certainly did not come from the head).

The East London Christian Mission

A few days later, the same street preachers knocked on our front door to ask William to preach at their tent meetings in Whitechapel. On Sunday, July 2, 1865, in a drafty tent pitched on an old graveyard, William conducted what was to be the first meeting of the Christian Mission (eventually the Salvation Army).[56] Soon, Rev. Booth was fully in charge. Others quickly recognized his natural leadership. The group never intended to form a church because there was a chapel or mission hall on every street in East London, yet with little effect. The idea of this new mission was to convert the people and send them to the churches. But this idea failed utterly. The people would not go when sent. It is easy to guess why this was so: They were not wanted. The poor did not dress properly or speak correctly; they were not perceived as equals to the better educated churchgoers. Moreover, the new believers were the hardest workers and most effective witnesses to the saving love of Christ at the mission. It was obvious that we needed these people as much as they need us. Our mission would be their spiritual home.

After the East London Christian Mission's only tent grew tattered, making it useless, a dance academy hall was purchased for a meeting place. For eighteen months, the two-story building was filled twice every Sunday. Local pubs were deserted when the meetings were on; their patrons' curiosity forced them to inspect what the fuss was all about. William instinctively knew that unusual methods were needed to attract the broken East Enders, who saw the church as harsh and irrelevant. It mirrored to them a frozen-hard God. Who wanted a cold heaven over a warm hell?

William's commitment to reach these souls was remarkable, but this challenge was far too great for one, two, or half-dozen workers. The first year, only sixty people enrolled as members in the Christian Mission, and the second year, three hundred did, yet in spite of this, the People's Market was purchased for thirty-five hundred pounds.[57] It was to be the People's Mission Hall, a place for offices, preaching, and an affordable food store for the poor.

No one ever had a direct revelation from God that there should be a Salvation Army. There was never a master plan or strategy by committee. Instead, the Army formed as a natural progression over many years.

Different people's ideas came together, with each new addition fitting perfectly into the whole. When God manifests a move upon the earth, he speaks to many people at the same time, giving different portions to each one, confirming his will to all. After several years, William realized that we were attracting more churchgoers instead of the poor to which we felt especially called. Something had to be done, something to breathe new life back into the cause.

I remember a Saturday in 1878 when the proofs for the yearly report of the Christian Mission were being reviewed in our living room. I was in the kitchen, elbow-deep kneading dough (one of my least favorite activities), when William called for me to join the discussion. Mission Annual Report in hand, William requested, "Listen to this." He began reading the opening line on the first page:

> The Christian Mission, under the superintendency of the Rev. William Booth, is a volunteer army recruited from amongst the multitudes that are without God and without hope in the world, devoting their leisure time to all sorts of labors for the salvation of others, from unbelief, drunkenness, vice and crime.[58]

William took a pen and crossed out the word "volunteer" and substituted the word "salvation." In Britain, those known as volunteers were part-time soldiers who were trained for emergency military duty.

My eldest son protested, "God's servants must be regular soldiers; we are not part-timers but full-time servants in God's army."

An Army Forms

William, turning to me, asked, "Do you think the Christian Mission, organized as a Christian army in a military fashion, would be scriptural? Would the Lord be pleased?"

I so appreciated how my husband valued my opinion. As he offered specific details, I listened, thought, and prayed. The warrior-king David fighting the Philistines came to my mind. I saw the Israelites at war with the Amorites and the Hittites, the Jacobites, the Moabites, the parasites, and the mosquito bites (I jest). While William talked of troops, bombardments, and battle plans, the vision of the Prophet Joel came vividly to mind, exciting my innermost being. I bid him wait until I found these Bible verses to read aloud:

Blow the trumpet in Zion;
sound the alarm on my holy hill. …
for the day of the LORD is coming.
The LORD thunders
at the head of his army;
his forces are beyond number. …
I will show wonders in the heavens
and on the earth,
blood and fire and billows of smoke.
And everyone who calls
on the name of the LORD will be saved.
(Joel 2:1, 11, 30, 32)

There it was. William was as excited as I was. It was right for us and right for England. The timing was perfect. An Army it would be, an Army of deliverance, and a Salvation Army! The new descriptive name was only part of the trend toward adopting military terms and tactics in this new approach to Christian warfare. William explained the new name of the mission in the Army's magazine: "We are a salvation people. We do not volunteer to serve God. We enlist by an act of our will. We are called; the Holy Spirit conscripts us. We do not choose God, he chooses us and we respond."[59] We love God, because he first loved us!

A fighting force should look distinctive. Uniforms were worn everywhere in the streets of London. Postmen wore red coats, Bobbies blue uniforms, and doctors' pageboys delivering medicine had white jackets bedecked with silver buttons. Should not the preachers of the Lord Jesus Christ in darkest England do likewise? I particularly liked the idea of a complete uniform for everyone. It would eliminate visual class distinction and boost the morale of the poor among us to don clothes of which they could be proud.

Furthermore, it became apparent to us that a real Army needed a real flag. In our street processions, the missionaries would carry banners bearing the name of their districts. It seemed altogether fitting that if the whole of England honored Queen Victoria with royal guards, banners, bands, and great pageantry, surely the King of Kings and Lord of Lords deserved the same. I was given the honor of presenting the first Salvation Army flag to the Corps of Coventry.

Though some in the Christian Mission found militarization hard to embrace and consequently departed, it was received for the most part with great enthusiasm. Journalists often asked my husband why we used a military form of government. The General frequently answered, "What better form was there for war?"

We explained that the Salvation Army is completely opposite to the armies of violence. Why should we go to war against nations when there is so much evil to combat in the neighborhoods? Our soldiers are trained to save, not to destroy. When we go to battle, it is not with men, but with God's weapons of love and mercy, food and medicine. Every Salvationist soldier knows our warfare is "not against flesh and blood, but against the rulers, against the authorities, against the powers of this dark world and against the spiritual forces of evil in the heavenly realms" (Eph 6:12).

"We Must Go"

Almost at once, the Salvation Army experienced a period of phenomenal growth, amazing everyone. Expansion did not occur because we had a flag to rally around, nor because the General was an autocratic leader, as some have suggested. The reason was the outpoured grace of God and our Holy Spirit-led people. The family of Amos Shirley is just one example. Mr. Shirley found it necessary to leave his home in Coventry to find employment in America. He became a foreman in a silk factory in Philadelphia, and eighteen months later, his wife, Anna, and daughter, Eliza, joined him.[60] Though only sixteen years of age, Eliza was a lieutenant in our Army, and being a minor, she was duty-bound to go with her parents. Before sailing, she received a promise from the General that if she were successful in beginning an unofficial work, he would send officers to establish a corps.

Eliza rented an old dirt-floor chair factory for ten dollars a month and began preaching. The Shirleys' efforts were so successful that every wooden seat and foot of standing room was occupied during their meetings. A few weeks later, an additional building had to be acquired. When report of this success reached London headquarters, *The War Cry*, the Army newspaper, responded with a printed statement: "We must go to America. This news has come upon us like a voice from heaven, and leaves us no choice."[61]

A fortnight later, George Railton and seven Hallelujah Lasses, only one of whom was over twenty years of age, set sail for America.[62] I have often been asked why one man and seven young women were sent together across the ocean. The reason is simple: They were the only ones who volunteered!

An unusually stormy season made what should have been a ten-day Atlantic crossing last twenty-five miserable days. When the eight seasick soldiers arrived in New York Harbor, the Shirleys were waiting on the dock to welcome them. The Salvationists soon discovered that it was against the law to preach in the streets in the United States, with or without a soapbox. The only place they could find to sing and preach was in a music hall as a vaudeville act, sandwiched between the dog show and the box trick. At first, the audience thought the presentation was a comedy routine. But that first day, James Kemp, who was infamous in New York City as Ash Barrel Jimmy, was sitting in the theater.[63] (Jimmy earned his moniker when he had been discovered drunk, upside down, in a barrel one morning by the police.)

The Word of the Lord preached from the stage reached deep into Jimmy's soul, and he gave his heart to the Lord Jesus. Overjoyed and invited to the stage at the next performance, Jimmy immediately began sharing his conversion testimony. Only three months later, these newly arrived Salvationists counted ten preaching corps stations, with two hundred services held every week, with five hundred new soldiers and sixteen officers scattered among the cities of New York, Newark, and Philadelphia.[64]

I marvel at those early days. The Salvation Army spread around the world so fast, it had to be the sovereign hand of God. There never was a grand scheme in the mind of the General to infiltrate every foreign continent. It simply began to happen. As immigrants move to other lands, many Salvationists were among them. In their new countries, Army soldiers either started corps or sought them out. The Armies in Sweden, Norway, and Germany began with visitors to England becoming converted and returned to their homelands to start new corps. As we worked in the back streets of darkest England, requests for Salvationist workers began to arrive at headquarters from around the world.

The Booth Children

Our dear children were also influential in the mighty quick march of the Army around the world. I cannot begin to tell you how very proud I am of each one of them. They largely supervised the Army during its beginning years. My husband and I believed parenthood is a God-given vocation of the highest order. We did not see the involvement in our children as a limitation to our own time or freedom; on the contrary, they were our privilege to raise. The children of the Christian worker should never take second place in family life. Instead, they should be included in the work of the Kingdom and made aware of the purpose of their parents' work. Before I was even married, I prayed for all my children. I said to the Lord, "They shall be Thine, down to the third and the fourth generation."[65]

We have been severely criticized for making the early Salvation Army a family dynasty. To that I say, spiritual things must be discerned spiritually, and not as the world sees them. The Army believes in heredity; it believes in training and in the extraordinary capacity of the whole family. Our children were consecrated from the cradle to the service of God, and where better to serve than with their extended family, their fellow Salvationists? All eight of our children lived an adult lifespan in an age when reaching seventy years of life was only accomplished by 6 percent of the population.[66]

Bramwell, our firstborn son, began serving the Christian Mission as its secretary when only sixteen years old; he then became the General at his father's passing. When he was newborn, I held him up to God as soon as I had strength to do so and asked the Lord to make him an advocate of holiness. God graciously answered my prayer and gave us eight more children. Could any mother ask for more? One would think not, but then God brought to us precious Harry, an exceptional child we adopted and affectionately called Little Georgie, who loved God and served the Army just as intently as our other children.[67]

Suffering and Persecution

The stories of hundreds of the early Army pioneers are so inspiring. The Army was too radically different for some people, a financial threat for others, and just plain scary for still more. I will never forget a visit to Sheffield in 1882. A very successful Sunday meeting angered a local gang known as the Blades, who disliked the Army because it had converted away some of its members. They laid in wait to attack the brass band when they marched home through the streets from a concert. Gang members suddenly began hurling all sorts of objects. Leading the march, Lieutenant Emerson Davison suffered a concussion from a rock that struck the back of his head. When William reviewed these returned troops coated with blood, mud, egg yolk, and tomato sauce, their band instruments battered beyond repair, he said, "Now, gentlemen, is the time to have your photographs taken!"[68] It was the perfect comment, reminding all present that it is an honor to suffer for the sake of Gospel of Jesus Christ.

Similar things happened throughout the British Isles and around the world. In America, Captain Joseph Garabed, an Armenian of Turkish descent, was arrested fifty-seven times for Jesus for his street singing and preaching.[69] In Brooklyn, Salvationists were attacked, with some receiving broken limbs. New Hampshire's Army hall was twice burned down, while in Connecticut, fifty drums were confiscated, one by one. Newfoundland marchers were chased by a mob of three hundred, armed with hatchets and knives. Similar things happened in Europe, as five Salvation Lassies were badly beaten in Switzerland. Across Germany, bandsmen and officers were regularly jailed for street marching and preaching. There were those who offered their Lord the ultimate sacrifice. In England, Mrs. Captain Susannah Beatty died after being assaulted.

A young cadet was brutally attacked by a gang as he monitored the door of a Paris hall and died a few hours later. Another doorkeeper was stabbed to death in San Francisco, and in St. Louis, a soldier was clubbed and stoned until he died. These I have mentioned were certainly not the first martyrs of Christ, and they will not be the last. Why should our reception as preachers of the Gospel be any different from the disciples of Jesus when they turned the world upside down? Innovation often meets with misunderstanding, and evil hates the sight of holiness. So, like the apostle Paul, these Salvationists loved as he loved and suffered as he suffered.

The Tide Turns

Fortunately, the tide of persecution turned with the dawning of the new century. Governments began to understand what the Army set out to do. Policemen saw the changed lives of former criminals and found their work made easier. Finally, members of other Christian churches, who at first scorned the General and his troops, joined with the person in the street in their reassessment. Why is it that churches are often the last ones to accept change? Persecution gave way to tolerance and then to understanding, which moved to respect and eventually praise. Truth is always revealed in the end. Right conquers wrong, good wins over evil, and God's ultimate will is accomplished. Is this not so? But first, the battle will rage. Our adversary is real and will not give up easily. Satan is the enemy of our souls, and sometimes, evil even seems to triumph.

During World War II, many Salvationists joined the service. In 1942, an entire Salvation Army band enlisted together in Melbourne, Australia. When the authorities saw the Salvationists' Christian standards, they allowed them to be trained together and formed into a battalion band. They were posted to New Guinea; when not performing, they served as stretcher-bearers. After two years, the band was taken prisoner. Some managed to escape due to their military training, only to die in the unforgiving mountains. The rest were being transported at sea to a new detention location when a torpedo hit their ship, and all aboard perished. These were beloved sons, husbands, and young fathers tragically lost, but they had used their war service as an opportunity to take the Christian message in music where it was particularly needed.

Caring for the Poor

In the name of Jesus, and for his sake, we must not ignore the conditions of people around us. "What is the use," William told his officers, "of preaching the Gospel to men whose whole attention is concentrated upon a mad, desperate struggle to stay alive? You might as well give a tract to a shipwrecked sailor who is battling the surf to come ashore to keep from drowning. He will not listen to you. The first thing to be done is to get him a footing on firm ground and then give him room to live."[70] It is useless to preach about a God of love without trying to improve the daily lives of those to whom you are speaking. William said, "No one ever got a blessing if they had cold feet or a toothache."[71]

Prostitution was very common in Victorian England, with poor girls as young as twelve being sold by their parents into what was called the white slave trade. In London alone, as many as eighty thousand prostitutes worked the trade; one in every fifty Englishwomen was a streewalker.[72] When the General saw prostitutes of the streets of London giving their hearts to God, but with no place to live, he sent Bramwell on an errand with a bold request. Mrs. Harriet Webb was a prominent, middle-class woman and Sergeant in the West London Corps. Would she be willing to move to the slums and open her home to these girls? How she convinced her husband and children to sell their fine house and move to an area with no sanitation, permeated by the stench of an open sewer, I do not know. Could I have done this? Could you? In 1890, the year William published his best-selling book, *In Darkest England and the Way Out*,[73] the Army had expanded Mrs. Webb's open home to thirty-five homes for prostitutes, five shelters for the homeless, and one for alcoholics. We must care about the living conditions of our fellow human beings. We must be in the world but not like it, relieving pain and suffering. The Christian must not hide inside church walls but be in the thick of spiritual battle, where poverty and injustice prevail.

I would not have you deceived. The world in which we live knows not God. Its order is not the divine order. The mores of society are not based upon the law of God. The world itself is very much out of joint. Therefore, we cannot accept things as they are, for we live in an evil, fallen state. We Christian believers, of all people, must make a difference in the world. Jesus said we are the salt of the earth. We are the leaven that makes the difference in the world, bringing forth its flavor and true life. Dear ones, what the world needs are denouncers of iniquity, those who are willing to speak truth plainly and suffer the consequence of an angry world that does not wish to hear of its own sin.

The Need of the Hour

Before I complete my remarks, I want to point out something to you. No one doubts that the Savior's heart ached in sympathy with the volume of human suffering he witnessed before him: hunger, sickness, violence, poverty, and more. Jesus could have fed the masses by miracles every day as easily as when he multiplied the loaves and fish. Perhaps he might have lectured and taught on science or government so perfectly as one to whom knowledge appears as an open book. But he did not. Instead, he showed us his scheme for alleviating sin and suffering in the world when he said, "I am the way and the truth and the life" (Jn 14:6).

Christ's very presence brought the heavenly Kingdom to this earthly kingdom, fulfilling the divine redemptive plan that was set in motion from the Fall of humankind. The great need, ladies and gentlemen, is as it was in Jesus's day: the salvation of souls. I learned that if I preached to the grand ladies in their fashionable parlors in the West End, or stood in a hovel speaking to a dozen drunkard's wives in the East End, the message was the same: The gift of God is eternal life through Jesus Christ. All other matters fade and disintegrate by comparison. Jesus became flesh and made his dwelling among us, and we have seen his glory, the glory of the one and only Savior. The truth is not that God so hated the world that his own Son was compelled to die in order to appease his wrath, as has been too often represented, but that God so greatly loved the world that he gave his only begotten Son.

I want to share with you a true story the General often told when preaching:

> Over a century ago, a steamer ship with a number of coal miners aboard was seen approaching San Francisco Bay. The voyage had been delightful and all aboard were in high glee at the near prospect of a new home. But suddenly, a fierce gale drove the ship into a rock as the treacherous currents and winds there are well known to do. The captain announced the ship was sinking and ordered it abandoned immediately. On the deck, a sunburned miner was buckling around his waist his gold and savings, when

> a little lassie of seven summers came along, tugged at his trouser leg, looked up into his face, and asked, "Please, sir, can you swim?"
>
> "Yes," said the miner, "I reckon so."
>
> "Then please, sir," asked the child with fearful eyes, "will you save me?"
>
> Quickly the miner saw that he could not save the child and his money as well. But he soon decided, and overboard went the gold.
>
> "Creep up me darling, put your arms tight around me neck." In the next moment, the miner was strapping the little legs, where a few seconds before he had been fastening the gold. Then, plunging into the billow below, he began to swim and swim, until a large wave landed him unconscious on the shore. Witnesses bore him to a cottage nearby to recover. Opening his eyes he asked, "Where am I?"
>
> Then the same little form, creeping across his chest, kissed him on both cheeks and said, "Please, sir, I'm so glad you saved me."
>
> All around you on the wastewaters of life, in their poverties and riches, in their miseries and sins, the people are sinking. Will you help them?[74]

What Will You Do?

Dear friends, today is the day of salvation, not tomorrow, but today. This is the acceptable hour. Jesus is the Savior, the one mediator between God and man. He is the way, the truth, and the life. No one comes to the Father but through him. I ask you, have you found the treasure? Is

Jesus Christ the most important thing in your life? Do you know him in the fullness of his Resurrection power? Have you given your all to Jesus? Is there anything at all that is holding you back from full surrender to his will? If money is your pride in life, overboard with it. It is nothing compared to the riches that are in Christ Jesus. He is the treasure, the Pearl of Great Price.

True saving faith is giving over your whole being to God. Take the step of faith, and remember that none of us are righteous, for all have sinned and fallen short of the glory of God. Commit your whole being to God, and the fire of the Holy Spirit will come upon you and seal you as his child; you will be empowered to live in righteousness before him. As my dear husband often said, and I with him, "It is the Divine will of God that every sinner become a Saint, every Saint a Soldier of the Cross, and every Soldier a Saver of Souls."

Those of you who call yourselves Christians, may I ask you, have you done all within your power to rescue those round you that need you? Have you gone not only to those who need you, but also to those who need you the most? Have you grown weary in well doing? Then come to Jesus, and be refreshed. Hear the General's plea: "Throw your arms around the perishing and swim and swim until on the by and by, when the kindly hand of death lands you on the golden shore, the Spirit by whom you are saved, shall bear you away on snowy wings to the feet of your Lord. Then you will hear the words, 'Well done, my good and faithful servant, enter into the joy of My Kingdom!'"[75] This is my prayer for you.

I am your servant in the love of Christ Jesus,
Catherine Booth

Conclusion

There can be no doubt that both William and Catherine Booth were each called and gifted as evangelists for sharing the Good News of the Gospel to the far-reaching corners of the earth. They would be the first to tell us that they didn't do it alone. By means of their passionate energy and commitment to their God-appointed mission, others were readily able to catch their vision and join them. By joining together with others, we can accomplish more, much more. The establishment of the Salvation Army was a process over time, building day by day, yet it is astonishing how much is accomplished in a relatively short period of time.

There were two major concerns that were the foundation upon which the Salvation Army stood. The first was inspired by John Wesley's core instruction to his preachers: the salvation of souls. The second was a consuming desire to relieve the terrible plight of the bodies and souls of the people living in abject poverty. The needs of the poor were so critical to William and Catherine that they were determined to do as much about it as they could. If we want our life to make a difference in the world around us, we have the popular expression that simply says, "Find a need and fill it." The Booth family and their extended faith community, the Salvation Army, did just that, and they continue to do it today.

The work of the Salvation Army continues on, after the passing of its beloved founders, with the same purpose and passion, but the need is enormously vast and overwhelming. A century after the Booths, after the damage of two world wars, natural disasters, famine, rapid population growth, and varieties of mores of different cultures, the numbers of the poor have substantially grown, but they are often ignored. In the mid-twentieth century, a middle-aged nun will abandon her contented convent life to fill the need she sees of the poor in the streets of her adopted city. Investigating further, we will learn how Mother Teresa became a catalyst for a new level of worldwide care for those known as the poorest of the poor.

Discussion Questions

1. Seeing the deplorable conditions of the East End of London, the Booths, like Jesus, had compassion on the crowds of people and decided to feed them physically and spiritually. With the conditions today of the poor around the world, what do you think you and your church can do to be more effective in addressing this growing problem?
2. Catherine Booth believed very strongly that women are called, equipped, and gifted by God to preach the Gospel to men and

women. Do you agree? Why or why not? What are the scriptures you would draw upon to support your position?

3. Mrs. Booth balanced her effective leadership ministry in the Army with the raising and successful discipling of her eight children. How can mothers today who are called to work outside the home maintain a balance between family and work responsibilities?
4. Catherine Booth's greatest passion in life was to bring people into a personal relationship with Jesus Christ. How do you share your faith with others? Do you feel equipped to assist someone to know that they have the assurance of salvation? How would you go about doing so?

Mother to the Poorest of the Poor

Introducing Mother Teresa of Calcutta

It is believed that the name Mother Teresa is known to two billion persons today, who find it synonymous with kindness and charity. Called the greatest humanitarian of the twentieth century and a living saint in her lifetime, Mother was the first non-native-born person to be given a state funeral in India. From humble beginnings in a volatile Balkan country, this short Catholic nun traveled the world, boldly speaking truth to power, according to her Christian beliefs.

Most corporate executives will tell you that growing an international business is very difficult. Before going global, they plan intensively, consider financial costs, identify a market, and analyze cultural issues that will affect their foreign workforce. Mother Teresa did none of these things. Yet she presided over one of the most thriving institutions in modern religious history. This unusual achievement was possible because in 1965, the Vatican had declared the Missionaries of Charity a society of pontifical right, thus making it answerable only to the pope, thereby freeing it to operate worldwide. With that spiritual covering, Mother became an international phenomenon, fulfilling a pledge she had made to God in 1949, to show compassion to the poorest of the poor. Her unspoken spiritual goal became a reality.

Invitations came from auxiliaries, foundations, and bishops to the Missionaries of Charity, asking them to set up a needed service. Mother's three-part process to handle these requests was simple: read the invitation, pray over it, and then decide. With the mobility of the order's philosophy of service, a work could start quickly anywhere in the world. All that was needed was a nun capable of overseeing the service, with a handful of sisters living together as contemplative workers. In 2017, there were 5,167 Sisters and 416 Brothers living in 758 houses (242 in India; 516 abroad), serving in orphanages, schools, and homes for lepers, AIDS patients and the dying, in 139 countries.[1]

Mother Teresa coined a few descriptive catchphrases and used them throughout her life, which redefined how the world understood charity. While countless organizations have worked with the poor, Mother identified the poorest of the poor as a new, urgent, and moral imperative.[2] Any loving, Christ-like activity was, for her, doing something beautiful for God. Quoting the words of Jesus to his disciples that whenever they helped "one of the least of these brothers of mine, you did it for me"(Mt 25:40), Mother Teresa counted off, one by one, on the fingers of her hand, the last five words of this quote to emphatically illustrate her belief that in serving one person, you were serving Christ himself.

Mother's unsolicited fame at first upset her, because she sought to be unknown, like the very poor to which she felt called. Within a short time, she realized that awards and fame enabled her purposes to be made known, acknowledged, supported, and even achieved. With the notoriety came some who were not part of her ministry; they wondered if they could do what she and her sisters were doing with the poor. So she encouraged others to use whatever gifts and talents they had to serve the needy, and God would use each person's service for good.

She wisely said, "What I can do, you cannot. What you can do, I cannot. But together, we can do something beautiful for God."[3]

(Note: Since Mother Teresa is a well-known contemporary of modern culture, the following letter, like all the others in this book, is fictitious, yet based on extensive research to be as accurate as possible.)

An Open Letter from Mother Teresa

Namaste, dear one! God bless you beautifully today.

I have never written an autobiography, though I have been asked to do so many times. I'd rather talk about Jesus and the people who are forgotten, than myself. Since I've been questioned about my life in interviews by all kinds of media people, you can easily piece together my life story; it is an open book. I have given many speeches around the world and never with any notes, because I don't like to give speeches. I just like to talk from my heart when I look into the beautiful faces of my audience. Apparently, I tell the same stories over and over, so those who have traveled with me can confirm these recollections I will share in this letter. One of my dear Charity Sisters has helped me put together the life events that I have shared publicly. Oh goodness, does that make it an autobiography? I don't know. (You will notice my English is not the best. It was not my first language.) I pray my life only pleases God and inspires you to love and live for him also.

My Beautiful Family

I am Albanian by birth, but I am a citizen of India. In my work, I belong to the whole world, but in my heart, I belong only to Jesus Christ.[4] My family belonged to the Albanian community in the Balkans, and my devout and most excellent papa was engrossed in politics. He was a member of the Community Council of our town of Skopje, which lies outside Albania in the Kosovo region of what is now Serbia (I should know because I taught geography for eighteen years). This little part of the world has a very sad history—a 250,000-square-mile triangle that's been a battleground since at least 2000 BC.[5] It is a major land route, because of a mountain range between Europe and Asia, and that caused a legacy of conquered peoples. When you have different cultures and religions collide, sadly, there will be conflict. Do you remember that it was the assassination of the Archduke Ferdinand of Austria by a Serbian national that started the First World War? I did not teach history; I lived it.

My earliest childhood memories are of my papa and mama praying together every night. My father, Nicola Bojaxhiu, was a good man with a big heart who gave generously to the poor. We never knew if a hungry stranger was coming home with him for a meal. My mother, named Dranafile but called Drana, truly loved God and went almost every day to the nearby chapel for Mass. My older brother, Lazar, and sister Agatha (Age), and I went to Sacred Heart Catholic School at our parish church. We laughed a lot when we were a whole family. My parents lived for God, and I can tell you we were a very happy household.

But our carefree lives changed when my papa suddenly died one night, after attending a political banquet. I was nine years, and it was so very sad. The townsfolk believed a rival party had poisoned him, but it was never proven. After months of crying daily in her bedroom, Mama began embroidering beautiful clothes and made wedding dresses to earn a living. We had an alcoholic neighbor, a young widow named Filé, for whom Mama cared; she had six children. When Filé died, all her children came to live with us, and they became our family.[6]

The Call of God

I was still very young, no more than twelve years old, when I experienced the desire to belong completely to God and become a nun. I wanted to go out and give the life of Christ to the people. The first time I said I wanted to devote my whole life to God, my mother opposed me, explaining that I was much too young to think about such things. I thought and prayed about my desire for six more years. At times, I had the impression that my vocation, that is, the call of God on my life to give myself completely to him, did not exist. I wanted to be sure that God had called me.

So I prayed to God and asked for guidance: "How can I know if God is calling me, and for what he is calling me to serve in the church?"[7] We all want to know God's will for our lives, do we not? I trusted God's Spirit would lead me step-by-step by his Word, as I sought him each day in every decision. I was reminded that it was more important to seek God than to seek what I was looking for *from* God. The more I sought to know him, the more his will would be revealed, even in spite of the difficulties.

When I was going to school, some of the town's Jesuit priests went to India as missionaries. They sent word to us of what they were doing for the people there. We heard beautiful descriptions about the experiences they had, especially with the children. My heart began to yearn for India. After much prayer, I learned of the Loreto Sisters of Ireland, who were the only Catholic order of women serving in India.[8] Through the efforts of these Jesuit missionary priests, I was put in contact with the Irish Sisters. When I turned eighteen, it was time for me to accept my vocation. I remember Mama's exact words to me after she had prayed alone, not leaving her room for twenty-four hours: "All right, my daughter, you go. But be careful to be always for God and Christ only."[9] She would ask me one day, "My child, have you lived only for God?"[10] Oh, may I say, "Yes!"

I remember well the trip to the abbey of the Loreto Sisters in Rathfarnham, just outside Dublin (a roundabout way to go to India, don't you think?). It seemed like the whole town came to the railway station in Zagreb to say good-bye: friends, schoolmates, neighbors, young and old from the church, my sister, and of course, Mama. Everyone wept. As the train pulled away from the platform, I watched my mother's sad face, unaware that I would never look upon her countenance again. The train sped through Austria, Switzerland, and France on my way through London to the Loreto Abbey in the Irish countryside, where I began to learn English and the ways of the religious life as a new postulate.[11]

After only six weeks in the Loreto Convent, we beginners sailed for India, where we would do our novitiate to learn the life of a nun. It was 1929, and the voyage was long and tiring. It took seven weeks to sail across the Irish Sea, through the Straits of Gibraltar, across the Mediterranean Sea, through the Suez Canal, down the Red Sea into the Indian Ocean. With no priest on board, we did not receive Communion—not even on Christmas Day; but we made a crib, prayed together, and sang Christmas songs. Our hearts were excited because we knew each day we were closer to the country of our dreams. On December 27, 1929, our steamer ship, the *Marchait,* arrived in Colombo, on the island of Ceylon (now Sri Lanka).[12] The next landing was the city of Madras, where I walked with my companions through the swarming streets.

Reaching the Land of my Dreams

I believed I was prepared for the sights I would encounter in India, but clearly I was not. The poverty of the people horrified my soul. The street dwellers were almost naked, their only shelter and bedding made of banana leaves. If only the people outside India could see this poverty, they might stop grumbling about their own misfortunes and offer thanks to God for their blessed lives.[13] I arrived in India at a time of great turmoil in the country. The British raj still ruled there, but millions rallied for independence, either under the Hindu movement by Mahatma Gandhi and Jawaharlal Nehru, or the Muslim league of Mohammed Jinnah.[14] There would be years ahead of political upheaval effecting millions of lives in India, but my focus had to be learning the life of a nun devoted to God.

The training for a Loreto Sister took place in the picturesque town of Darjeeling, where all the wonderful tea is grown. The religious life is one of pure joy for those who are called to it. It is not a sacrifice, dear friend; it is a life of blessedness. A few months after my twenty-first birthday, on May 24, 1931, I took my First Vows of Poverty, Chastity, and Obedience. In the heart of the ceremony, one lies prone on the floor in an attitude symbolic of death—death to one's flesh and selfish desires. In that place, one leaves behind all worldly things and one's former life, and rises to a new covenant relationship with God in a new life. I've never had any regrets. A photo taken on the day with my class of new Loreto Sisters has been published. If you ever want to find me in that picture, just look for the shortest one with the biggest nose. That will be me.

Final Vows, I Now Belong

I took Final Vows in the year of our Lord 1937, also in the month of May and in the same city as before. The ceremony repeated the First Vows; only this time, I became a professed nun, fully dedicated to God for the rest of my life. Words can never express the inner joy that commitment brought to my heart. My work was as a teacher at St. Mary's High School for upper, middle-class Bengali girls. I couldn't say whether I was a good teacher. This, my pupils would know better … but I loved teaching. I taught geography and religion eighteen blissful years, and I was the happiest nun in the world. When I was twenty-seven years old, I was made principal of St. Mary's, and with it came the title change from Sister to Mother.[15] My Loreto Sisters-in-Christ were my spiritual family. Our convent was filled with flowers and birds, songs and prayers. It was a comfortable, contented, simple life. But when I walked outside the convent compound, there was the smell of decay and suffering. From my second-story classroom window in Darjeeling, I could see the rooftops of *Motijhil*, a famous *bustee* or slum;[16] *Motijhil* means "Pearl Lake."[17] But the pearl lake was a pool of brown filthy water in the center of a sprawling slum. Disease and death were everywhere.

You may wonder why there was so much poverty in Calcutta. Throughout the war years, Bengal suffered tremendous devastation, after Britain drew them into the conflict without being consulted. A great famine occurred in 1934, which was intensified by the confiscation of riverboats that brought rice and goods in and out of the city. Several million people lost their lives, and many more came to the city seeking food and a way to earn a living. War babies were left on our doorstep. Our school and compound were taken over by the British military for use as a hospital. Then, in 1946, there was even more death due to the partition of India, between Hindus and Muslims, because of the problematic independence from England. Our city, after partition, was a city of three thousand bustee slums of human misery.[18] Even they could not contain the two million more destitute people seeking help. It would take years for any visible recovery.

The Call within a Call

My Sisters of Loreto were all teachers, which is a most worthy apostolate for Christ. But quite unexpectedly one day, I was riding on a small-gauge train from Calcutta to Darjeeling for an annual spiritual retreat. As we passed by bustees of muddy lanes with open sewers and wretched hovels teeming with ragged, starving children, one after another, I heard God's inner voice. It was a call to renounce everything I knew and follow Christ Jesus into the slums to serve the poorest of the poor.[19] It was the tenth of September 1946, and it was by the hill train station at the base of the Himalayas. I felt God wanted something more from me. In quiet prayer with my beloved Lord Jesus, "the call within a call" was quite clear. I was to love him in the distressing disguise of the poorest of the poor.[20] Who are the poorest of the poor? They are the unwanted, unloved, uncared for, hungry, forgotten, naked, homeless, alcoholic, and leper. My call to them was like a second vocation. Jesus wanted me to be poor with the poor, and that meant actually living among them. Like a personal command from God, the desire in my soul was compelling. To leave the life in my Order was a great sacrifice; the hardest of my whole life. What I didn't leave was my condition of being a nun. The change would only be in the work. I knew right then where I belonged, but I did not know how to get there.

My call was also an order in more ways than one, a command, and a congregation. To my great surprise, God also gave me a divine impression that others would join me, and we would become a new congregation of Sisters. It would not be easy, however. On top of that, I would need permission to leave my Order. After much prayer, I requested *exclaustration* from the hierarchy of the church.[21] I waited two years for permission from the Vatican to have the right to keep my vows and leave my convent and Order to serve and live among the very poor. My priest supporters and my superiors determined my desire was God's will. With that discernment, there was confirmation about my call. I learned later that I was the first Catholic nun in three hundred years granted the privilege to remain a nun and work outside the convent.[22] Not bad, eh?

But seriously, I didn't have to give up anything; a vocation is belonging to Christ, and my belonging to him had not changed. My new work was only another way for me to put love for Christ into action.[23] Making the sacrifice to leave the Society of my Loreto Sisters only deepened my love for Christ Jesus.

Slum Life

The slums of Calcutta are among the worst in the world, dear friends, because it takes many years to overcome the effects of wars, famines, and prejudices. While packed with the dispossessed and the extreme poor, bustees exist alongside well-maintained, prosperous neighborhoods. Often a million people live inside one square mile of land. I saw unwanted babies thrown onto garbage piles in which children search for something to eat, and people on the streets too sick to move, eaten by insects and rats. These Indians need a lot of imagination to survive and ingenuity to earn a few rupees. Some women carry buckets of coal; others carry bricks on their heads up to the twenty-fifth story of a building for two rupees a day after eight hours of work.[24] Many children are orphans who have nothing else to do but beg or steal to keep alive. Other children have loving parents but are still homeless and do not go to school. Yet I can tell you that you do not need to have a house to be at home. Hundreds of thousands of people live on railway platforms, because when it rains, the water drains off, and they don't have to live in the mud. The space on the platform is home, because parents and children are together.

My problem was how to actually help the starving, dying, and dispossessed. Two important decisions were made. First, my superiors decided I would need some training in basic nursing techniques. Second, I felt that I should dress in a sari, as the Indian women do. I was sent to the city of Patna to study nursing at a missionary hospital. After four months of instruction, I went back to Calcutta where my priest, Father Van Exem, blessed my new habit of a plain white sari trimmed in three simple blue bands.[25] This was a common design worn by the poorest Bengali women who live in the region. For me, the white represents truth and purity, while the three blue bands each signify the vows that the nuns of the Order take: the first band represents poverty, the second obedience, and the third broad band represents the vows of chastity and of "Wholehearted Free Service to the Poorest of the Poor."

What to Do?

When I started walking the streets of Calcutta in December of 1948, there was no shelter, no money, no guarantee, and no security. So I prayed and affirmed my wholehearted trust in God and his promises. I trusted his call and knew he would not let me down.[26] I decided to start in Motijhil, the slum I knew best.

Father Julian Henry, our priest and spiritual director at St. Mary's School, had encouraged the students to go among these people and assist them. Those weekly trips into this bustee greatly affected our souls. On one of my trips in the streets, around noon, a priest I did not know came up to me. He asked me to give a contribution to a Catholic collection. I had left the convent with five rupees and had given four of them to the poor already.[27] I hesitated and then gave the priest the one that remained. Now rupee-less, I was truly one with the poor.

That very afternoon, the same priest came searching for me, to give me an envelope. He told me that a man had given him the envelope that day because he had heard about my project in the slums and wanted to help me. Inside the envelope were fifty rupees! Five rupees became fifty. Five is 10 per cent of fifty; a tithe. I knew at that moment God had begun to bless the work and would never abandon me,[28] and he never has. God is good, and he knows our every need. It is his good pleasure to give us what we need. Does he not tell us to ask him?

I needed a roof to shelter the abandoned people of the streets, so I started to search. Day after day, I walked and walked and walked, until I couldn't walk anymore; my arms and legs ached. Then, I understood better the exhaustion of the really poor, always in search of a little food, of shelter, of medicine, of everything. I experienced what many Christians call the Dark Night of the Soul.[29] In the sixteenth century, the Spanish mystic, St. John of the Cross, coined the term. (I would face these dark uncertainties many times in my life, but no matter. We trust and obey God rather than be guided by our feelings. Maybe this is real faith.) The memory of the material security that I enjoyed in the Convent of Loreto came to me as a temptation that I would need to pray to overcome. After much struggle and prayer, I was sure the Lord wanted me to be where I was, and therefore, he would offer me a solution.

School under a Tree

Orphaned street children have nothing to do all day but beg for food or steal it. Seeing the same children in my walks each day, it finally came to me what to do. I asked a few street children to follow me and had them sit under a big tree. I took a long stick and drew in the dirt the letters of the Bengali language. (This would not be an easy task, as there are eleven vowels, thirty-three consonants, and thirteen vowel/consonant combinations, totaling fifty-seven symbols to learn.)[30] The tree would be a schoolroom and the ground a chalkboard. The next day, there were more children, and the next day, more still. On the fourth day, some chairs and tables were waiting under the tree, brought there by the neighbors. Each day, more supplies appeared; we had a school.

Poor people care about each other very much, and God cares even more. At noon the children got a cup of milk, and if they came three days in a row, a piece of soap. I taught reading first and then hygiene because they knew nothing about it, and then I taught them about God's love as the only three subjects at our open-air school. Some locals were suspicious of a white woman in a sari, and they believed I just wanted to convert Hindus to Christianity.

To this accusation, I had an answer: "*Ami Bharater Bharat Amar,*" which means, "I am Indian and India is mine."[31] I could say this because I had become an Indian citizen. Beside Bengali, I also learned to speak Hindi, because when you speak to someone in their own language, they will believe you care about them and can be trusted.

One by One, They Came

On the first of March 1949, there was a knock at my door. I opened it and stood still. My heart beat faster as I looked at the little figure facing me. It was Agnes, one of my students. She told me that she had come to join me in his work. I told her it would be a hard life and asked if she was prepared for it. She confirmed she knew it would be hard and that she was prepared, and then she calmly stepped inside.[32] She replied that she was waiting only for a date and time. I suggested March 19, which was St. Joseph's feast day. Agnes could hardly wait. On that day, she entered into her new life. Years later, Agnes shared joyfully with me that ever since that special day, she has experienced only happiness in serving God.

That night, though, we talked over a cup of tea, and then I sent her home to think more about what she was saying. A month later, she came again, this time empty-handed and wearing no jewelry, just a plain simple sari. Then I turned to our Lord at that moment and thanked him for sending her. Because she came to me, I knew others would follow. Jesus kept the promise that he made me when he called me to the poor. I can only praise him for his incredible goodness.

The first ten Sisters to join me were students I had taught at St. Mary's Convent School.[33] One by one, I saw young girls arrive after 1949. They wanted to give everything to God, and they were in a hurry to do it. They took off their expensive saris with great satisfaction in order to put on our humble cotton ones. They came fully aware of the difficulties. When a girl who belongs to a very high caste comes to place herself at the service of the outcast, we are talking about a revolution, the biggest one, the hardest of all: the revolution of love. By the time our congregation was established in 1950, we were twelve in number. On October 7, the Constitution for the Missionaries of Charity was approved. Glorious day! The official vows of our new order were: Poverty, Chastity, Obedience, and one additional vow from all other Orders, "Wholehearted and Free Service to the Poorest of the Poor," which some call charity. Charity does not mean a hand-out; it means love. I pray often for these heroic sisters that Christ will be glorified through his love that we freely share with others. I ask God that when others see our works, they may see Jesus and acknowledge his Majesty. My heart's desire is that my Sisters may all be one, as the Father and Jesus are one, that they may live and serve through his Holy Spirit.[34]

Missionaries of Charity Begin

Pope Pius XII officially approved our new congregation, called the Missionaries of Charity, in a two-year process, which seemed like a long wait to me, but we must all learn patience. Our name came out of the call. In the Muslim country of Yemen, the Sisters are called Carriers of God's Love. The name means what we are meant to be. We are the only Christians allowed to be there, because they do humble work with so much joy and happiness that the people see it. Since our official beginning, girls from all over the world have joined us, reaching over four thousand Sisters forty years later.[35] I can only thank God. From that same time, things began to happen at an astonishing rate by normal standards. Along with several schools in the bustee districts, we opened dispensaries for the distribution of needed medicines, but these were just the start.

The need for orphanages for street children was so great. My heart was thrilled when we opened *Shishu Bhan,* a children's home.[36] In just a few short years, there would be five homes in Calcutta all called the same name. Then, whenever a new Motherhouse somewhere around the world was founded, it would create a Shishu Bhan as close in location to them as possible. I have lost count of these orphanage schools, but there is always a need for more.

The Sanctity of Life

I am very passionate about the plight of children around the world. It is no surprise to anyone that I believe in the sanctity of life. There is no doubt in my heart that human life begins at conception. God gives us life, and we are created in his image. For me, no human hand should be raised to end life.[37] In the same speech I have given before powerful people when accepting awards on behalf of the poor, I have said this from my heart:

> And today the greatest means, the greatest destroyer of peace is abortion. And we who are standing here—our parents wanted us. We would not be here if our parents would do that to us.
>
> Our children, we want them, we love them. But what of the other millions? Many people are very, very concerned with the children of India, with the children of Africa where quite a number die, maybe of malnutrition, of hunger and so on, but millions are dying deliberately by the will of the mother. And this is what is the greatest destroyer of peace today. Because if a mother can kill her

> own child, what is left for me to kill you and you to kill me? There is nothing between.
>
> And this I appeal in India, I appeal everywhere, "Let us bring the child back"—and this year being the child's year: What have we done for the child? At the beginning of the year, I spoke everywhere, and I said: Let us ensure this year that we make every single child born, and unborn, wanted. And today is the end of the year. Have we really made the children wanted?
>
> I will tell you something terrifying. We are fighting abortion by adoption. We have saved thousands of lives. We have sent word to all the clinics, to the hospitals, police stations: "Please don't destroy the child; we will take the child." So every hour of the day and night, there is always somebody—we have quite a number of unwedded mothers—tell them: "Come, we will take care of you, we will take the child from you, and we will get a home for the child." And we have a tremendous demand for families who have no children; that is the blessing of God for us.[38]

What does God say to all of us? He says, even if a mother could forget her child, I will not forget you. I have carved you in the palm of my hand (Isa 49:15, 16). We are carved in the palm of his hand; that unborn child has been carved in the hand of God from conception. God can never forget us. Let us not forget the least among us (Mt 25:40), from the unborn child to the sick beggar on the street.[39] We have a tremendous demand from families who have no children. Adoption is a beautiful thing for a mother, father, and a child. True love begins at home.

Home for the Dying

What we see every day in the slum streets is difficult to bear. About two years after we were approved as an Order, something happened that made me extremely angry. Close to our Motherhouse, on a street next to

Campbell Hospital, we came upon a man dying in pain. We carried him inside the hospital, but they refused to accept him for two reasons: He had no money, and he was going to die anyway. We went to a drugstore to get medicine for him, but when we returned with it, the man was dead, outside in the dirt. I could not hide my disgust; it appeared they look after a dog or a cat better than another person. They would not allow this to happen to their pets.[40] I told my Sisters,

> Let each sister see Jesus Christ in the person of the poor: the more repugnant the work or the persons, the greater also must be her faith, love, and cheerful devotion in ministering to our lord in this distress. When I first picked up that woman who was eaten up by rats— her face, legs, and so on—if I had just passed by when I had seen and smelt her, I could not have been an MC, but I returned, picked her up, and took her to Campbell Hospital. If I had not, the Society would have died. Feelings of repugnance are human and if in spite of it we still give all our wholehearted free service, then we are on the right path and will be a holy sister.

I went to the commissioner of police to complain about this state of affairs, then to the city managers. I begged the authorities to simply provide me with a roof, and I would do the rest. They knew the problem was great, and so they responded.

Inside the temple of the goddess Kali, I was given a *dharmashala*; that means two large rooms designated as dormitories for temple pilgrims.[41] The temple was a center of Hindu cult devotion, yet I accepted the rooms happily. We finished cleaning the rooms in twenty-four hours and placed low cots and some mattresses on the ledges that ran along the sides of the great rooms. At once we took in the most desperate cases of the sick and dying. That was the origin of the Kalighat Home for the Dying, which we named in Bengali, *Nirmal Hriday*. Translated into English, it is A Place of the Pure Heart,[42] referring to the pure heart of Mary. Now there was a place where the homeless could die with some dignity, rather than being alone in the street.

The priests of the goddess Kali did not look favorable upon our intrusion. They watched us continuously, and one actually planned to kill me. The issue of the Kalighat Home for the Dying came up at the Calcutta Municipal Corporation meeting.[43] Some people objected on religious grounds to destitute people being brought there to die. But no one offered to provide a better place. After much discussion, a resolution was passed that allowed us to remain until another suitable place was found to accommodate the dying.

I thought I must look for a new place right away, but a friend chided me to stop wasting time worrying. She explained that the objection had been duly registered and put into cold storage, so we would never have to leave. We never have.

This was a big lesson for me in politics. One of the priests of the Kali Temple caught a contagious disease, and no hospital would take him, so we attended him day and night until he got well. From then on, the priests stopped spying on us and became, instead, our good friends and supporters.

At times, the poor we serve arrive in a most terrible condition: filthy, covered with sores and maggots, eaten away by syphilis. We wash them all. When a case is really bad, I want to take care of them myself. First, we ask the person their name and their religion, so that we can respect their faith and burial wishes. When they die, we record their name, religion, and the date. For many, it is the only evidence anywhere that they ever existed. Well over a hundred thousand names appear in the Sacred Heart records.

People often ask, "Why bother with the dying when you can't help them get better?"

We say, "No one should die alone."[44]

When we serve the dying, we want them to know that they are loved. We want them to die with God. This is why we started looking after the dying, that we might help them think of God in their last moments and make an act of love to him. I distinctly remember one old man who told me he never slept in a bed in his life.

Clutching the metal side of his simple camp bed frame, he proclaimed with a radiant smile, "Now I can die like a human being."[45]

We cannot do what we do with a long face. The whole of our society is engaged in feeding the hungry Christ, clothing the naked Christ, taking care of the sick Christ, and giving a home to the homeless Christ.

Come and See

It is very beautiful to see our young people so fully devoted with love for God's poor. To be able to understand the poor, we freely choose to be poor ourselves. We just choose not to have things that we could easily have. If a young girl wishes to join the Missionaries of Charity, there are four things she must do:

- be healthy of mind and body
- have the ability to learn
- have plenty of common sense
- possess a cheerful disposition[46]

Without these things, she could not do what we do. If she meets these four conditions, then she comes and sees the work, just like in the Gospel when our Lord said, "Come and see," to John and Andrew (Jn 1:39). The young lady goes to one of our houses and comes into close contact with the poor and with the Sisters. She works with them, prays with them, and stays with them. Then she decides if this is what God wants from her. If she joins, she spends six months as an aspirant, one year as a postulant, two years as a novice, then six years with temporary vows. One year before Final Vows, she goes home for a fortnight, back to her parents, to decide if she really wants to make this commitment. Then she goes to the Tertianship to prepare for Final Vows. At the end of that year, she takes her Final Vows. We have very few girls who leave. Some become ill before they are professed, but most who leave do so for family reasons. Otherwise, God has been very good to us.

Poverty, Chastity, Obedience, Charity

The four vows we take are of first importance to each Sister. They are designed to streamline our life for greater service to God and help us imitate Jesus, who chose to be poor, chaste, and obedient to his Father. The first three are these:

1. Poverty: freedom from worry over possessions since everything is held in common
2. Chastity: the freedom to love many people with abandon
3. Obedience: freedom from self-interest in order to do the will of God in all things[47]

The fourth vow for each Missionary Sister is Wholehearted and Free Service to the Poorest of the Poor.[48] The vow means that we cannot work for the rich, nor can we accept any money for the work we do. Ours has to be a free service. We exist as a society to bring Christ to the people and people to Christ; ours is a mission of love. Our particular message simply says God loves the world and the poor. He shows his love for the poor through us, and we show our love for God by putting our love for him into what I call living actions, by serving the poorest of the poor.[49]

All over the world, we dress as I do, and we always go in twos. Our sari habit is the visible sign of our consecration to God. The habit we wear draws respect from people. Though people are what they are sometimes, and do what they will do, still they know who belongs to God the Lord. Every Missionary of Charity owns the same few things: two saris, one to wash and one to wear (I like to think we were first to invent wash-and-wear). We have a pair of sandals, a toothbrush, and (if we are old) a sweater. We also have a rosary and a Breviary for prayer times, where we pray the Divine Hours, read scripture passages, and say beautiful prayers. Heaven and earth will pass away, but the Bible, God's Word, shall never pass away. It is the one thing that will last for all eternity. Finally, every Sister has her own bucket with which to wash her clothes. She can also place all her personal belongings inside it on a moment's notice, and her suitcase is packed. This is how we can mobilize with speed when there is a natural disaster somewhere in the world. Our Sisters are eager to go wherever they are most needed.

Calcutta Sisters' Daily Life

We begin every day at 4:40 in the morning. Naturally, we start with prayer and meditation. We take one and a half hour for this, while we sit on the floor in our life of simplicity. Our community is very closely woven together, so we do everything together: We pray together, we eat together, we work together. A typical day in the life of the Sisters of the Missionaries of Charity in Calcutta would be as follows:

4:40 a.m.	Rise and dress.
5 a.m.	Morning prayers and meditation.
6 a.m.	Holy Communion Mass, kneeling on floor.
6:30 a.m.	Breakfast and washing of clothing, alternating in two groups (we are so many, so while one eats, the other group washes).
7:30 a.m.	Sisters leave for work/service (some to the Home for the Dying or homes of lepers, others for the slum schools. Some prepare food, some teach Catechism, some distribute medicine in dispensaries, and so on across the whole city.).
12:15 p.m.	Sisters return to Motherhouse.
12:30 p.m.	Lunch, all together.
1:15 p.m.	Housework (whether we want to or not, because it's there).
1:45 p.m.	Rest time (because Sisters are on their feet all day).
2:15 p.m.	Examination of conscience, the divine office, and spiritual readings.
2:45 p.m.	Sipping a lovely cup of Darjeeling tea (doesn't that sound good?).
3 p.m.	Professed Sisters go out; novices and postulants remain for classes.
6:15 p.m.	Return to Motherhouse.
6:30 p.m.	Chapel, meditation, and adoration.
7:30 p.m.	Dinner, all together.
8:10 p.m.	Preparation of work assignments for next morning.
8:30 p.m.	Recreation (a happy time; everyone talks at the top of their voice because they have been working all day and have much to share).
9 p.m.	Chapel, night prayers.
10 p.m.	Bedtime (alas: 4:40 a.m. comes on time).[50]

Once a week, we have what is called a Day of Recollection. On this day, the first-year novices go out, because they do not go out all day during the week. The professed Sisters stay in for the day. This is a very beautiful time when we can regain our strength to fill up the emptiness again. It is a day of confession and adoration. Just as the earth needs to be replenished with fresh rain, so do we. That's why this day is so very beautiful. Did not our God have a day of rest after he created all things? What we are doing in the slums, maybe you cannot do. What you are doing in the place where you are called—in your family, in your college, in your work—we cannot do. But you and we together are doing something beautiful for God, if it is done in love.

Mobile Missionaries

We go any place in the world where we are invited. We have been asked by religious leaders and by government officials to come to their homeland. What we have learned is that there is no great difference in the reality of one country from another. People may look different, or dress differently, or have different positions and levels of education. But they are all the same. They are all people to be loved. An AIDS patient in Cambodia could be an AIDS patient anywhere. They and we, every one of us, are hungry for the same things: love and care. Yet people say that what we do is nothing but a drop in the ocean. I agree, but if we didn't do it, the ocean would be one drop less.[51] We have no reason to be despondent, discouraged, or unhappy because what we do, we are doing to Jesus. Even with all the humanitarian efforts we hear about, I think the world today turns its back on the poor, and this is turning its back on Christ himself.

We have absolutely no difficulty working in countries with many faiths, like India. We treat all people as children of God. They are our brothers and sisters because we are created in God's image (Ge 1:27). We show great respect to them. They know very well that what I have is a treasure that I'd like to give them, and I am not afraid to tell them so. But I also tell them that faith is a gift of God (Eph 2:8).

I was told recently that there are one and a half billion people living in poverty in the world. But I think of only one at a time. If I saw a crowd, I wouldn't know where to start. Jesus was only one, and I take Jesus at his word when he said in Matthew's Gospel, "You did it for me" (Mt 25:40). I have used this parable in speeches before presidents, kings, ambassadors, and religious leaders to explain our purpose for being and doing what we do in this way:

> On the last day, Jesus will say to those at his right hand, "Come, enter the joy of my Kingdom. For I was hungry and you gave me food, I was thirsty and you gave me drink, I was sick and you visited me."
>
> Then Jesus will turn to those on his left hand and say, "Depart from me, for I never knew you. I was hungry and you did not feed me, I was thirsty and you did not give me drink, I was sick and you did not visit me."
>
> These will ask, "But Lord, when did we see you hungry, or thirsty, or sick, and did not come to help you?"
>
> And Jesus will answer them, "Whatever you neglected to do to one of the least of these, you neglected to do it unto me!"[52]

I believe Jesus meant these words. When he says, "You did it for me" (Mt 25:40), it means we have been created to love as he loves us; Jesus makes himself the hungry one, the naked one, the homeless one, the unwanted one, and he says, "You did it to me."[53] Dear sisters and brothers, I take one person, one individual person at a time, because I have seen that you can only feed one at a time, only save one at a time, and only love one at a time.

Nobel Peace Prize

Our society has received many humanitarian awards, both religious and governmental. One of the first, on January 6, 1971, was the Pope John XXIII Peace Award, presented in Rome by Pope Paul VI. I did not want an award because the poor are not given rewards, and I want to identify with them. After much pressure, I said I would receive it only on behalf of my Sisters and in honor of the poorest of the poor. Besides, Pope Paul VI was my pope, and I must obey him. Can you see me saying no to my Lord Pontiff? Not in my lifetime. The pope declared on the occasion,

> Humble Mother Teresa, in whom we like to see the thousands and thousands of people dedicated full time to the personal service of the most needy, becomes an example and symbol of the discovery, in which lies the secret of world peace, which we are all seeking. It is the discovery, ever so up-to-date, that man is our brother and she who comes to us as a Missionary of Charity is the apostle of brother-hood and the messenger of peace.

Years later, after receiving the Nobel Peace Prize, I said, "When I was given the Nobel Peace Prize, I accepted it for the glory of God and the good of our poor people, not for myself—otherwise I don't take it, I do not accept it."[54] However, my colleagues convinced me that this award could bring attention to the many needs of the poor. So I accepted the prize in the name of the poor people of the world.

In 1979, I received the Nobel Peace Prize in the Great Hall of Oslo University from the King of Norway; I then gave a speech that was heard throughout the world. What a grand occasion it was, with many international luminaries. I spoke to well-dressed men and ladies laden with jewels, about the terrible details of the lives of the poor of Calcutta. Traditionally, a lavish banquet follows the award ceremony to honor the recipient. I was so pleased when I asked them to cancel the banquet and give the money to feed those who had nothing to eat. God bless them, they did.

There was a standing reception afterward, and I remember I drank a cool glass of water. It was delicious. I also took the cash award of $250,000. Are you surprised? I must explain. I had been praying for the financial means to build a home (a whole town actually) where the lepers of India could come to live in peace, earn their own living, and receive medical care. Lepers are the most forgotten of the poor and the most in need. I believe this money was God's answer to that prayer.

We have Sisters who have been specifically taught to take care of lepers. We take all the precautions possible to protect them. When they are properly trained, there is very little possibility of infection. We have many lepers to look after, thousands of them. When we ask our new Sisters, "Who would like to go and work with the leper?" every hand goes up. We give a Christmas party every year in Calcutta for the sweet lepers. One Christmas, I went and told the lepers that God has a very special love for them, and they are very dear to him. I also said that the disease they have is not a sin, and it is not a punishment from God.

An old man who was completely disfigured struggled along the floor to come near me and cried, "Repeat that once more. It did me good. I have always heard nobody loves us. It is good to know that God loves us. Please say that again!"[55]

I was overjoyed to oblige him. What lepers need (even more than the sulphone drug, Dapsone, that can stop the process of the disease in two years)[56] is a way to make their own living. We called the first colony built for lepers *Shanti Nagar*, which means the "Town of Peace."[57] When the government of India saw what we were doing for these dear souls, they gave us a thirty-four-acre plot of land on which to build, and we did just that.

Some think I accept these awards to become famous so I can influence the world politically. I am not that smart. Awards have brought fame, but with fame come other things, like cameras. They can be like gnats buzzing, yet the notoriety has opened doors to the Missionaries of Charity to places no one else can go. Not just to the slums or declining inner cities, but also to regions beset by famine, natural disasters, and even war.

I remember one trip into Lebanon. We set out for Beirut because we heard that crippled children were trapped in a hospital, surrounded by crossfire.[58] The only way we could enter was by sea from the Isle of Cypress, because Syria, Israel, and Turkey would not allow us to pass, fearing it was too dangerous for us. Still we went, not to side with either faction, but to bring supplies and Sisters to do work with the refugees and victims of the fighting. Without Jesus, we could not do the things we do, like going into a war zone. Certainly, we could not continue for a whole lifetime; one year, two years, perhaps, but not for a whole life. Without Jesus Christ, our life would be incomprehensible. Jesus explains our life.

Brothers of Charity

After some time, I realized that there were aspects of our work to which men were best suited. Male volunteers were most helpful with older orphan boys, elderly lepers, and others, so I saw a need for a branch of Brothers for the Missionaries of Charity's worldwide services. According to church law, a woman could not start a male order, but by God's divine providence, help arrived at just the right time. Dear Brother Andrew, an Australian Jesuit priest who had been in India for many years, co-founded the Order with me and served as its capable leader. In 1963, the Brothers of Charity took over several leprosy centers after being established as a branch order of the Missionaries of Charity.[59] These hard-working, godly men wear ordinary shirts and trousers, with a little crucifix pinned to their shirts. On this day of sharing with you, there are four hundred Brothers in eighty-eight communities in thirty countries, with seventy applications requesting new communities.[60] These communities are like towns where the lepers learn skills and have dignity through their daily work, like weaving or woodworking, while caring for themselves despite their medical conditions.

Operating Finances

One day, a Sister of another order criticized me for distributing free food to the poor. She said that I spoiled the poor with acts of charity. I responded to her and the group by saying,

> There is great talk going on all over the world that Mother Teresa is spoiling the people by giving them things free. In Bangalore, once at a seminar, in the name of the whole group, one nun got up and said to me, "Mother Teresa, you are spoiling the poor people by giving them things free. They are losing their human dignity. You should take at least ten naya paisa for what you give them, then they will feel more their human dignity." When everyone was quiet, I said calmly, "No one is spoiling as much as God Himself. See the wonderful gifts He has given us freely.

> All of you here have no glasses, yet you all can see. Say, if God were to take money for your sight, what would happen? We are spending so much money for Shishu Bhavan to buy oxygen for saving life, yet continually we are breathing and living on oxygen and we do not pay anything for it. What would happen if God were to say, 'You work four hours and you will get sunshine for two hours.' How many of us would then survive?" Then I also told them: "There are many congregations who spoil the rich, then it is good to have one congregation in the name of the poor, to spoil the poor." There was profound silence; nobody said a word after that.[61]

Do not be deceived, my friend; free food is not really free. Someone has to pay for it. I have been asked about our budget for our many services around the world. As for money, it always comes. The best I can tell you is the Lord sends it. We do his work. He provides the means. If he does not give us the means, that tells us he does not want us to do that work. So why worry? One day, Mr. Thomas, the chairman of Hindustan Lever, came to offer us a property in Bombay.[62] He first asked me, "Mother, how is your work financed?" Later, he wrote about my reply,

> At the end of that visit I asked her whether she had a budget for her work. She looked at me and asked with a smile "Mr. Thomas, who sent you here?" I was somewhat taken aback and said "no one in particular. I just wanted to come and see." Then she said something very profound: "You are my budget! People like you come and I ask them for help."[63]

Many famous and not-so-famous people come to see our work, and they give. Whenever a visitor comes to our Motherhouse, I take them immediately to the chapel to pray for a while. I invite them to greet the Master of the house, because Jesus is always here. We accept all gifts to feed the poor. We do not judge the giver. There must be a reason why some people can afford to live well. I only feel angry when I see waste, when I see people throwing away things that we could use. I hope you are not giving to God only from your surplus. You must give what costs you. Giving out of your surplus is like giving the banana peel instead of the banana. I urge you to make a sacrifice; go without something you like so that your gift may have value before God. It will satisfy your soul, and then you will be a true brother and sister to the poor, who do not have even small things they need.

Poor People Want to Love and Share

It is so beautiful that there is the International Association of Co-Workers who serve with us. This provides an opportunity for laypeople to work and grow in the likeness of Christ through humble acts of service to their own families and next-door neighbors. I ask them to first start in the city in which they live and then to venture into the world. These people share in the spirit of our society and work alongside the Missionaries of Charity Sisters and Brothers. They are carriers of God's love and compassion. The work is to encourage Christians and non-Christians alike to do acts of love. You see, every work of love, done with a full heart, always brings people closer to God.

I'll never forget when a gentleman came to our Motherhouse during a famine disaster in Bangladesh and said, "Mother, there is a Hindu family who has not eaten for many days. There are eight children. Do something for them."[64]

I took some rice and went to find them. I saw the children, their eyes shallow with hunger. (I don't know if you have ever seen hunger, but I have seen it very often.) The mother of the family took the rice, divided it into two bowls, took one bowl, and went out.

When she came back, I asked her, "Where did you go?"

She gave me a very simple answer: "They are hungry also."

What struck me was that she knew. And who were they? A Muslim family with six children, and she knew. I didn't bring any more rice that evening, because I wanted them, Hindus and Muslims, to experience the joy of sharing. There were those little children, sharing the joy and peace with their mother because she had the love to give until it hurt. One's giving or offering need not be confined to money. I would like more people to give their hands to serve and their hearts to love, to recognize the poor in their own homes, towns, and countries.

Poor people are often very great people, very lovable people. Many of them are new to the experience of poverty. There are new refugees every day somewhere in the world. I remember very well the terrible year of 1947, when India and Pakistan were divided, and so many people were displaced and forced to migrate to a new home; thousands died in that terrible process. Then again, my friend, people are displaced and become refugees every single day. These are people in great distress, and they are often very good people, like this one man I will tell you about.

We have a home for homeless alcoholics in Melbourne, Australia. One of them was very badly beaten by another. I thought this was a case for the police. So we sent for the police, and they came and asked that gentleman, "Who did this to you?"

He started telling all kinds of lies, but he wouldn't tell the truth. He wouldn't give the name, and the policemen had to go away without doing anything.

Then I asked him, "Why did you not tell them who did this to you?"

He said, "His suffering is not going to lessen my suffering."[65]

He hid the name of his brother to save him from suffering. We call them poor, but they are rich in love.

The Deepest Hunger

In places like Ethiopia and Bangladesh, the people are hungry for bread: physical hunger. But there is a much deeper, much greater hunger. There are desperately lonely people sleeping on the back streets of Paris, and there are desperately lonely people shopping in the exclusive boutiques on the Champs Élysées. The biggest disease today is not leprosy or cancer or AIDS; it is the feeling of being unwanted, unloved, uncared for, and abandoned.[66] The greatest evil in the world today is the lack of love and charity; it is indifference towards one's neighbor.

I remembered receiving a letter from my dear mama that touched me and stayed in my mind. She wrote, "Do you remember our neighbor Filé? She was covered in sores, but what caused her more suffering was the knowledge that she was all alone in the world. We did what we could for her but the worst thing was not the sores, but the fact that her family had forgotten her."[67]

No one expects hunger in the great Western countries. Terrible loneliness is not expected there, either, but there is great hunger for love and hunger for God. Nakedness means not only a need for a piece of clothing but also a need for human dignity, which we have stolen from our poor people. We treat them as good for nothing, as thieves, and as lazy people, but who chooses to be poor?

I want to say something to you. Please do hear my heart. Once a journalist asked me what I thought about being called a living saint on the cover of *Time* magazine. I said, "Oh, please, let me die first! I am no one special."

Believe me, this is true. I do not even make important decisions on my own. I wait on God before I move. Once, after our Order was spreading around the world, I longed for us to go to China. Personally, I was ready to go right then, yet I knew the wise thing was to wait for God's timing. He decides; I don't decide. Just like for China, He will decide the time. It is not the time now, but we have done our best. We are his vessels to be used as he desires. I describe it like this:

> I am nothing but a little pencil in the hands of God. It is He who writes, it is He who thinks, it is He who decides. That's all. He does the thinking. He does the writing. The pencil has nothing to do it. The pencil has only to be allowed to be used.
>
> We have seen many sacrifices, many prayers; everybody, I am asking to pray but, the last word is with Him. He decides.[68]

We all are meant to be instruments in the hand of God that he can use as he wills. Is this not a beautiful thing? I have met many great people in my life. They are among the poorest of the poor, and you will never know their names. There are many great and good people in the world, but the greatest one you can ever meet is Jesus Christ, the Word of God who became flesh and lived among us.

> Sometime ago, about forty professors came from the United States, and I think our house has become a tourist house. Anyway, they all came there and we talked, and at the end one of the professors asked me, "Mother, please tell us something that will help us to change our lives—to make our lives more happy." And I said to them "Smile at each other, make time for each other, enjoy each other." One of them asked me, "Are you married?" Of course, I said, "You don't know what you are talking about" and I said, "Yes." I find it sometimes very difficult to smile at Jesus. He can be very demanding and so this is something, a living reality. We must help each other—we need that.[69] This is really something true. It is where love comes in—when it is demanding, and yet, we can give it to him with joy.[70]

Become a friend of Jesus. This is my prayer for you. Begin at home. Love Jesus. Love Jesus in people.

Loving Jesus Joy

I have often been asked who Jesus is to me.

> **Who Is Jesus to Me?**
> Jesus is the Word made Flesh.
> Jesus is the Bread of Life.
> Jesus is the Victim offered for our sins on the Cross.
> Jesus is the Sacrifice offered at the Holy Mass for the sins of the world and mine.
> Jesus is the Word—to be spoken.
> Jesus is the Truth—to be told.
> Jesus is the Way—to be walked.
> Jesus is the Light—to be lit.
> Jesus is the Life—to be lived.
> Jesus is the Love—to be loved.
> Jesus is the Joy—to be shared.
> Jesus is the Sacrifice—to be offered.

Jesus is the Peace—to be given.
Jesus is the Bread of Life—to be eaten.
Jesus is the Hungry—to be fed.
Jesus is the Thirsty—to be satiated.
Jesus is the Naked—to be clothed.
Jesus is the Homeless—to be taken in.
Jesus is the Sick—to be healed.
Jesus is the Lonely—to be loved.
Jesus is the Unwanted—to be wanted.
Jesus is the Leper—to wash his wounds.
Jesus is the Beggar—to give him a smile.
Jesus is the Drunkard—to listen to him.
Jesus is the Retarded—to protect him.
Jesus is the Little One—to embrace him.
Jesus is the Blind—to lead him.
Jesus is the Dumb—to speak for him.
Jesus is the Crippled—to walk with him.
Jesus is the Drug Addict—to befriend him.
Jesus is the Prostitute—to remove from danger and befriend.
Jesus is the Prisoner—to be visited.
Jesus is the Old—to be served.[71]

To Me:
Jesus is my God.
Jesus is my Spouse.
Jesus is my Life.
Jesus is my only Love.
Jesus is my All in All.
Jesus is my Everything![72]

May he be your everything, too!

Namaste,

Mother Mary Teresa of Calcutta,
Missionaries of Charity

Conclusion

Mother Teresa told the world of her all-encompassing love for God. The foundation for her life's work to serve the poorest of the poor was based on her spiritual understanding that every person is created in the image of God and reflects the Creator and his glory. For that reason, when she looked into the eyes of any person, she saw Jesus Christ in them. Mother believed if you truly loved God, you would naturally love people and want to care for them. Her vertical relationship with God was expressed in a horizontal relationship with all people. In so doing, she was following the mandate of Jesus Christ when he unified the Ten Commandments down to only two, saying, "'Love the Lord your God with all your heart and with all your soul and with all your mind.' This is the first and greatest commandment. And the second is like it: 'Love your neighbor as yourself'"(Mt 22:37–40). Mother's vision of serving others was caught by young and old, high and low, wherever she ventured, by her spoken precepts and daily example.

(The writings of Mother Teresa of Calcutta © all used with permission by the Mother Teresa Center, exclusive licensee throughout the world of the Missionaries of Charity for the works of Mother Teresa.)

Discussion Questions

1. Jesus said, "The poor would always be with us," but not because it should be so; he knew that mankind would turn their backs on God and on one another. Mother Teresa reached out to the poor, abandoned and dying. What things do you observe that prompted her to attend to these forgotten people?
2. Mother Teresa never campaigned for money for her projects of relief for the poor. What do you think of her method of relying on God for the finances required to care for the outcast, poverty-stricken and dying?
3. Mother said she disliked giving speeches, yet, she did so for decades because she believed it would raise awareness of the plight of the poor around the world. Are there things you could do for the sake

of the Gospel, even though you think of yourself as unqualified or incapable?

4. Have you ever received guidance from God that seemed in any way similar to Mother Teresa's experience of her "call within a call?"
   How did that happen for you and what was the result?
5. In what different ways have you "shared a cup of cold water in Jesus name" with the poor, lonely, sick, or imprisoned?
   What effect did your experience have on you?

Conclusion

Seven Church Mothers

The women whose stories are presented in these pages loved God first and foremost; they demonstrated that love with intentional actions to care for their neighbor, as if for themselves. Doing this was never easy, yet each was undaunted in their vibrant quest to represent the cause of God and his absolute love for each individual person. All through biblical history, women, as well as men, have passed on the message of redemptive salvation with faith and actions, not counting the cost to themselves. Historically speaking, it has only been recently that women have been more widely accepted as preachers and leaders within the church. None of our seven historical figures were ordained as pastors or priests in their particular place in Christianity's story, but neither did any of them seek out this distinction, nor did they care. We can admire them for courageously addressing an overlooked need of those suffering around them, in spite of cultural or physical obstacles stalling them from doing so. What mattered to them more than human recognition and organizational titles was to discover the will of God and then do it with all their hearts. May women and men today rise up and follow their footsteps of faith!

These seven notable church mothers have been chosen to represent countless other women who, like them, deserve honor and recognition for their devotion to God and serving people. These other spiritual women could have names that are well known, but most will remain nameless outside the history books. The lives, leadership, and contributions of these seven women, and innumerable female believers through history, clearly demonstrate that since ancient times, God has effectively called, gifted, and empowered women to send them out into his vineyard to bear fruit for his Kingdom. This historical reality springs from the biblical teaching of the spiritual equality of all believers and that the Holy Spirit was, is, and will continue to be poured out on both male and female alike. We are all one in Christ Jesus, in whom there is neither male nor female (Gal 3:28).

Whether or not women are accepted as preachers or deemed worthy to be ordained within the church, each of us needs to earnestly seek the face of our Beloved Lord and find our special place of service in the Family of God. Christ has called his people to do great things for him through the power of his Holy Spirit. My fellow believer, you and I have a unique story to tell. As the scriptures urge us, we must work out our own salvation with earnestness and then share his story and ours as an undeniable witness to the Goodness of Almighty God.

Epilogue

"Women Don't Do That!"

At seventeen, I found myself at a church high school Easter camp. Not having been raised in the church, I was quite ignorant of Christianity. The five days of being with born-again believers in God challenged my understanding of the world. All the adult counselors and kids there were very different from other people I had met. They seemed to actually love, not only each other, but me as well. I could tell they authentically loved me, and I hadn't done anything to deserve it. They were happy and kind, and they apparently had something I didn't have. They talked about knowing God and Jesus, and what the Bible had to say. Actually envious, I asked how I could be like them. They said to ask God to forgive me for my sins and by faith choose to believe and trust in Jesus as my Savior and Lord.

There wasn't much logic in that answer, for my way of thinking. Then I heard someone at camp say that praying for Jesus to come into my heart would be like jumping off a tall cliff and falling through the air, but being caught before reaching the bottom. Somehow, that picture made sense to me; I decided to take a leap of faith, and it worked. Jesus Christ became real to me, and all I wanted to do was read the New Testament and learn as much as I could about Jesus's life and the beginning of the church. I was disappointed when I finished reading the book of Acts because I wanted to know what happened next in church history, which I mistakenly assumed should have been the next book in the Bible.

Where Do I Belong?

My new Christian friends took me to church services every Sunday morning and evening, and to midweek youth group and Friday night prayer meetings. About two months later, after a Sunday morning church service, I entered the back door of my home to find my mother sitting alone in the kitchen, waiting for me. She stood up, began wagging her finger at me (something she never did), and said, "Young lady, you get any idea out of your mind about becoming a pastor, because women don't do that!"

I was utterly shocked. How did she know what I was thinking? I never said a word to her about what I had decided at the church camp. All she saw was my desire to be with Christians, yet she knew. Within days of my decision to wholeheartedly embrace the Gospel of Jesus Christ, I bemoaned the reality that I was a female and not a man. I thought if I was a man, I could go to seminary and become a pastor, so I could tell others the truth, that Jesus is the Savior of the world. Yet I couldn't do that because I thought women weren't ministers. I had never heard of a woman being a pastor. Women pastors were serving in pulpits, but I did not know that. So I decided I would try to be a missionary in a foreign country because, at least, women could do that.

It takes time, study, and many experiences of testing to become a mature Christian. In my excitement of being a new believer, I told the Lord I would go anywhere in the world as a missionary, as long as it wasn't Africa. I didn't know what I said just so happened to be a common statement heard in Christian circles. My local church sponsored missionaries in different parts of the world, and one particular Sunday, a missionary couple on furlough came to preach to our congregation. Where were they from? Africa, of course.

They gave an altar call, asking young people to go to the mission field as volunteers to assist the current workers. Something came over me; I ran out of the church and flung myself on the lawn, crying, but I didn't know why. A year later, three of us college students were sent by our church as short-term, volunteer missionaries to Kinshasa, Congo, the same mission field as the visiting missionary couple.

Unexpected Changes

The Christian life is not a mere body of knowledge but a vertical relationship with God and a horizontal relationship with other people, both believers and nonbelievers, like-minded and dissimilar. The third-world experience in Africa was eye-opening for me and thoroughly exciting. I fell in love with the African people and decided to finish my education in the States and return to the Congo as a missionary for the rest of my life. A scholarship to Oral Roberts University allowed me to attend that Christian college to prepare myself. My dream of Africa faded when I fell in love again, this time with Gene Hunt, a fellow student who grew up as a missionary kid in Venezuela. Heading for the continent of Africa or South America didn't matter to me, as long as I was with Gene and sharing the Good News of Salvation in Christ with others.

Gene wanted to be a missionary pilot, flying supplies and missionaries to ministry stations, like he had seen in the field growing up. Because paying for private flying lessons was so expensive, his instructors advised him to go into the military and let the service teach him to fly while serving his country. He could build up flight hours there. Besides, they said he would have to compete with retired military pilots for a position in the missionary flying organizations anyway. Soon he was in Naval officer training and flight school in Pensacola, Florida.

After three years of marriage, we discovered that I was expecting (doctors had told us that I was unable to have a child). Our life was on schedule, according to our plans, and we were ecstatic, praising God for his goodness to us. One week before the officers' commissioning ceremony and on Gene's last training flight, I was holding up dinner because he was late coming home. A few more hours passed, and then two officers appeared at my front door. There had been a plane crash, and both pilots were killed.

I looked into the sad eyes of the men and said, "He's fine, and he's seeing heaven for the first time."

A peace came over me I had never experienced before. In my mind's eye, I saw Gene walking with friends, wide-eyed viewing heaven. Reality soon set in, and my sister and I accompanied my husband's casket to San Diego for burial. Four months later, our son was born in the Navy hospital in Balboa Park.

Overcoming Grief

I never knew the vast emotional depths the human spirit can experience. If the depth of grief pangs can be measured, I felt my grief dropped to the bottom of the deepest seafloor. Time doesn't heal painful agony by itself. Time is not a healer. I remember praying, asking God to let me sleep for two or three years, and then I would wake up, and this intense pain would be gone. God spoke to me with a clear impression, the kind of awareness when you know you are hearing God's voice, because you would never have thought of the insight yourself. God's still, small voice also rings true and brings comfort and his *shalom* (peace). I learned I had to progress through the grieving process in order to get to the years when the pain of grief no longer overshadows one's life. Even when you don't want to do anything, you still have to get up and put one foot in front of the other and move.

What does a widowed mother with a brand-new baby do? At twenty-seven with a son and port-a-crib in tow, we flew to five cities across America, praying for God to show me what I should do and where we should live. As an officer's widow, I had the GI Bill to cover education costs beyond my BA degree. I was choosing between getting a nursing degree and attending seminary, so I could study theology because it interested me. I was grateful to get honest advice along the way. The head of admissions at John Hopkins nursing school in Baltimore was emphatic: "You don't want to be an RN with a baby, by yourself, because the working hours in hospitals are terrible." In response, I chose my heart's desire: seminary.

A Visit with Santa

I also knew that I wanted to be married again. To me, marrying again was not saying I didn't love Gene anymore. Instead, wanting to marry again was a compliment to him, because the years we were married, though few, were so very happy and fulfilling. Besides, I soon realized that seminary was a great place for a woman to find a Christian husband who was called to the ministry. I reasoned if I couldn't be a pastor myself, I could be a pastor's wife.

One day on Christmas break, while attending Fuller Theological Seminary, I decided to take Wesley, my three-year-old son, to Knott's

Berry Farm in Buena Park to visit Santa Claus. The amusement park had a large igloo display with Santa's workshop nearby for children to watch while waiting in line to see Santa. Mr. Claus wore a microphone so the public could hear from loudspeakers what the children wanted for Christmas. Parents stayed at the entrance of the igloo so children could sit alone on Santa's lap.

When Santa asked my little Wesley what he wanted, he said sheepishly, "A fire truck."

"Is there anything else?" Santa probed.

My son nodded his head.

"What is that?"

"A daddy," Wesley answered.

An emotive gasp went through the crowd, and all eyes turned to look at the woman standing at the head of the line, me. It was as if I heard the people say, "How could that woman not have a daddy for that adorable child?"

At bedtime that evening, I told my son that Santa Claus could not bring him a daddy, but Jesus could, if we prayed for one. So we did just that, and three weeks later, I got a phone call from a stranger who asked if she could come over to meet me. A half-hour later, Barbara Johnson was at my door. I soon learned she was the Christian humorist-author who had published many books with Zondervan and would become a regular speaker for the "Woman of Faith" conferences around the country.

She interviewed me for what seemed like hours, asking what I believed and what kind of wife I wanted to be again. When satisfied with my answers, she pulled out a photo of a tan "surfer dude" and proceeded to sing his praises.

When I could get a word in, I told her unequivocally, "Good-looking, tan, blond surfers were never interested in me. I was the girl that guys took home to meet their mother."

But within the year, with my son's approval, Wesley Eugene Hunt served as ring bearer at my wedding to Todd Ehrenborg, a Fuller Seminary theology student. I can now say with confidence, I have been twice blessed with two excellent Christian husbands in my lifetime.

God Answers Prayer

Being a new wife and mother, while taking a full-course load of theological classes with my husband, was certainly challenging but truly exhilarating. Studying the Bible together as newlyweds was as meaningful as praying together as a couple. My husband's skill in how to correctly interpret scripture passages encouraged me, and his knowledge of the Bible caused me to call him my "walking concordance."

After much examination and study, I realized there is no biblical mandate baring women from leadership in the church or from preaching the Gospel. It was Catherine Booth's particular words that finally sealed the dilemma for me when she wrote, "A mistaken application of the passage, 'Let your women keep silence in the Churches,' has resulted in loss to the church, evil to the world, and dishonor to God." Despite some fervent opinions and strong opposition to the contrary, the Bible and history adequately document that God has been calling, equipping, sending, and blessing women in spiritual leadership for thousands of years. God's people owe a debt of gratitude to courageous and faith-filled women who ignored cultural restraints and chose instead to be obedient to his call on their lives for his glory.

For thirty-four years, I found it was never easy to juggle a home and family with all the responsibilities of co-pastoring a church with my husband. Nevertheless, I find standing in the pulpit to preach God's Word to a congregation is not just a noble responsibility, but a privilege and great joy. I have heard it said, "You do best what you like to do, and you like to do what you do best." For Christians, there is more to it than that. Followers of Jesus Christ find the best fulfillment in life is doing what God has called us and designed us to do, even before we were knit together in our mother's womb. There is nothing like living in the center of God's will for our lives and completing the tasks that he has set before us. That place is true fulfillment, peace, and indescribable joy.

My prayer for you is that you and all those you are called to love and serve will flourish with much happiness and fruitfulness as you wholeheartedly follow Christ.

Endnotes

Introduction: Church Fathers and Church Mothers

1 Canon of the Bible (Grk: kanon was a ruler, staff, or measuring rod; used to mean a standard, rule, or norm. The Canon of the Bible is the standard or rule used to recognize and collect the God-inspired, authoritative books of the sacred scriptures). Norman Geisler and William Nix, *A General Introduction to the Bible* (Chicago: Moody Press, 1974), 127.

2 Crimean War (1853–56): Russian aggression against Turkey led to war in 1853, with Turkey's European allies intervening to destroy Russian naval power in the Black Sea in 1854; eventually, the allies captured the fortress city of Sebastopol in 1855, after a lengthy siege. *Oxford Dictionary*, "Crimean War." Posted May 21, 2020. https://www.britannica.com/event/Crimean-War

3 "The dark night of the soul" is a type of spiritual depression. This phenomenon describes a malady that the greatest of Christians have suffered from time to time. It was the malady experienced by King David (Ps. 6:6) and Jeremiah, "the Weeping Prophet." "This is no ordinary depression, but is linked to a crisis of faith, a crisis that comes when one senses the absence of God or gives rise to a feeling of abandonment by Him." R. C. Sproul, "The Dark Night of the Soul." *Tabletalk Magazine*, February 1, 2008. Ligonier Ministries. https://www.ligonier.org/learn/articles/dark-night-soul/

4 Poor Clare Colettines, Ellesmere, UK, "The Rule of Life of St. Clare." Little Plant of St. Francis. Posted July 6, 2012. https://littleplantofstfrancis.blogspot.com/2012/07/rule-of-life-of-saint-clare.html

5 The Peasants War (1524–25) was a peasant uprising in Germany. Inspired by changes brought by the Reformation, masses of peasants invoked divine law to demand agrarian rights and freedom from oppression by nobles and landlords. Some hundred thousand peasants were killed. *Encyclopaedia Britannica*, "Peasants War." Posted April 11, 2017. https://www.britannica.com/event/Peasants-War.

6 The Second Great Awakening was a Protestant religious revival in America from about 1795 to 1835, during which meetings were held in small towns and large cities throughout the country. The unique frontier institution known as the camp meeting began, causing churches to experience a vast increase in membership. Soul-winning became the primary function of ministry and stimulated several reforms, including temperance and the emancipation of women. *Encyclopaedia Britannica*, "The Second Great Awakening." Posted May 8, 2019. https://www.britannica.com/topic/Second-Great-Awakening
7 Trevor Yaxley and Carolyn Vanderwal, *William & Catherine, The Life and Legacy of the Booths* (Minneapolis: Bethany House, 2003), 185.
8 The Missionaries of Charity is one Catholic religious order with nine branches: Missionaries of Charity Sisters, Missionaries of Charity Brothers, Missionaries of Charity Contemplative Sisters, Missionaries of Charity Contemplative Brothers, Missionaries of Charity Priests, Missionaries of Charity Co-Workers and Sick and Suffering Co-Workers, Missionaries of Charity Volunteers, Lay Missionaries of Charity, Corpus Christi Movement (for Diocesan Priests).

Chapter 1: Judge Deborah, a Mother of Israel

1 Fuchsia Pickett, *Deborah* (Lake Mary, FL: Creation House, 1999), 9.
2 Pickett, *Deborah,* 18.
3 Lawrence O. Richards, *The Bible Reader's Companion* (Owings Mills, MD: Ottenheimer Publishers, 1991), 16.
4 Herbert Lockyer, *All the Women of the Bible* (Grand Rapids, MI: Zondervan, 1967), 42.
5 James L. Garlow, *The Covenant.* (Kansas City: Bacon Hill Press, 1999), 11.
6 Garlow, *The Covenant*, 50.
7 Garlow, *The Covenant*, 50.
8 Garlow, *The Covenant*, 42.
9 Garlow, *The Covenant*, 64.
10 R. A. Torrey, *Difficulties in the Bible* (Chicago: Moody Press, 1907), 59.
11 Gilbert V. Beers, *The Victor Handbook of Bible Knowledge* (Wheaton, IL: Victor Books SP Publications, 1981), 144.
12 Beers, *The Victor Handbook*, 144.
13 Randall Price, *Rose Guide to the Temple* (Torrance, CA: Rose Publishing, 2012), 9.
14 David Howard Jr., *Fascinating Bible Facts* (Lincolnwood, IL: Publication International, 1997), 8.
15 Price, *Rose Guide to the Temple*, 9.
16 Price, *Rose Guide to the Temple*, 40.

17 Price, *Rose Guide to the Temple*, 40.
18 Price, *Rose Guide to the Temple*, 41.
19 Howard, *Fascinating Bible Facts*, 14.
20 Howard, *Fascinating Bible Facts*, 153.
21 Miriam F. Vamosh, *Women at the Time of the Bible* (Herzlia, Israel: Palphot Ltd., 2007), 88.
22 Edith Deen, *All the Women of the Bible* (New York: Harper and Row, 1982), 69.
23 Pickett, *Deborah*, 2.
24 Vamosh, *Women at the Time of the Bible*, 15.
25 Pickett, *Deborah*, 11.
26 Lockyer, *All the Women of the Bible*, 41.
27 Sylvia Charles, *Women in the Bible* (Tulsa, OK: Virgil Hensley, 1995), 96.
28 James Harpur, *Great Events of Bible Times* (New York: Doubleday, 1987), 62.
29 Robert Huber, *The Bible through the Ages* (New York: Reader's Digest, 1996), 50.
30 Huber, *The Bible through the Ages*, 50.
31 Ernest Wright, *Great People of the Bible and How They Lived* (New York: Reader's Digest, 1974), 116.
32 Deen, *All the Women of the Bible*, 70.
33 Deen, *All the Women of the Bible*, 70.
34 Talbot, John Michael, "God Alone Is Enough." Album, *Simple Heart*. Troubadour of the Lord: Original Release Date: January 1, 2000.
35 Wright, *Great People of the Bible*, 116.
36 Harpur, *The Bible through the Ages*, 62.
37 Jacques Duquesne, *Women of the Bible* (Paris: Flammarion, 2010), 80.
38 Pickett, *Deborah*, 28.
39 Wright, *Great People of the Bible*, 116.
40 Harpur, *The Bible through the Ages*, 64.
41 John Michael Talbot, "Only in God (Psalm 62)." Album, *Signatures*. Troubadour of the Lord: 2003.
42 Caroline Masom and Pat Alexander, *Picture Archive of the Bible* (Batavia, IL: Lion Publishing, 1987), 54.
43 Jean-Pierre Isbouts, *The Biblical World* (Washington DC: National Geographic, 2007), 150.
44 Merrill Tenney, *The Zondervan Pictorial Encyclopedia of the Bible*, Vol. 3 (Grand Rapids, MI: Zondervan, 1977), 747. Note: The six tribes were Naphtali, Zebulun, Ephraim, Benjamin, Machir, and Issachar.
45 Tenney, *Zondervan Pictorial Encyclopedia*, Vol. 3, 747.
46 Tenney, *Zondervan Pictorial Encyclopedia*, Vol. 5, 432.
47 Melville Bell Grosvenor, *Everyday Life in Bible Times* (Washington DC: National Geographic, 1964), 337.
48 Harpur, *The Bible through the Ages*, 64.

49 Duquesne, *Women of the Bible*, 80.
50 Richards, *The Bible Reader's Companion*, 163.
51 Beers, *The Victor Handbook*, 147.
52 Charles, *Women in the Bible*, 101.

Chapter 2: Mary of Nazareth, the Mother of Jesus

1 David Howard Jr., *Fascinating Bible Facts* (Lincolnwood, IL: Publication International, 1997), 9. The personal name for God, Yahweh (Exodus 6:3), written as Y-H-W-H, was so holy to the Jews that they eventually stopped pronouncing it because they felt unworthy. When God's name was encountered in scripture while reading aloud, they substituted one of God's titles, Adonai ("the LORD").
2 Edith Deen, *All the Women of the Bible* (New York: Harper & Row, 1982), 162.
3 Mark Galli, "The Life and Times of Jesus of Nazareth" (*Christian History,* Issue 59, Vol. XVII, No. 3, 1998), 32.
4 Galli, "The Life and Times of Jesus of Nazareth," 15.
5 Melville Bell Grosvenor, *Everyday Life in Bible Times* (Washington DC: National Geographic, 1964), 324.
6 Galli, "The Life and Times of Jesus of Nazareth," 20.
7 Galli, "The Life and Times of Jesus of Nazareth," 21.
8 *Elohim* is the most common name for God in Hebrew writing. It is used thirty-two times in the first chapter of Genesis alone.
9 Grosvenor, *Everyday Life in Bible Times,* 324.
10 Howard, *Fascinating Bible Facts,* 8.
11 Vicki Weber, *Traditions! Celebration and Ritual in Jewish Life* (Hong Kong: Berman House, 2000), 208.
12 Weber, *Traditions! Celebration and Ritual,* 208.
13 Galli, "The Life and Times of Jesus of Nazareth," 25.
14 Howard, *Fascinating Bible Facts,* 148.
15 Galli, "The Life and Times of Jesus of Nazareth," 24.
16 Galli, "The Life and Times of Jesus of Nazareth," 25.
17 Galli, "The Life and Times of Jesus of Nazareth," 25.
18 Galli, "The Life and Times of Jesus of Nazareth," 24.
19 Galli, "The Life and Times of Jesus of Nazareth," 25.
20 Galli, "The Life and Times of Jesus of Nazareth," 24.
21 Galli, "The Life and Times of Jesus of Nazareth," 25.
22 Galli, "The Life and Times of Jesus of Nazareth," 25.
23 Tim Dowley, *Everyday Life in Bible Times* (Grand Rapids, MI: Kregel Publications, 1998), 14.

24 Miriam F. Vamosh, *Daily Life at the Time of the Bible* (Herzlia, Israel: Palphot, 2007), 57.

25 Vamosh, *Daily Life at the Time of the Bible*, 57.

26 Miriam F. Vamosh, *Women at the Time of the Bible* (Herzlia, Israel: Palphot, 2007), 5.

27 Dowley, *Everyday Life in Bible Times*, 10.

28 Galli, "The Life and Times of Jesus of Nazareth," 17.

29 Vamosh, *Women at the Time of the Bible*, 25.

30 Vamosh, *Women at the Time of the Bible*, 25.

31 Gilbert V. Beers, *The Victor Handbook of Bible Knowledge* (Wheaton, IL: Victor Books SP Publications Inc., 1981), 338.

32 Lucien Deiss, *Joseph, Mary, Jesus* (Collegeville, MN: The Liturgical Press, 1998), 15.

33 Beers, *The Victor Handbook of Bible Knowledge*, 338.

34 Vamosh, *Women at the Time of the Bible*, 25.

35 Vamosh, *Women at the Time of the Bible*, 25.

36 Vamosh, *Daily Life at the Time of Jesus*, 59.

37 Howard, *Fascinating Bible Facts*, 160.

38 Federico Suarez, *Mary of Nazareth* (New York: Scepter Publishers, 2003), 38.

39 Vamosh, *Women at the Time of the Bible*, 36.

40 Vamosh, *Women at the Time of the Bible*, 36.

41 Howard, *Fascinating Bible Facts*, 197.

42 Dowley, *Everyday Life in Bible Times*, 14.

43 Deiss, *Joseph, Mary, Jesus*, 6.

44 Dowley, *Everyday Life in Bible Times*, 14.

45 Deen, *All the Women of the Bible*, 174.

46 Chris Armstrong, "'All Generations Will Call Me Blessed': Mary in the Imagination of the Church" (*Christian History & Biography* Issue 83, Summer 2004), 29.

47 Deen, *All the Women of the Bible*, 173.

48 Lockyer, *All the Women of the Bible*, 30.

49 Lockyer, *All the Women of the Bible*, 32.

50 Howard, *Fascinating Bible Facts*, 41.

51 Howard, *Fascinating Bible Facts*, 41.

52 Beers, *The Victor Handbook of Bible Knowledge*, 334.

53 Howard, *Fascinating Bible Facts*, 196.

54 Deiss, *Joseph, Mary, Jesus*, 86.

55 Galli, "The Life and Times of Jesus of Nazareth," 15.

56 Howard, *Fascinating Bible Facts*, 149.

57 *Ruach* is Hebrew for "Spirit." *Ruach Hakodesh* means "the Holy Spirit." Ruach is also described as the "Breath" of God and as the "Spirit of God."

58 Beers, *The Victor Handbook of Bible Knowledge*, 348.
59 Beers, *The Victor Handbook of Bible Knowledge*, 469.
60 Beers, *The Victor Handbook of Bible Knowledge*, 469.
61 Galli, "The Life and Times of Jesus of Nazareth," 16.
62 Galli, "The Life and Times of Jesus of Nazareth," 17.
63 Lockyer, *All the Women of the Bible*, 98.
64 Armstrong, "All Generations Will Call Me Blessed," 34.
65 Garlow, *The Covenant*, 18, 19.
66 Vamosh, *Daily Life at the Time of Jesus*, 72.
67 Galli, "The Life and Times of Jesus of Nazareth," 41.
68 Howard, *Fascinating Bible Facts*, 82.
69 Howard, *Fascinating Bible Facts*, 82.
70 Lockyer, *All the Women of the Bible*, 99.

Chapter 3: St. Clare of Assisi, the First Franciscan Mother

1 Ingrid Peterson, "Francis's Tenacious Lady" (*Christian History*, Issue 42, Vol. XIII, No. 2, 1994). Mark Galli, editor.
2 Peterson, "Francis's Tenacious Lady," 34.
3 Chiara Augusta Lainati, *Saint Clare of Assisi* (Assisi, Italy: Edizioni Porziuncola, 1994), 90.
4 Peterson, "Francis's Tenacious Lady," 35.
5 Nesta De Robeck, *St. Clare of Assisi* (Chicago: Franciscan Herald Press, 1980), 17.
6 Lainati, *Saint Clare of Assisi*, 10.
7 Bret Thoman, *St. Clare of Assisi, Light from the Cloister* (Charlotte, NC: TAN Books, 2017), 2.
8 Lainati, *Saint Clare of Assisi*, 12.
9 Carol Lee Flinders, *Enduring Grace* (San Francisco: Harper Collins, 1993), 17.
10 Lainati, *Saint Clare of Assisi*, 9.
11 Lainati, *Saint Clare of Assisi*, 54. "Madonna" is a title of respect given to a highborn lady in the Middle Ages and Renaissance times.
12 Thoman, *St. Clare of Assisi*, 3.
13 Mark Galli, "Five Who Knew a Saint" (*Christian History*, Issue 42, Vol. XIII, No. 2, 1994), 22.
14 Julien Green, *God's Fool: The Life and Times of Francis of Assisi* (San Francisco: Harper & Row, 1983), 144.
15 Green, *God's Fool*, 14.
16 Green, *God's Fool*, 24.
17 Thoman, *St. Clare of Assisi*, 12.

18 Regis Armstrong and Ignatius Brady, *Francis and Clare: The Complete Works* (New York: Paulist Press, 1982), 3.

19 Green, *God's Fool*, 56.

20 Green, *God's Fool*, 56.

21 Madeline Nugent, *Clare & Her Sisters* (Boston: Pauline Books and Media, 2003), 21.

22 Green, *God's Fool*, 62.

23 Thoman, *St. Clare of Assisi*, 35.

24 Green, *God's Fool*, 77.

25 Johannes Jorgensen, *Saint Francis of Assisi* (New York; Image Books, 1955), 49.

26 Jorgensen, *Saint Francis of Assisi*, 49.

27 Penance is an action showing regret for one's wrongdoings.

28 St. Luke's Productions (1983). "Saint Francis, Troubadour of God's Peace" (DVD; available from www.stlukeproductions.com).

29 Thoman, *St. Clare of Assisi*, 35.

30 Green, *God's Fool*, 91.

31 Jorgensen, *Saint Francis of Assisi*, 57.

32 De Robeck, *St. Clare of Assisi*, 4.

33 Green, *God's Fool*, 97.

34 De Robeck, *St. Clare of Assisi*, 17.

35 Marco Bartoli, *Clare of Assisi* (Quincy, IL: Franciscan Press, 1993), 37.

36 Green, *God's Fool*, 118.

37 Jorgensen, *Saint Francis of Assisi*, 83.

38 Green, *God's Fool*, 121.

39 Jorgensen, *Saint Francis of Assisi*, 86.

40 Green, *God's Fool*, 122.

41 Jorgensen, *Saint Francis of Assisi*, 85.

42 St. Luke's Productions, "Saint Francis, Troubadour of God's Peace."

43 Flinders, *Enduring Grace*, 25.

44 De Robeck, *St. Clare of Assisi*, 32.

45 Thoman, *St. Clare of Assisi*, 60.

46 Thoman, *St. Clare of Assisi*, 65.

47 Bartoli, *Clare of Assisi*, 46.

48 Murray Bodo, *Clare: A Light in the Garden* (Cincinnati, OH: St. Anthony Press, 1992), 15.

49 Gloria Hutchinson, *Six Ways to Pray from Six Great Saints* (Cincinnati, OH: St. Anthony Messenger, 1982), 34. The Divine Hours observed by the Poor Ladies followed a centuries-old pattern: Matins and Lauds (middle of the night), Prime and Terce (early morning), Sext and None (noon, early afternoon), Vespers (late afternoon), Compline (early evening).

50 “Life of Penance” includes the pattern of actions that show regret for one’s wrongdoings, usually consisting of prayer, fasting, work, and so on, undertaken voluntarily to show remorse.

51 De Robeck, *St. Clare of Assisi*, 93.

52 De Robeck, *St. Clare of Assisi*, 93.

53 Lainati, *Saint Clare of Assisi*, 59.

54 Raphael Brown, *The Little Flowers of St. Francis* (New York: Image Books, 1958), 72.

55 Brown, *The Little Flowers of St. Francis*, 73.

56 Brown, *The Little Flowers of St. Francis*, 195.

57 Armstrong, *Francis and Clare*, 4.

58 Mark Galli, “Did You Know,” (Christian History, Issue 42, Vol. XIII, No. 2) 1994), 2.

59 Green, *God’s Fool*, 203. Al-Malik al-Kāmil (born 1180, died 1238), a sultan (from 1218) of the Ayyūbid line, ruled Egypt, Palestine, and Syria during the Fifth and Sixth Crusades. On his accession to the sultanate, al-Kāmil engaged the armies of the Fifth Crusade and eventually negotiated their withdrawal from Egypt in 1221. During this conflict, he had an interview with St. Francis of Assisi, who tried to convert him to Christianity. In 1229, al-Kāmil ceded Jerusalem and other Palestinian towns to Emperor Frederick II, leader of the Sixth Crusade. *Encyclopaedia Britannica*, July 20, 1998. https://www.britannica.com/biography/al-Malik-al-Kamil

60 Thoman, *St. Clare of Assisi*, 192.

61 Green, *God’s Fool*, 210.

62 Green, *God’s Fool*, 210.

63 Thoman, *St. Clare of Assisi*, 195.

64 Jorgensen, *Saint Francis of Assisi*, 244.

65 Green, *God’s Fool*, 252.

66 Brown, *The Little Flowers of St. Francis*, 190.

67 Lawrence S. Cunningham, “Tattered Treasure of Assisi” (*Christian History,* Issue 42, Vol. XIII, No. 2, 1994), 16.

68 Cunningham, “Tattered Treasure of Assisi,” 40.

69 Green, *God’s Fool*, 255.

70 Bodo, *A Light in the Garden*, 51.

71 Green, *God’s Fool*, 256, 257.

72 Brown, *The Little Flowers of St. Francis*, 318.

73 Thoman, *St. Clare of Assisi*, 167.

74 Cunningham, “Tattered Treasure of Assisi,” 17.

75 Thoman, *St. Clare of Assisi*, 180.

76 Thoman, *St. Clare of Assisi*, 181.

77 Lainati, *Saint Clare of Assisi*, 78.

Chapter 4: Katharina Luther, Mother of the Reformation

1 Merle Severy, "The World of Luther" (*National Geographic*, Vol. 164, No. 4, 1983), 418.

2 Roland H. Bainton, *Women of the Reformation in Germany and Italy* (Minneapolis: Augsburg, 1971), 23ff. "Katharina ministered to her husband's diseases, depressions, and eccentricities. She had great skill with diet, herbs, poultices, and massages. Her son, later a distinguished physician praised her as half a doctor. Luther frequently suffered tortures from the stone. On one such occasion he would neither eat nor drink, and Katie besought him to take some sustenance. 'Very well,' said he, 'roast beef, peas, and mustard and be quick before my fancy fades.' She complied and he ate heartily. His doctors called and were aghast. They returned in the morning to see the corpse and found him at his desk. He had passed a stone." For further reading, see John Warwick Montgomery, *The Life of Paul Luther, Physician*, in *Christ as Centre and Circumference, Essays Theological, Cultural, and Polemic* (Eugene, Oregon: Wipf and Stock Publishers, 2012), 314.

3 Severy, "The World of Luther," 426.

4 Dolina MacCuish, *Luther and His Katie* (Fearn, Scotland: Christian Focus Publications, 2017), 23.

5 Roland H. Bainton, *Here I Stand* (New York: Abingdon, 1950), 93.

6 Bainton, *Here I Stand*, 113.

7 Bainton, *Here I Stand*, 113.

8 Bainton, *Here I Stand*, 119.

9 Bainton, *Here I Stand*, 443.

10 Kathleen Benson, *A Man Called Martin Luther* (St. Louis: Concordia, 1980), 77.

11 MacCuish, *Luther and His Katie*, 25.

12 Bainton, *Here I Stand*, 286.

13 Bainton, *Women of the Reformation* (Boston: Augsburg, 1974), 23.

14 MacCuish, *Luther and His Katie*, 26.

15 Ewald M. Plass, *This Is Luther* (St. Louis: Concordia, 1984), 252.

16 MacCuish, *Luther and His Katie*, 26.

17 Bainton, *Here I Stand*, 286.

18 MacCuish, *Luther and His Katie*, 27.

19 Benson, *A Man Called Martin Luther*, 7.

20 Bainton, *Here I Stand*, 26.

21 Benson, *A Man Called Martin Luther*, 14.

22 Bainton, *Here I Stand*, 25.

23 Ewald M. Plass, *What Luther Says*, Vol. 1, No. 420 (Saint Louis: Concordia, 1959), 142.

24 Benson, *A Man Called Martin Luther*, 19.

25 Benson, *A Man Called Martin Luther*, 30.
26 Herbert F. Brokering, *Celebrating a 500th Birth Day* (Minneapolis: Lutheran Brotherhood, 1982), 1.
27 Bainton, *Here I Stand*, 34.
28 Benson, *A Man Called Martin Luther*, 34.
29 Benson, *A Man Called Martin Luther*, 36.
30 Peter Manns, *Martin Luther: An Illustrated Biography* (New York: Crossroads, 1983), 32.
31 Marshall Shelley, ed., "Jan Hus: The Incendiary Preacher of Prague" (*Christian History*, Vol. XIX, No. 4, Issue 68, 2000), 35. Hus also stated at this time, "Today you will roast a lean goose [his nickname was "the goose"], but a hundred years from now you will hear a swan sing, whom you will leave unroasted and no trap or net will catch him for you."
32 Bainton, *Here I Stand*, 296.
33 Bainton, *Here I Stand*, 45.
34 Roland H. Bainton, *Where Luther Walked* (Worcester, PA: Gateway Films Vision Video, 1992).
35 Benson, *A Man Called Martin Luther*, 41, 42.
36 MacCuish, *Luther and His Katie*, 10, 11.
37 Benson, *A Man Called Martin Luther*, 48.
38 Benson, *A Man Called Martin Luther*, 49.
39 Brokering, *Celebrating a 500th Birth Day*, 1.
40 Severy, *The World of Luther*, 438.
41 Benson, *A Man Called Martin Luther*, 55.
42 I recommend this book by Alister E. McGrath: *Luther's Theology of the Cross: Martin Luther's Theological Breakthrough* (Malden, MA: Blackwell Publishers, 1985).
43 Severy, *The World of Luther*, 442.
44 Severy, *The World of Luther*, 442.
45 "August 11, 1519: Death of Tetzel in Leipzig, "neglected, smitten in soul, and full of misery." A hawker of indulgences, he had been a relentless foe of Luther. After indulgences had fallen into disrepute through Luther's teaching, Tetzel complained to Rome that he was safe nowhere, but Luther, when he heard of his illness, had written him a kind letter, forgiving him" (*Christian History*, August 11, 2020, devotional email, https://us1.campaignarchive.com/?e=8b62aa3c88&u=8afcbca846220ea5008858654&id=e2847ecdfc; info@christianhistoryinstitute.org).
46 John Warwick Montgomery, *In Defense of Martin Luther* (Milwaukee: Northwestern Publishing, 1970), 19.
47 Severy, *The World of Luther*, 442.
48 Severy, *The World of Luther*, 442.

49 Bainton, *Here I Stand*, 82.
50 Bokering, *Celebrating a 500th Birth Day*, 2.
51 Kevin Miller, "Martin Luther: The Early Years" (*Christian History*, Issue 34, Vol. XI, No. 2, 1992), 16.
52 Benson, *A Man Called Martin Luther*, 86.
53 Bainton, *Here I Stand*, 288.
54 Bainton, *Women of the Reformation*, 26.
55 Severy, *The World of Luther*, 454.
56 Bainton, *Women of the Reformation*, 26.
57 Bainton, *Here I Stand*, 288.
58 Plass, *This Is Luther*, 265.
59 Charles Ludwig, *Queen of the Reformation* (Minneapolis: Bethany House, 1986), 156.
60 Miller, *Martin Luther: The Early Years*, 40.
61 Clara S. Schreiber, *Katharina: Wife of Luther* (Milwaukee: Northwestern Publishing, 1972), 101.
62 Schreiber, *Katharina: Wife of Luther*, 178.
63 Ludwig, *Queen of the Reformation*, 126.
64 Ludwig, *Queen of the Reformation*, 126.
65 Plass, *This Is Luther*, 255.
66 Bainton, *Women of the Reformation*, 39.
67 Plass, *This Is Luther*, 260.
68 Bainton, *Here I Stand*, 302.
69 Plass, *What Luther Says*, Vol. 1, 142.
70 Schreiber, *Katharina: Wife of Luther*, 115.
71 Bainton, *Here I Stand*, 304.
72 Bainton, *Here I Stand*, 304.
73 Bainton, *Women of the Reformation*, 37.
74 Bainton, *Women of the Reformation*, 37.
75 Plass, *What Luther Says*, No. 400, 137.
76 Bainton, *Here I Stand*, 300.
77 Bainton, *Here I Stand*, 301.
78 MacCuish, *Luther and His Katie*, 40.
79 Severy, *The World of Luther*, 452.
80 MacCuish, *Luther and His Katie*, 42.
81 Bainton, *Women of the Reformation*, 29.
82 MacCuish, *Luther and His Katie*, 42.
83 Bainton, *Women of the Reformation*, 43.
84 Severy, *The World of Luther*, 444.
85 Martin Luther, *Three Treatises* (Philadelphia: Fortress Press, 1973), 261.
86 Severy, *The World of Luther*, 429.

87 Bainton, *Here I Stand*, 170.
88 Severy, *The World of Luther*, 449.
89 Bainton, *Here I Stand*, 181.
90 Bainton, *Here I Stand*, 183.
91 Bainton, *Here I Stand*, 184.
92 Bainton, *Here I Stand*, 185.
93 Bainton, *Here I Stand*, 185.
94 Bainton, *Here I Stand*, 186.
95 Gregg Quiggle, "Martin Luther Challenges Us to Read Our Bibles." Dr. Quiggle, Church History Instructor, Moody Bible Institute. Lecture Handout Notes, 1.
96 Severy, *The World of Luther*, 462.
97 Severy, *The World of Luther*, 462.
98 The "Battle for the Bible" refers to the controversial issue in the last century of the debate concerning inerrancy and errancy. Recommended Reading: Harold Lindsell, *The Battle for the Bible* (Grand Rapids, MI: Zondervan, 1981).
99 Historical criticism, also known as the "historical-critical method" or "higher criticism," is a branch of literary criticism that investigates the origins of ancient texts to understand "the world behind the text." This new type of biblical interpretation has its roots in deism, rationalism, and the Enlightenment. In contrast, the grammatico-historical hermeneutic has its roots in Luther and the Reformation of 1517. This method maintains that the words of scripture must be taken as simple, clear, natural, and literal truth, as intended by the original author, as opposed to the subjective opinions of interpreters. For a scholarly refutation of the historical-critical method biblical hermeneutic and an excellent presentation of Luther's belief in inerrancy, see *In Defense of Martin Luther*, Essays by Dr. John Warwick Montgomery (Milwaukee: Northwestern Publishing House, 1970). See Chapter 1, "Luther's Hermeneutic vs. the New Hermeneutic," pp. 40–85. ("For him [Luther], unlike both medieval Roman and contemporary Protestant hermeneutics, the objective message of God's written Word must stand forever over the corporate and the individual conscience—judging them, not in any sense being judged by them," p. 69.)

Chapter 5: Susanna Wesley, the Mother of Methodism

1 Charles Ludwig, *Susanna Wesley, Mother of John and Charles* (Milford, MI: Mott Media, 1984), 179.
2 W. Le Cato Edwards, *Epworth … the Home of the Wesleys* (Gainsborough, England: G. W. Belton), 29.
3 G. Elsie Harrison, *Son to Susanna* (Nashville: Cokesbury, 1938), 23.

4 *The Journal of John Wesley*. 1770.

5 Edwards, *Epworth*, 31.

6 Robert E. Coleman, *"Nothing to Do but to Save Souls," John Wesley's Charge to His Preachers* (Grand Rapids, MI: Francis Asbury, 1990), 16.

7 Wilson Engel, "John Wesley, Revival and Revolution" (*Christian History*, Vol. II, No. 1, 1983), 7.

8 Rebecca Lamar Harmon, *Susanna, Mother of the Wesleys* (Nashville: Abingdon, 1984), 32.

9 Mary Greetham, *Susanna Wesley, Mother of Methodism* (Peterborough, England: Foundery Press, 1994), 4.

10 Arnold A. Dallimore, *Susanna Wesley, the Mother of John and Charles Wesley* (Grand Rapids, MI: Baker, 1993), 15.

11 Carolyn Nystrom, *The Wesleys Amazing Love* (Downers Grove, IL: InterVarsity, 2002), 13.

12 Harmon, *Susanna, Mother of the Wesleys*, 20.

13 Dan Noorlander, Wesley Heritage Study Guide, *An Introduction to the World of John Wesley* (Orlando: Educational Opportunities Tours, 1998), 11.

14 Dallimore, *Susanna Wesley*, 22.

15 Greetham, *Susanna Wesley*, 6.

16 Dallimore, *Susanna Wesley*, 34.

17 Donald L. Kline, *Susanna Wesley: God's Catalyst for Revival* (Lima, OH: C.S.S. Publishing, 1980), Preface, xii.

18 Edwards, *Epworth*, 1.

19 Harmon, *Susanna, Mother of the Wesleys*, 48.

20 Harmon, *Susanna, Mother of the Wesleys*, 49.

21 Dallimore, *Susanna Wesley*, 68.

22 Harmon, *Susanna, Mother of the Wesleys*, 49.

23 Harmon, *Susanna, Mother of the Wesleys*, 50.

24 Harmon, *Susanna, Mother of the Wesleys*, 11.

25 Dallimore, *Susanna Wesley*, 70.

26 Dallimore, *Susanna Wesley*, 70.

27 Ludwig, *Susanna Wesley*, 136.

28 Harmon, *Susanna, Mother of the Wesleys*, 52.

29 Harmon, *Susanna, Mother of the Wesleys*, 52.

30 Harmon, *Susanna, Mother of the Wesleys*, 53.

31 Harmon, *Susanna, Mother of the Wesleys*, 53.

32 Harmon, *Susanna, Mother of the Wesleys*, 53.

33 Harmon, *Susanna, Mother of the Wesleys*, 77.

34 Harmon, *Susanna, Mother of the Wesleys*, 47.

35 Lynette Danskin, *Portrait of Susanna* (Video. Mike Fairman, Director; Leah Gallardo, Producer, Pasadena: Media Center, UMC Cal-Pac Conference, 2000).
36 Dallimore, *Susanna Wesley*, 61.
37 Dallimore, *Susanna Wesley*, 60.
38 Dallimore, *Susanna Wesley*, 57.
39 Ludwig, *Susanna Wesley*, 148.
40 Kline, *Susanna Wesley*, 8, 9.
41 Danskin, *Portrait of Susanna.*
42 Edwards, *Epworth*, 15.
43 Kline, *Susanna Wesley*, 18.
44 Kline, *Susanna Wesley*, 17.
45 Ludwig, *Susanna Wesley*, 154.
46 Greetham, *Susanna Wesley*, 8.
47 Greetham, *Susanna Wesley*, 20.
48 Harmon, *Susanna, Mother of the Wesleys*, 161.
49 Greetham, *Susanna Wesley*, 22.
50 Charles Wesley, "Ode to Music." Poem composed for Charles's mother, Susanna Wesley. Poem in the public domain, original publication undetermined.
51 Kline, *Susanna Wesley*, 2.
52 Edwards, *Epworth*, 15.
53 Engel, "John Wesley," 32.
54 Nystrom, *The Wesleys*, 17.
55 Nystrom, *The Wesleys*, 17.
56 Albert C. Outler, *John Wesley* (New York: Oxford University Press, 1980), 17.
57 Marshall Shelley, "The Wesleys, Charles & John" (*Christian History*, Vol. XX, 1, Issue 69, 2001), 21.
58 Outler, *John Wesley*, 66.
59 Coleman, *"Nothing to Do but to Save Souls,"* 27.
60 Engel, "John Wesley," 4.
61 Engel, "John Wesley," 4.
62 John Wesley's great contribution was in opposing the Anglican theological rationalism of the Enlightenment and in his stress on evangelism. He also correctly emphasized that a true, authentic Christian conversion experience was not merely a moment-in-time event. He believed, like Luther, that the "new birth" began an ongoing process of daily transformation into the image of Christ, called sanctification. It must be acknowledged, however, that Wesley's critical theological error was to think that sanctification was the heart of the believer's experience rather than justification.

Chapter 6: Catherine Booth, the Army Mother

1 The Salvation Army International, International Statistics (as of January 1, 2017), https://www.salvationarmy.org/ihq/statistics, accessed March 1, 2017.

2 Kevin A. Miller, "William and Catherine Booth" (*Christian History*, Issue 26, Vol. IX, No. 2, 1990), Preface.

3 Helen K. Hosier, *William and Catherine Booth, Founders of the Salvation Army* (Uhrichsville, OH: Barbour Publishing, 1999), 176–77.

4 Charles Ludwig, *Mother of an Army* (Minneapolis: Bethany House, 1987), 48.

5 Ludwig, *Mother of an Army*, 49.

6 W. T. Stead, *Mrs. Booth of the Salvation Army* (London: James Nesbit, 1900; reprinted, Oakville, Canada: The Trumpet Press, 1979), 10.

7 Ludwig, *Mother of an Army*, 10.

8 Stead, *Mrs. Booth of the Salvation Army*, 20.

9 Hosier, *William and Catherine Booth*, 33.

10 Kenneth Lawson, "Jesus Christ and Him Crucified" in *Catherine Booth—Her Continuing Relevance*, Clifford W. Kew, ed. (London: Campfield Press, 1990), 35.

11 Stead, *Mrs. Booth of the Salvation Army*, 31.

12 Catherine Bramwell Booth, *Catherine Booth: The Story of Her Loves* (London: Hodder and Stoughton, 1973), 33.

13 Ludwig, *Mother of an Army*, 32.

14 Roger J. Green, *Catherine Booth* (Grand Rapids, MI: Baker Books, 1996), 31.

15 Stead, *Mrs. Booth of the Salvation Army*, 38.

16 David Guy, "This Life of Trust," in *Catherine Booth—Her Continuing Relevance*, 25.

17 William Booth, "The Founder Speaks," The Salvation Army, Audio Recording (Rancho Palos Verdes, CA: Salvation Army Western Territorial Museum), Ms. Frances Dingman, historian.

18 Barbara Bolton, "A Denouncer of Iniquity," in *Catherine Booth—Her Continuing Relevance*, 139.

19 Ludwig, *Mother of an Army*, 57.

20 Ludwig, *Mother of an Army*, 58.

21 Miller, "William and Catherine Booth," 5.

22 Miller, "William and Catherine Booth," 6.

23 Trevor Yaxley and Carolyn Vanderwal, *William & Catherine: The Life and Legacy of the Booths* (Minneapolis: Bethany House, 2003), 51.

24 Hosier, *William and Catherine Booth*, 21. (The nickname reflected William's fiery personality and his strong opinions.)

25 Yaxley and Vanderwal, *William & Catherine*, 61.

26 Milton Agnew, *Manual of Salvationism, Instructors' Book*, Rev. ed. (Verona, NJ: The Salvation Army, 1985), 155.
27 Yaxley and Vanderwal, *William & Catherine*, 160.
28 Hosier, *William and Catherine Booth*, 32.
29 Christine Parkin, "A Woman's Place?," in *Catherine Booth—Her Continuing Relevance*, 9.
30 Green, *Catherine Booth*, 121.
31 Parkin, "A Woman's Place?," 2.
32 Parkin, "A Woman's Place?," 2.
33 Anna Pickup, *Broken Alabaster Jars: Portraits of Women in Ministry* (Mukilteo, WA: Winepress Publishing, 1998), 21.
34 Parkin, "A Woman's Place?," 11, 12.
35 Ludwig, *Mother of an Army*, 141.
36 Green, *Catherine Booth*, 135.
37 Pickup, *Broken Alabaster Jars*, 23.
38 Green, *Catherine Booth*, 136.
39 Miller, "William and Catherine Booth," 9.
40 Yaxley and Vanderwal, *William & Catherine*, 185.
41 Ludwig, *Mother of an Army*, 127.
42 Ludwig, *Mother of an Army*, 129.
43 Ludwig, *Mother of an Army*, 130.
44 Ludwig, *Mother of an Army*, 130.
45 Richard Collier, *The General Next to God* (Glasgow: Fontana Books, 1985), 33.
46 Yaxley and Vanderwal, *William & Catherine*, 97.
47 Hosier, *William and Catherine Booth*, 12.
48 Hosier, *William and Catherine Booth*, 13.
49 Ludwig, *Mother of an Army*, 157.
50 Miller, "William and Catherine Booth," 20.
51 Collier, *The General Next to God*, 18.
52 Collier, *The General Next to God*, 15.
53 Collier, *The General Next to God*, 19.
54 Ludwig, *Mother of an Army*, 174–75.
55 David Bennet, *William Booth* (Minneapolis: Bethany House, 1986), 13.
56 Yaxley and Vanderwal, *William & Catherine*, 117.
57 Cyril Barnes, *God's Army* (Colorado Springs: David C. Cook, 1987), 16.
58 Barnes, *God's Army*, 20.
59 Barnes, *God's Army*, 21.
60 Bennet, *William Booth*, 61.
61 Barnes, *God's Army*, 38.
62 Miller, "William and Catherine Booth," 10.
63 Bennet, *William Booth*, 69.

64 Bennet, *William Booth*, 73.
65 Stead, *Mrs. Booth of the Salvation Army*, 54.
66 Ludwig, *Mother of an Army*, 10.
67 Yaxley and Vanderwal, *William & Catherine*, 143.
68 Green, *Catherine Booth*, 227.
69 Barnes, *God's Army*, 54.
70 Barnes, *God's Army*, 8.
71 Yaxley and Vanderwal, *William & Catherine*, 131.
72 Yaxley and Vanderwal, *William & Catherine*, 202.
73 Miller, "William and Catherine Booth," 33. (The book sold 90,000 copies in its first month, 200,000 in its first year, and more than a million in Booth's lifetime.)
74 William Booth, "Please Sir, Save Me!," Classic Audio Recordings of Sermons by General William Booth. Broadcast on VTM: 1910. www.sermonindex.net.
75 William Booth, "Please Sir, Save Me!"

Chapter 7: Mother Teresa of Calcutta, Mother to the Poorest of the Poor

1 Mother Teresa Center, 3835 National Avenue, San Diego, CA 92113, USA
2 David Van Biema, "Mother Teresa, the Life and Works of a Modern Saint" (USA: Time Specials, 2016), 37.
3 Jose Luis Gonzalez-Balado, *Loving Jesus* (Ann Arbor, MI: Servant Publications, 1991), 54.
4 Jose Luis Gonzalez-Balado and Janet Playfoot, *My Life for the Poor* (New York: Ballantine Books, 1985), 1.
5 Mother Teresa was born August 26, 1910 into an Albanian family in Skopje (Uskub in Turkish), then part of the Kosovo Vilayet of the Ottoman Empire (from 1392-1912). Skopje is now the capital of the Republic of North Macedonia. Encyclopaedia Britannica, February 23, 1999. https://www.britannica.com/biography/Mother-Teresa
6 Kathryn Spink, *Mother Teresa: A Complete Authorized Biography* (San Francisco: Harper Collins, 1997), 7.
7 Sam Wellman, *Mother Teresa Missionary of Charity* (Uhrichsville, OH: Barbour Publishing, 1997), 29.
8 Joanna Hurley, *Mother Teresa: A Pictorial Biography* (Philadelphia: Courage Books, 1997), 27.
9 A&E Home Video, *Biography: Mother Teresa: A Life of Devotion* (1999, DVD, available from www.amazon.com).
10 Spink, *Mother Teresa*, 11.

11 Wellman, *Mother Teresa*, 49.
12 Wellman, *Mother Teresa*, 41.
13 Spink, *Mother Teresa*, 14.
14 Hurley, *Mother Teresa*, 31, 213.
15 Hurley, *Mother Teresa*, 38.
16 Spink, *Mother Teresa*, 34.
17 Navin Chawla, *Mother Teresa* (Rockport, MA: Element Books, 1996), 33.
18 Chawla, *Mother Teresa*, 17.
19 Malcolm Muggeridge, *Something Beautiful for God* (New York: Harper & Row, 1971), 85.
20 Gonzalez-Balado, *Loving Jesus*, 73.
21 Hurley, *Mother Teresa*, 56.
22 Hurley, *Mother Teresa*, 56.
23 Gonzalez-Balado, *My Life for the Poor*, 7.
24 Georges Gorree, *Love without Boundaries* (Huntington, IN: Our Sunday Visitor, 1978), 18.
25 Hurley, *Mother Teresa*, 59.
26 Gonzalez-Balado, *My Life for the Poor*, 10.
27 Muggeridge, *Something Beautiful for God*, 88.
28 Gonzalez-Balado, *My Life for the Poor*, 9.
29 David Van Biema, "The Secret Life of Mother Teresa" (*Time*, September 3, 2007), 38.
30 Wellman, *Mother Teresa*, 62.
31 Wellman, *Mother Teresa*, 101.
32 Spink, *Mother Teresa*, 39.
33 Muggeridge, *Something Beautiful for God*, 90.
34 Gonzalez-Balado, *My Life for the Poor*, 13.
35 Hurley, *Mother Teresa*, 116.
36 Hurley, *Mother Teresa*, 73.
37 Spink, *Mother Teresa*, 253.
38 Spink, *Mother Teresa*, Nobel Peace Prize Lecture, Appendix B, 296–97.
39 Mother Teresa of Calcutta, MC, "Love Always Hurts" Lecture (Washington DC: National Prayer Breakfast, Shoreham Hotel, February 4, 1994).
40 Gonzalez-Balado, *My Life for the Poor*, 28.
41 Spink, *Mother Teresa*, 54.
42 Courtney Tower, "Mother Teresa's Work of Grace" (*Reader's Digest*, December 1987), 220. Kalighat is one of the oldest and densely populated neighborhoods located in the southern part of Calcutta (now called Kolkata).
43 Spink, *Mother Teresa*, 56. Calcutta Municipal Corporation, now Kolkata Municipal Corporation, is the local government of the Indian city of Kolkata, the state capital of West Bengal.

44 A&E Home Video, *Mother Teresa: A Life of Devotion.*

45 Spink, *Mother Teresa*, 55.

46 Spink, *Mother Teresa*, 73, 214.

47 David Van Biema, *The Life and Works of a Modern Saint*, 23.

48 Spink, *Mother Teresa*, 120.

49 Gonzalez-Balado, *Loving Jesus*, 33.

50 Gonzalez-Balado, *Loving Jesus*, 34–36.

51 Edward Le Joly and Chaliha Jaya, *Mother Teresa's Reaching Out in Love* (New York: Barnes & Noble, 2002), 122.

52 Mother Teresa of Calcutta, "Love Always Hurts" Lecture 2-4-1994 (*Good News Magazine*, November/December 1997, pp. 18–19; see Endnote # 42).

53 Mother Teresa of Calcutta, "Love Always Hurts."

54 Wellman, *Mother Teresa,* 177.

55 Chawla, *Mother Teresa*, 212.

56 Spink, *Mother Teresa*, 67.

57 Wellman, *Mother Teresa*, 105.

58 Le Joly, *Mother Teresa's Reaching Out in Love*, 112.

59 Wellman, *Mother Teresa*, 153.

60 Tower, "Mother Teresa's Work of Grace," 233.

61 Le Joly, *Mother Teresa's Reaching Out in Love,* 134–5.

62 Le Joly, *Mother Teresa's Reaching Out in Love*, 138.

63 Le Joly, *Mother Teresa's Reaching Out in Love*, 32.

64 Le Joly, *Mother Teresa's Reaching Out in Love*, 12.

65 Le Joly, *Mother Teresa's Reaching Out in Love*, 56.

66 Muggeridge, *Something Beautiful for God,* 73.

67 Spink, *Mother Teresa*, 10.

68 Marcel Bauer, *The Testament of Mother Teresa* (1996; DVD, available from Kultur Video, www.kultur.com).

69 Spink, Nobel Peace Prize Lecture, Appendix B, 302.

70 Spink, Nobel Peace Prize Lecture, Appendix B, 302.

71 Gonzalez-Balado, *My Life for the Poor*, 113.

72 Fr. Brian Kolodiejchuk, *Jesus Is My All in All* (San Diego: Knights of Columbus, 2004), 7.

About the Author

Rev. Gwen Ehrenborg is a gifted storyteller who has an energetic style of sharing biblical truths with a warmth and relevance upon a sound theological foundation. Her heart's desire is to inspire people to know Jesus Christ well as they joyfully fulfill God's plan for their lives. Gwen has been writing, speaking, and performing compelling, dramatic stories for over thirty-five years through her pastoral ministry and nonprofit drama ministry, Living Witnesses. Pastor Gwen served five California congregations with her clergy husband and also travels with her drama ministry, portraying seven leading women of church history. Beginning in 1984, these well-researched, one-women dramatizations have been enthusiastically received by Catholics and Protestants alike across America.

Pastor Gwen is an ordained minister and general evangelist in the United Methodist Church, which allows her to represent the denomination throughout all nations. She brings to her teaching and preaching a variety of life experiences, having served in the Democratic Republic of Congo as a single missionary and then in Mexico with her late husband. Suddenly widowed at age twenty-seven while expecting her first child, she soon attended Fuller Theological Seminary to earn a master's of divinity degree. Seminary served her very well because after three years, she met and married a fellow student, Todd Ehrenborg. Gwen said that rather than staying a widow, she has been twice blessed by God with the gift of two amazing husbands in her lifetime.

In 2004, Rev. Ehrenborg founded a second nonprofit organization, Supporting Women In Ministry International (SWIM), which is a support network for Christian women of all ages and backgrounds. After fourteen years of serving as president of the board of directors, she now travels as the ministry's International Ambassador.

Gwen's creative gifts and research skills have enabled her to write accurate scripts for dramatic presentations, which have been highly praised by pastors for their masterful ability to educate, entertain, and inspire their congregations. Over the years, Rev. Ehrenborg has written and taught many biblical program series for church conferences, retreats, and study groups. She thoroughly enjoys travelling, especially when leading tour groups to historic Christian sites in Europe and the Holy Land. She loves to play her piano and can be found spontaneously singing silly songs in a "Cinderelli" mouse voice. Gwen lives on Camano Island, Washington, with her husband, and they have three adult children and the cutest granddaughter.

Other Resources from Living Witnesses Ministries

The letters contained in this book are inspired by the dramatic presentations Gwen has written and performed over the years. You can enjoy more of Gwen's creative gifts through her DVDs.

Judge Deborah: A Mother of Israel

Portrayed by Rev. Gwen Ehrenborg and filmed in the Holy Land on the sites where Judge Deborah lived and served God as the leader of the nation of Israel. Produced by Jerusalem Vistas, Dr. Jay and Daniel Rawlings.

Katie Luther: First Lady of the Reformation

Portrayed by Rev. Gwen Ehrenborg, this live production dramatizes the story of how God used Martin and Katie Luther to change the course of history. Produced by Ernie Fosse and Rev. Don Brekas.

All of us at Living Witnesses Ministries appreciate the opportunity
to help bring you and your organization into a deeper and
more intimate understanding of our Christian faith.

Living Witnesses Christian Drama and Teaching Ministry

Live dramatic portrayals of seven great women of church history, portrayed by Gwen Ehrenborg: Judge Deborah; Mary of Nazareth; Lady Clare of Assisi; Katie Luther; Susanna Wesley; Catherine Booth; Mother Teresa of Calcutta.

Conference/Retreat Speaker, Gwen Ehrenborg

Three-day retreats designed for women or for mixed audiences
Conference speaking, pulpit supply, TV/radio interviews

We welcome any and all communication. Please direct all
communication or for inquiring about booking Gwen at:

Website: https://www.livingwitnesses.org
Email: livingwitnesses@sbcglobal.net

To order Living Witnesses resources by mail,
use the order form on the next page

Living Witnesses Ministries

Order Form

Name: ____
First and Last

Shipping Address: ______________________________________
Street and Suite/Apartment number if applicable

____
City, State, and Zip

Phone: ____
Area code and number

Email Address: ____

Please provide a phone or email address in case there is a question about filling your order.

† **Signed copies of:**	**Quantity**	**Subtotal**
Our Church Mothers, Letters from Leaders at Crossroads in History		
Paperback $19.95	______	$______
Hardback $35.99	______	______
† **DVDs**		
Judge Deborah, A Mother of Israel $10.00	______	______
Katie Luther, First Lady of the Reformation $10.00	______	______
Washington Residents add 8.7% sales tax:		______
Add $3.00 postage for each book		______
(Shipping limited to the United States)		
GRAND TOTAL:		$______

Please send this form with your check or money order payable to:
Living Witnesses Ministries, 167 Vista Del Mar St., Camano Island, WA 98282-7254